W9-AOL-895

DARK MOUNTAIN

DARK MOUNTAIN

Issue 17 · Spring 2020

The Dark Mountain Project

Published by the Dark Mountain Project 2020
dark-mountain.net

ISBN 978-0-9955402-8-6

Editors
Neale Inglenook
Eric Robertson
Steve Wheeler

Poetry Editor
Cate Chapman

Art Editor and Producer
Charlotte Du Cann

Proofreader
Mark Watson

Editorial Assistant
Ava Osbiston

Assistant Readers
Hattie Pierce
M.E. Rolle

Associate Publishers
Erik Jacobs and
Dina Rudick

Typesetting
Christian Brett,
Bracketpress

Printed and bound by
TJ International Ltd.,
Padstow, PL28 8RW

MIX
Paper from
responsible sources
FSC® C013056

Cover Art
by Kate Williamson
Violet Storm
Acrylic on canvas

Violet Storm celebrates the powerful, regenerative forces in nature. It is the chaos of a storm bringing scouring rains to assist new growth, natural erosion and the dispersal of seeds. Native to New Zealand, the seeds of the *kōwhai* tree have a hard outer coating allowing them to float in the water. In a 'Violet Storm' the kōwhai seeds would be swept away by the deluge, scraping against rocks before they settle on a distant riverbank. The gentle battering they receive enables water to penetrate the seed casing and begin the entire germination process. What in nature has the power to destroy also has the power to restore.

ISSUE 17 · SPRING 2020

Contents

Resistance

Restitution

Retreat

Redemption

CONTENTS

JULIE WILLIAMS
Photographer Unknown
Gelatin silver photograph

EDITORIAL

From the Ashes

What is there left to say?

When *Uncivilisation: the Dark Mountain Manifesto* was launched a little over a decade ago, the mainstream rhetoric around environmental destruction and political breakdown was blandly complacent. Climate change was acknowledged as a problem, but one to which new technologies and the good sense of political elites were sure to eventually find a solution. The financial crisis had shaken confidence in the global political and economic system, but the conventional thinking was that, once we weathered the storm, it would be back to business as usual. Few were willing to hear about the lack of an imaginal and mythic dimension in our public discourse, and those who did were likely to dismiss it as irrational, aesthetic frippery.

Things look very different at this end of the decade. After another ten years of broken environmental and climatic records, after a year and a half of Extinction Rebellion protests and school strikes, after the worst bushfires in Australian history devastated over 170,000 km^2 of land and killed an estimated billion animals, after the 'insect apocalypse' and the endemic microplastics and the die-off of the Great Barrier Reef, there are signs that the full dismal horror of our environmental situation is beginning to penetrate the public consciousness.

Meanwhile, a wave of reality-smashing political grifters – appealing to the most troubling elements in the public psyche to a degree few anticipated – has swept across the Western world and beyond, while the global economy continues to stagger on, average incomes flatlining while the wealthiest get ever richer. As establishment thinkers cast about for expla-

[opposite] The artist, in mourning for a wounded landscape, utilises lens-based self portraiture to explore our vulnerability as a species in a collapsing world. She enters the eucalypt forest on a mountain plateau and encounters a tree sculpted by bushfire. Drawing upon the burned tree's steadfast ability to maintain deep roots in a regenerating landscape, the duo make first contact and vow to collaborate: to conjure the past to the present to envision the future.

nations, they are beginning to suspect that their model of the human psyche as a rationalist, unfeeling agent is itself a fantasy.

With the terms of discussion having shifted so decisively, there is a sense, here at the dawn of the 2020s, of a change of chapter. As we said in the editorial of the 10-year anniversary issue, 'we are not going anywhere' – in the simple sense that we intend to carry on doing what we do, and also in the sense that 'going anywhere' has never really been the point of the Dark Mountain Project. Rather, it has always been a space held open for voices that would otherwise have gone unheard, for perspectives that do not fit the accepted frames, and for stories that speak to the reality of being human in these strange times. And, in these terms, we still see plenty of work to be done.

There is still a need, for example, for art and writing that helps us grieve for all that is being lost and will yet be lost regardless of where our course now takes us – whether musing on the shadowed lessons of a Dark Goddess, or pausing in contemplation over the corpse of a lone rabbit or fox. There is still a value in hearing the quiet voices of particular places, learning of the regenerative power in an abused piece of ex-industrial ground and the resilience of the human spirit in times of flood, war or sickness.

But this is also a space to explore new aspects of our global predicament, foregrounding fresh ideas, images and insights that might yet provide us with the hope that arises once the grieving has been honoured. One hundred years ago, the notorious German thinker Oswald Spengler wrote that he had chosen the title of his epic work *The Decline of the West* at a time when 'the European-American world was infused with the trivial optimism of the Darwinist age' – but that, 'if I had to choose again now, I would try with another formula to strike at today's equally trivial pessimism.'

So it is that, while the Western world clothes itself in the latest gothic apocalypticisms, we present to you a volume loosely themed on 'restoration'. Perhaps the most interesting questions now, once we have accepted the true state of things, are: How should we live? What can be saved? What beauty and life might yet grow from the fallen trunk of this civilisation?

In these pages, you will read of the ways in which that very same mechanistic ideology that has caused so much harm has also blinded us to the ways in which ecosystems can be repaired. You will hear of how rivers can be helped to run again and hearts helped to heal; landscapes rewilded and broken bowls mended. Testimony will reach you from Iraqi marshes, Berlin parks, Canadian forests and Japanese dormitories, alongside tales of rebellious communities, revivifying storms and rejuvenated pigs. You will be invited to consider the peregrinations of ancient peoples as they sought refuge and revelation, and to take an astronomical perspective on our small world's happenings.

Restoration is not a call to believe in techno-fixes or the triumph of human supremacy. Nor is the idea of restoration a way to deny the damage that has been done, or to pretend that we can reverse or replace the losses that have been visited upon this planet's human and more-than-human peoples.

Rather, it has its roots in humbleness, in the ability to attend to the reality of these times so that we might see what useful action can be taken. At its best, restoration is a way to see opportunity within the grim crises that are unfolding; to find useful work to be done in service of life and truth; to tend the much-abused garden of our world back towards health and wholeness with careful and circumspect actions, always alert to the realisation that what we had dismissed as weeds were actually the first shoots of new growth.

– Dark Mountain Editors,
Spring 2020

Dark Mountain would not exist without the support and generosity of its readers. There are many ways to get involved with the project, but the simplest and most direct form of support you can offer is to become a subscriber. For more information, visit: dark-mountain.net/subscribe

ERIC NICHOLSON

No Longer

Darwin's frogs no longer leap in the shrinking wetlands of Chile
the Formosan clouded leopard no longer hunts in the mountains of Taiwan
the Sri Lankan spiny eel no longer swims in the rivers of Sri Lanka
the Eskimo curlew no longer calls over the snowy grasslands of Greenland
the Santa Cruz pupfish is extinct   to be confirmed
the western black rhinoceros no longer trundles across African plains
the angel shark no longer swims in the Black Sea   latest data 2023
the crescent nail-tailed wallaby no longer lopes across the Australian outback
the giant golden-crowned flying fox no longer gorges on figs in the forest
    of Panay
the spectacled cormorant no longer fishes in the polluted rivers or toxic lakes
    of Russia
the Labrador duck is extinct   dead as a dodo
the Javan lapwing no longer flaps its wings in Indonesian skies
the Tahiti sandpiper no longer plaintively pipes on the river banks of Tahiti
even our house sparrows   are in the shit

there's a sapient product of natural selection who
no longer harnesses wind-power or utilises solar energy
no longer holidays in the Bahamas or Thailand
no longer cultivates his own garden
no longer considers the categorical imperative
no longer gets the bullet train to work
no longer measures the rise in average temperature
no longer checks in at the inter-city-airport Terminal
no longer rushes home to watch the World Cup
no longer develops a military capability second to none
no longer speculates as to whether she is a brain-in-a-vat
no longer does the school run before nine o'clock
no longer views the Holocaust exhibit of discarded shoes
no longer speculates whether the table still exists if there is no one to see it
no longer does the night shift on the maternity ward
no longer prepares ingenious explosive devices
no longer validates cogito ergo sum
no longer orders 'seed potatoes' early from a first-rate suppliers in London
no longer tackles the problem of social isolation among the elderly
no longer checks in at the local gym or does press ups before breakfast
no longer sets a moral compass in line with the Golden Rule
no longer scans next year's seed catalogue for new variety perennials
no longer formulates any messages of reconciliation or peace
no longer takes the dog for a walk in the park
no longer asks if the 'free-will defence' is adequate to account for
the problem of evil
no longer speculates what it is like to be a bat
no longer puts flowers on the family headstone

ROB LEWIS

Walking to the Restoration

A few months ago, the word *restoration* took up residence in my mind and began setting roots there. In the manner of an oak in a field, it rose above the other words around it, kin to wider things, like the horizon and the Earth's turning. It was sure of itself, this word, spreading in a constellation of directions, commanding my thoughts, bearing the energy and authority of something whose time has come.

Perhaps what drew me is what it's not – new or technological. Restoration is no one's innovation. It's also not 'environment', a word I find problematic. If the aim of a word is to speak for its subject, to lend an appropriate feeling for it, environment fails. Try as it might, it can't reach beyond its political confines into the depths of the actual living world. Instead, it functions like an ideological marker, partitioning people onto one side or another of an increasingly dangerous divide. Perhaps it's the vacuum left in the wake of this unfortunate word that allows *restoration* to emerge so succinctly, to be the oak in the clearing.

The more I circled it, the more it revealed its universality. There is no end to what you can restore. In addition to land, you can restore health, trust, balance, justice, democracy, civility, vision: all of which seem broken today. You can restore a river and you can restore a Model T. A farmer distrustful of 'environmentalism' might welcome a conversation about restoring fertility to his or her soil. A building contractor may not think he has much in common with an 'environmentalist', but both might equally appreciate the craft in an old Victorian home and agree the building should be restored. With restoration, political identity becomes a little less predictive, its borders more porous.

It also has a bridge-like quality. You can imagine divergent peoples meeting at the middle of such an intention, approaching it from different directions but agreeing on its suitability, its rightness. It could sit as easily in a conservative conversation as a liberal one and, in today's fractured world, that is no small thing.

One day, while walking down a country road I made it a noun and capitalised it. I called it 'the Restoration', a coronation it accepted rather nobly, I thought. Now I felt myself apprehending not just a resonant phrase, but a potential human era, an organising principle capable of competing with capitalism itself, as though its natural successor. Is that too grandiose? A few feet overhead, a sharp-shinned hawk floated over, the scalloped dark and light design on the undersides of its wings clearly discernible. The soundlessness of the passage stopped me. Whether coincidence or not, I felt an affirmation. Nature approved, I decided, and kept walking.

*

That journey soon took a more practical turn when I came across a notice about the Global Earth Repair Conference taking place near where I live in the north-west corner of the US Pacific Northwest. The conference promised a four-day exploration into every imaginable aspect of restoration, and I signed up immediately.

Looking for a broad overview, The first sessions I attended were 'Earth Repair in India', delivered by Rajendra Singh – known as 'the water man of India' – and 'Earth Repair in Africa', by Precious Phiri.

Singh is credited with bringing water back to over a thousand villages and resurrecting numerous dried-up rivers throughout some of India's most desiccated landscapes. Though he started out doing medical work, he was challenged one day by an indigenous farmer who told him that if he really wanted to help the villagers he would bring them water. Then this farmer explained to him the old ways of harvesting the rains; ways largely undone by subsequent British colonial rule. The principle was simple: hold the rainfall on the land, not with industrial-scale dams, but small, traditional catchments called check dams, or *johads*. Once held, the water would drain down, recharging aquifers, feeding vegetation and calling back long lost weather patterns.

It worked, almost magically, as it had worked for centuries before the British imposed centralised engineering. Not only did the old methods restore land previously barren, they also prevented flooding, moderated droughts and cooled the local climate by a rather auspicious 2°C. In time, forgotten rivers began flowing again, and young people, who had fled the region, began returning. Villages revived, farming resumed, wildlife reappeared.

Phiri's presentation, 'Earth Repair in Africa', began like Singh's, with photos of cracked and barren landscapes. Then pictures of the miracle: chest-high pasture grass, wildlife browsing, children playing in a river. Like Singh, Phiri didn't bring new knowledge, imposed from outside, but instead restored something pre-existent which had been lost. In this case, it was the once-teeming herds of wildlife, ungulates such as zebra and wildebeest, which had fertilised and hoof-tilled the landscape for millennia. Phiri and her team, using grazing techniques pioneered by Zimbabwean ecologist Allan Savory, began moving cattle in patterns similar to the ancient herds, to which the land responded exuberantly, as though remembering itself. Forgotten shrubs and grasses appeared again, and, as in India, a local river once thought extinct started to flow.

Along with wildlife, human culture returned too. Cow herding had lost status against the advance of technology, coming to be considered work for high school dropouts. But as the land returned to health, more and more young people showed up, wanting to learn the trade.

I could have also attended 'Reforesting Scotland', 'Mycorrhizal Fungi and Jamaica', 'Wetland Restoration with Ranchers in Harney Basin, East Oregon', 'Agroforestry in the Pacific Northwest', 'Earth Repair after Hurricanes', 'Earth Repair in War-Torn Areas', and would probably have heard the same basic story: not only is the land renewed but so too are the people, and the relationship between them. But it was 'Ecosystem Restoration for Climate' that caught my attention. I'd brought a question with me, and I was hoping this panel might answer it. The question, or questions, went something like this: *If climate projections are modelled on a current baseline of ruined landscapes, biocidal farming and collapsing ecosystems, what would they predict on a planet that was healthy, or being restored to health? Doesn't the Earth have a say in this?*

Apparently, I wasn't the only one with questions. The room was packed and I found a place against the wall with about twenty others. A panel of eight presenters from various parts of the world had been pulled together; most Skyped in remotely.

Professor Millán M. Millán, who began his career as an aeronautical engineer (and who also happened to design the metal detectors we pass through at airports) got things started by referencing a 1971 MIT publication called *Inadvertent Climate Modification*. This early scientific treatise on climate change reflected what the modern climate narrative seems to have forgotten: that there is more to climate than the build-up of carbon gases. There is also a local and regional basis moderated by hydrologic cycles. In fact, the most significant driver of climate, both in terms of heating and cooling, by volume and weight, isn't CO_2 but H_2O, water. It affects climate in all its various phases: as a potent greenhouse gas, as heat-reflecting ice and cloud, through cooling by evaporation, amongst others. 'Back then,' he said, 'the idea was that there were two legs to the climate, one being carbon gases and the greenhouse effect, the other land use and hydrology, because whenever you alter land surface you immediately change critical hydrologic cycles, from very small-scale to very large.' And that profoundly affects climate.

This was news to me. In years of climate activism, I had never heard much about land use – urbanisation, industrial agriculture, deforestation and the like – or the hydrologic cycle. It was always about atmospheric carbon. Millán wasn't dismissing atmospheric carbon, it was just that for him the carbon that mattered most was the carbon in the soil and vegetation, for through them ran the prize – water.

'Water begets water, soil is the womb, and vegetation is the midwife', continued Millán. Apparently, when scientists go down the restoration road, they start talking like poets. Unlike the common perception that rain originates over large water bodies like lakes and oceans – which to some degree it does, depending on the location – it mostly develops *and regenerates itself* over living landscapes, via hydrologic cycles which are profoundly local, cycling through watersheds large and small. 'Clouds begin in the ground', he said, calling to mind what Singh and his indigenous guide accomplished in India. Through various, local means of holding water on land, they 'planted' future clouds in the ground and eventually 're-grew' lost rain patterns, cooling their local climate as they did so. Not surprisingly, in India they say, 'Water is climate, climate is water.'

Vegetation is the midwife because it delivers moisture from the soil to the atmosphere via transpiration, thus feeding the formation of clouds. Like this, plants help water propagate itself through soil, landscape and atmosphere, cooling all three on its journey. We've seen in India and Zimbabwe that rain can be convinced to return to an area it seems to have abandoned. Millán is now working to re-establish lost summer storms over arid regions of the Mediterranean, which in Roman times were wetlands. He hopes to accomplish this with the strategic planting of woodlands. Since rain there is now scarce, he must hold what little falls on the land as long as possible. The means for this is soil, but not just any kind will do. It has to be living soil, capable of creating what he called the 'soil sponge'.

Didi Pershouse, a soil sponge strategist, author and educator, described the soil sponge as 'the basic infrastructure that makes life on land possible.' She demonstrated with a plate heaped with dry flour. The flour represented the degraded soils of modern agriculture, heavily tilled and chemically sterilised. She poked holes in the bottom of a cup to simulate rain and 'rained' over the flour. The water slid off as if repelled, or carved deep gouges and ravines, before flooding the plate. What remained resembled a classically eroded landscape.

Then she did the same onto three slices of bread. The bread represented living soil, or soil 'leavened' with carbon-based microorganisms into a living, sponge-like matrix. This 'soil' absorbed nine times as much water as the flour, and the water that did drain through sank downward, seeping out of the bottom into what – in a natural system – would be an aquifer, getting filtered both physically and biologically along the way.

Then she gestured to the two plates, asking, 'In a dry climate, with infrequent rain and strong wind, which would you rather have? In a wet climate with heavy and frequent rain, which would you rather have? If you were a seed trying to grow, where would you rather make your home? If there were hazardous chemicals in the soil that you wanted to keep out of local rivers and streams, which would you want?' Another question one could ask: 'If you were trying to draw carbon out of the atmosphere, which would you need?'

The difference between these two soils is life, or, chemically speaking, carbon. One has it, the other doesn't. Or you could say, one has vegetation, the other doesn't. When plants pull carbon out of the air they essentially make themselves out of it, mixing it with mineral nutrients drawn up from the soil, making carbohydrates, or carbon sugars, which they then feed to the soil microbial community, down through their roots but also when they decompose into the ground. Like this, you could say, plants 'sweeten' the soil with carbon.

The equation is simple: SSC (sand, silt, clay) plus C (carbon) = soil sponge. The carbon in this equation comes as life: mycelia, fungi, bacteria, nematodes, earthworms, other soil microorganisms and the slimes and glues they exude. Only this mixture, fed by plants sipping carbon out of the air, can produce the soil sponge, of which she showed us a highly magnified photograph. You could see the individual mineral particles and clumped aggregates and, between them, translucent slimes and threads holding the particles both together *and* apart. This created spaces that Pershouse, who also tends toward the poetic, called 'cathedrals'. It is where the water is held, much like the air pockets in bread. This stored water feeds more vegetation, which draws down more carbon, while feeding the clouds more moisture to spread more life, and around and around it goes.

'It's a very, very elegant, natural system,' added Walter Jehne, a renowned Australian soil scientist and UN climate advisor. He referred to the soil sponge as the soil-carbon sponge, emphasising its carbon-sequestration capabilities. Like Millán and Pershouse, he took a broader view of carbon, presenting it as a necessary element in the cycle of life. Also like them, he didn't speak much in numbers, but the few he offered were illuminating. At present, 130 billion tonnes of atmospheric carbon are produced on the planet each year through various oxidative processes, such as forest fires, modern agricultural practices and the burning of fossil fuels. However, 120 billion of those tonnes are then re-absorbed by the various processes of life and sequestered in soil, plants and animals. It's this second number that turns the lens, bringing the nature of our present crisis into clearer view. This is a crisis of balance – not just of chemicals in the atmosphere, but in the overall functioning of life on Earth. The planet, if allowed, and even helped, to flourish, can cool itself naturally, absorbing carbon along the way. If we weren't busy paving, tilling and poisoning its living membrane of soil, it would be turning the excess carbon in the atmospheric into more life.

Here Jehne reminded us that while sequestering carbon is important and necessary, we need to go beyond that and begin to cool the planet. This has become increasingly important as the oceans, which have been steadily absorbing our excess heat, are now full, and will begin throwing heat back out, with future land-based warming baked into the proverbial cake. Cooling the planet may sound like a mammoth undertaking, but according to Jehne, it is quite doable. He estimates that restoring one per cent of the planet's natural cooling capacity through restored hydrologic cycles would offset the heating effects of current anthropogenic carbon gases. At two per cent we are cooling down.

Pershouse provided a visual explanation, showing a fence-line photo of barren, rocky soil next to a section of land restored to rangeland grasses and shrubs, both under the same blazing sun. She then asked us to imagine standing on one side, and then the other, in bare feet. Not only would our feet feel cooler on the grassy side, but so would our heads. The air temperature above vegetated landscapes is cooler than that over bare soil or pavement by as much 11.6°C.

We started burning life off this planet long ago, Jehne explained. Through deforestation, the draining of marshes and exhaustive agricultural practices, we've not only been heating the Earth, we've been desiccating it, with a trail of over 20 self-made deserts left in our wake. They reach around the globe on virtually every continent, not to mention the once heavily forested Middle East. The obvious opportunity – and this spoke directly to my question – is in bringing all those places back to life, with all the extra carbon in the atmosphere helping to feed the growth, and all that growth helping to cool the atmosphere. Restore soil and nature does the rest. As though speaking in the voice of the planet, he said, 'I can run a monsoon, I can re-green continents.'

*

The Q&A session at the end was dominated by questions like 'why isn't anybody talking about this?' It was as though we found ourselves standing in a new conceptual geography. Zach Weiss, who runs an ecological restoration firm, laid out this new terrain. Carbon, he pointed out, is invisible, and its cycling is so slow we can never see the results of our work with it. With water, though, the results are almost immediate, occurring within a single rainy season. And when people witness the rebirth of their landscapes, they no longer need convincing, he said. 'They come running.'

Charles Eisenstein, the philosopher on the panel and author of *Climate: A New Story*, flipped the narrative completely, pointing out that when he googled the term 'effect of biodiversity on climate', the results always came back for the opposite request: the effect of climate on biodiversity. He encountered the same with soil erosion. He was researching what he called his 'living Earth hypothesis', that the climate is a product of a living biosphere, and discovered how skewed we are towards seeing it the other way around. He brought up the classic image of the 'cracked field'. We've all seen versions of it alongside articles about climate change. The image implies that global warming, or anthropogenic carbon gases, caused the field to dry and crack, when actually abusive land use practices likely did that by ruining regional hydrologic cycles. The same is true of most flooding, where the soil sponge has been destroyed and the land can't hold and store the rain when it falls. And as Millán pointed out, our forests are drying out mostly because of damaged hydrologic flows. 'I think,' said Eisenstein, 'we are just beginning to understand how this planet actually works, and the role of life in maintaining climate.'

The role of life in maintaining climate. I hadn't before considered the notion, but felt its validity immediately, and it came as a relief. For years I've watched the climate narrative gradually push the non-human sphere to the side and place us, our technological innovations and economic interests, at the centre. We've been peering skyward for invisible carbon, fixating on abstract numbers, predicting far futures based on ice cores from deep pasts, all the while somewhat blind to the saws, roads, bulldozers and industrial farms busily dismembering the living remnants of what ultimately creates and maintains the climate. Now we turn to face a scale of ecological collapse we scarcely possess the vocabulary to describe.

How ironic, and even mysterious, that it's the places we've most injured that now look back with such profound capacity to help us. There is forgiveness in that, a generosity that is nearly unaccountable, and yet it's here, all around us, vibrant with potential. Somewhere during the discussion, the host joked about the need for a new bumper-sticker phrase: 'Make Carbon Life Again'.

*

I had more than enough for my brain to process at this point, but as I was to find out at the closing ceremony, the restoration story isn't to be fully comprehended with the mind alone.

We had gathered in a large circle, and an elder of the Rogue River People, Grandmother Agnes Baker-Pilgrim, invited us to drop from the intellectual mind to the heart-mind, that place from which we truly meet the world and each other. A Lakota man – who 'comes from a place also surrounded by seas; seas of grass' – spoke of flying over the Arctic and seeing vast cracks in the ice below him, and the deep grief the sight produced in him. He then sang a song, an old song, and you could hear the sadness in it. It stretched all the way back to the days of invasion and massacre, an ancient grief singing through a present one.

Another elder, a white elder, slowly tapping a drum, invoked the place itself: the giant madronas branching overhead, the grass and soil beneath our feet, the surrounding hills and ocean-fed breeze. The sun was warm on our faces. Birds sang into the silence. I rarely tear up, especially in public, but all the grief I'd been holding for this Earth suddenly started to move. I felt my chest beginning to shake, and, though surprised, I welcomed it, and let my eyes brim. Water again, salt water, like the water in the ocean so near I could smell it.

*

A few weeks have passed since I returned home, and I realise I no longer see the climate the same. Or perhaps more accurately, I've actually begun to *see* the climate, in the soils, the waters, in the flows and cycles of life. Before, it was always a featureless abstraction. I imagined a kind of vast atmospheric bubble, which one could presumably stick a thermometer into for a temperature reading. But I've since learned global temperatures are actually averages of thousands of individual local readings, each from specific landscapes. One is out my window, another yours.

Look around. Imagine seeing, say, 20 miles in all directions. How much of the land is covered in concrete, gathering heat? How much is laid out as monocrop, vast tracks of chemically sterilised soil, bare much of the year, sequestering and transpiring nothing? If there is grassland, how much is wrongly grazed? If there are mountains, how desiccated are they from not receiving moisture from the lowlands, which have been crippled of their hydrologic function, dammed at their own headwaters?

Looking out my window I see a clouded fragment of the Salish Sea, the inland waters between the US and Canada. Seen from overhead it resembles a bodily organ, spreading lung-like, north and south into inland bays fed by a densely veinous tapestry of streams and rivers. There its apex predators, the Southern Resident orcas, are starving. They're not starving because of carbon in the air, but because we've dammed the rivers that once fed them massive runs of salmon. We can decarbonise the entire global economy and they will still likely slip into extinction. So it is with so many creatures and remnant ecosystems. In many ways, the last thing they need is for us to embark on a new industrial revolution, however green it proposes to be. What they need from us is far more obvious and immediate – to repair the damage we've already done. And then join in the renewal.

Here is the nexus, the spark point. It's where the human hand and the living Earth, our intention and the regenerative genius of life, meet. Magic happens here, and points to the first thing we need to restore – our relationship with the rest of life. We are human, after all, as in *humus* – of the Earth – and so also 'humility'; which I would offer as the operative demeanour of the Restoration: to humbly restore our place as humans among, not over, the greater life community. If we could accomplish that simple grace, we would find ourselves hitched to the will of the planet itself, on the side of the very forces that can save us. Our human ship, tossing about in self-made gales, might find a compass point, a common destination by which to reach calmer waters. The Restoration could be just that at first, a directional bearing.

Where is it pointing? It's pointing here, where we've always been, toward vast landscapes hungry for life again, lost rivers ready to flow again. Here soils are building, not washing away, and restored farmlands are calling displaced peoples back home. Here, no miracle technologies come to save us, and the tech billionaires are surprised to find they're no longer at the centre of the story. The Earth has taken their place, and each day it grows back a little more skin, breathes a little more cooling water, lends a little more credence to the idea of hope.

Does this mean we can go on indiscriminately burning carbon? Of course not. Carbon gases do trap heat, frustrating the planet's already degraded ability to cool itself. They're also turning the oceans to vinegar. And they remain in the atmosphere for as long as centuries, subjecting all life to planetary changes of geologic scale, an epically irresponsible thing to do.

But there are two legs to the climate – CO_2 and H_2O. We can think of the carbon-gases leg as the pushing-off leg, the one that says *no*: to our reliance on fossil fuels, to the pipelines, the drilling, the concentrated greed, the asthmatic kids. Stepping forward is the land use and hydrology leg, saying *yes*: to rebuilding soils, repairing rivers, rehydrating forests, reviving land-based economies, restoring human respect for the Earth and each other. Together they provide a stride we can maintain for the long haul, twin determinations with a common confidence, on the Earth and toward life.

JENNIFER CASE

Animals on the Eve of Extinction

Once upon a time, I read my daughter a bedtime story in which dinosaurs and humans coexisted, living together sustainably in cities as well as on farms. They grew crops together, raised young together, and made decisions together. They ate only what they needed and carried no weapons. When they greeted each other and said their goodbyes, they used the phrase, 'Breathe deep, seek peace.'

For a month each evening, following our reading, my daughter nestled into her pillow, along with 16 plastic dinosaurs and one plush brachiosaurus, and asked if what happened to the dinosaurs would happen to us. 'Will we go extinct?'

For a month each evening, I paused and said, 'Maybe. Eventually. But you don't need to worry about that.' I kissed her forehead and told her goodnight, but when I left the room I was still thinking about dinosaurs. I was a mother grazing with my children in a wide, open pasture, and when I suddenly looked up, I saw the meteors fall.

EMPEROR PENGUIN · RINGED SEAL · ARCTIC FOX · BELUGA WHALE · ORANGE CLOWNFISH · KOALA BEAR · LEATHERBACK TURTLE · FLAMINGO · WOLVERINE · MUSK OX · POLAR BEAR · HAWAIIAN HONEYCREEPER · BAIRD'S SANDPIPER · IVORY GULL · WESTERN GLACIER STONEFLY · TUFTED PUFFIN

In my mid-20s, I began to desire a child. And so I had a child. She was born in a hospital in the middle of December, and she is beautiful, and every day, even when her burgeoning stubbornness forces me to count to ten in my head, her beauty astonishes me. The sharp cut of her jaw. The spark in her eyes. The moles, appearing in greater and greater quantities on her body. She has a zoo of imaginary pets, and she is starting to ask questions about death, and she tells me before bed that she thinks we should all – my husband, me, her and her baby brother – die together, at the same time, so that we won't be alone. In those moments, when her face opens, asking for something I cannot give, a fear the size of her pupils sears into my chest: that the pain she will experience in her future will not be the pain of a life – of a first love, of love lost, of grief for dying relatives – but a grief so much larger. Lost worlds. Lost lands. Lost species. Lost nations. As the Earth destabilises, as the climate destabilises, what will her culture become? What will life become? When we are focused so much on adapting, on reacting to the next thing, on wars over resources, what room will there be for joy?

SINAI BATON BLUE · PLICATE ROCKSNAIL · MEKONG GIANT CATFISH · PHILIPPINE CROCODILE · RESPLENDENT SHRUBFROG · JAVAN RHINOCEROS · PYGMY HOG · VARIEGATED SPIDER MONKEY · HAINAN GIBBON · OSGOOD'S ETHIOPIAN TOAD · TOYAMA'S GROUND GECKO · MARBLED GECKO

These of course are anxious thoughts. They are the thoughts of someone occasionally on the brink of despair. The thoughts of a mother, a parent, late at night. Someone trying to wrest control over an uncontrollable future. And surely, I think, my fears are no different than anyone's when the world tips toward instability. During the Vietnam War, didn't parents fear for their sons? In Europe and Asia, on the eve of World War II, didn't families fear for their children? In Sudan and El Salvador, now, doesn't the bringing of life into the world carry with it a risk that surpasses the risks of childbirth itself? Only in this case, the threat isn't nations, or even continents. It covers the planet.

MAGDALENA RIVER TURTLE · TITICACA WATER FROG · BANAT GRASSHOPPER · PLOUGHSHARE TORTOISE · MONGOOSE LEMUR · GOLDEN BAMBOO LEMUR · ADRIATIC STURGEON · RICORD'S ROCK IGUANA · GREAT PALAU TREE SNAIL · BLACK-BREASTED PUFFLEG · GLAUCOUS MACAW · GASTLETON'S FLIGHTLESS KATYDID · PARNASSOS GREEK BUSH-CRICKET · NORTHERN MOSS FROG

Sometimes, out of necessity, I want to turn it all off. I want to wake up, bring my children to their respective daycares, teach my students how to write, pick up my children, boil water for pasta and toss a green salad.

Eat at the table. Play evening games and then go on a walk. Tuck them in with a bedtime story and a sippy cup of water. I want those small routines, the comfort of them, to be everything. I want to not have to think about anything else. Not: what will this world look like in 30, 40, 50 years. Not to know that, by then, 50% of the species on the Earth right now will be lost.

WHITE-HEADED VULTURE · HOODED VULTURE · SLENDER-BILLED CURLEW · CALIFORNIA CONDOR · RAPA FRUIT-DOVE · SOCIABLE LAPWING · BLUE-EYED GROUND-DOVE · LESSER ANTILLEAN IGUANA · OKINAWA WOODPECKER · TAPANULI ORANGUTAN · EASTERN GORILLA · HIMALAYAN QUAIL

In my son's first year, the US government tried to repeal the Endangered Species Act. The Clean Air Act. The Clean Water Act. The White House reduced Bears Ears National Monument by 85 percent. They changed the image on the Bureau of Labor Resources' website from a family hiking to a wall of coal. They filled the cabinet with corporations. They slashed the budget of the Environmental Protection Agency.

On the day of the election, when I was nine months pregnant with my son, I drove to work in Arkansas. The Lawn of Peace Lutheran Church, next to a designated polling place, was slathered with Trump signs.

TRANSYLVANIAN PLUMP GRASSHOPPER · CANTERBURY KNOBBLED WEEVIL · THREE FORKS SPRINGSNAIL · BAMBOO LEMUR · BLACK-AND-WHITE RUFFED LEMUR · LIVINGSTON'S FLYING FOX · CORAL PINK SAND DUNES TIGER BEETLE · MCCORD'S BOX TURTLE · PAINTED TERRAPIN · HOODED GREBE

In downtown Little Rock, my daughter runs across the benches of the Central Arkansas Nature Center, her fingers tracing the long line of aquariums. 'Look, that one has teeth!' she says of the albino gar, and her joy is great.

Watching her watch the fish, I can't help but imagine the roles reversed. Some alien creature is watching us, a teeming, frothing force of humans, specimens in a vast glass world, and we are coupling. Reproducing.

Eating. Desecrating. Taking from the soil. Taking over resources. Like termites, only worse. Or maybe just like termites, only with more tools. Some of us have a god and believe we will be saved. Some of us do not. And it doesn't really matter, but I am just one of them. One specimen, who birthed two more specimens, and from above I move through the routines in my life, and the aliens know what is coming, know the brink my species is bringing itself to, will watch the impending environmental apocalypse, which will not be the end of all life – the Earth will remain – but will certainly be the end of a great deal of life, and perhaps even the end of our own.

IBERIAN GREY BUSH-CRICKET · HAWAIIAN CROW · LONG-BILLED FOREST-WARBLER · RED-FRONTED MACAW · NEW CALEDONIAN LORIKEET · YELLOW-BREASTED BUNTING · ORANGE-BELLIED PARROT · CELEBES CRESTED MACAQUE · BLEEDING TOAD · LA GOMERA GIANT LIZARD · CUBAN CROCODILE

Yesterday, it stormed. The sirens went off at 1pm. I was at work. My children both at school. I imagined my son's daycare teacher rolling all their small cribs against the safest wall in the infant room. I imagined my daughter's preschool, the teachers guiding the students to all make 'tents' with their hands beneath the tables. The rain poured down, horizontal. The sky turned green and black. I ached for my children.

That evening, after safely picking my children up, my daughter insisted on a rain walk. She put on her red rain boots and pulled out her children's umbrella. She hopped from foot to foot while I zipped my sweatshirt. Once outside, I lifted my face to the hazy, grey sky, and the wind puffed us with its humid breath, and my daughter sloshed through the gutters, the curbs, kicking and skipping through puddles, pointing with delight whenever she saw an even bigger puddle ahead. The neighbours smiled at her and waved – her pleasure in puddles a simple delight for us all – and we slowly made our way halfway around the block. But then the wind picked up, and the sky began to spritz a colder, stinging rain. My daughter's eyes widened. When a gust caught her umbrella, it pulled her 40-pound body backwards. 'Let's go back inside. Quick. The wind will take us away,' she said. Nothing I could say would ensure her she was safe.

WHITE-BELLIED HERON · MINI BLUE BEE SHRIMP · RED ORCHID BEE · SMALLTOOTH SAWFISH · BLACK RHINOCEROS · PYGMY THREE-TOED SLOTH · LEAF-SCALED SEA SNAKE · EUROPEAN MINK · FINE STAINED-GLASS LEAFHOPPER · SAN JOSE BUSH RABBIT · SOCORRO DOVE · BAWEAN DEER · IVORY-BILLED WOODPECKER · PURPLE-WINGED GROUND-DOVE · GOLDEN-EYED STICK INSECT · ANGELSHARK

I come from a culture that has shortened the Mississippi River by 150 miles, and birth and labour to 24 hours. A culture that in its quest for wealth and convenience has mined the mountains and eradicated the prairie and plundered the topsoil until conventional farmers can no longer grow crops without dousing the ground with fertiliser made from oil. A culture that has spewed CO_2 into the atmosphere at a rate faster than during previous great extinctions and then hid the facts to protect corporate wealth.

RED-THROATED LORIKEET · KAKAPO · BORNEAN ORANGUTAN · GIANT IBIS · SIBERIAN CRANE · JEYPORE GROUND GECKO · INDOCHINESE BOX TURTLE · BUTTERFLY SPLITFIN · YELLOW-SPOTTED TREE FROG · TENERIFE SPECKLED LIZARD · RED-BELLY TOAD · VANCOUVER ISLAND MARMOT · NASSAU GROUPER

I begin to plant a native prairie in our backyard. I bring my children to a native plant nursery, where we pick out tickseed, switchgrass and big bluestem. I sign us up for a CSA (Community Supported Agriculture) and brainstorm ways to minimise our use of cars. On weekends, we go to local parks where my daughter gazes at tadpoles and my son digs his hands in the sand.

All the while, I'm aware that parents have a psychological need to believe they can keep their children safe, and that climate change threatens that illusion.

I'm aware that the greatest reduction to a family's carbon footprint is to have fewer children.

I'm aware that I decided to have one child, but unintentionally had a second.

I'm aware that there are no guarantees for my children.

JENNIFER CASE

PHILIPPINE EAGLE · NEW CALEDONIAN OWLET-NIGHTJAR · GALAPAGOS PETREL · TRUE WEEVIL · GREAT INDIAN BUSTARD · YELLOW GOLDFLAKE · PEACOCK TARANTULA · DEVIL'S HOLE PUPFISH · MYANMAR SNUB-NOSED MONKEY · BLACK CRESTED GIBBON · POLYNESIAN TREE SNAIL · STELLATE STURGEON

In the late days of my pregnancy and the early days of my son's life, I sometimes could not watch the news. I couldn't bear to see what was happening. Or rather, what was happening had the power to make me lose hope. To stare at his small body – his belly button still weeping because the bit of tissue from the umbilical cord had not fully died – and feel so fully that our country was headed in the wrong direction. What was I to do? I nursed my infant. I ate bowls full of fruit. I took baths in herbs. I let my body heal. I lay down in the afternoon when others were around to watch my son. I went on walks outside. I carried him to the porch. I watched him squint in the sun. I opened the shades of our home. I snapped the edges of his cloth diapers. I pressed my forehead against the cool window of the door at night, when we were both awake, in need of something to drink.

SPENGLER'S FRESHWATER MUSSEL · WHITE-TIPPED GRASSHOPPER · SOUTHERN EVEN-FINGERED GECKO · ROSE'S MOUNTAIN TOADLET · RED-CRESTED TREE RAT · RIVERINE RABBIT · SIBILLINI MOUNTAIN GRASSHOPPER · LITTLE GLAND FROG · WHITE-TIPPED GRASSHOPPER · GREEN SAWFISH · RED WOLF

It is despair. It is hope. It is a long O. An om. A prayer. A praising. Sometimes a pleading. Sometimes nothing at all but my steps moving forward. One day at a time. One waking at a time. One night at a time. Life, right now, with small children, when climate change looms large, and our country is not doing enough about it, is my hands open, asking. My hands on tree trunks. On babies' bodies. On grass. On laundry. On the washcloth as I wash bottles and the valves of my breast pump. On student papers. On this keyboard, now. My hands, reaching out, saying sorry, and please, saying can't we be tender? Compassionate? Can't we break through something with our elbows? Can't we heave our bodies against what is stopping us from changing our mindsets, our ideologies? Can't we get past these simple comforts? Can't we give up something so that they, in the future, will have something too? I know what fear is, and I know how hard it is to think about changing our lives, and I know we all feel small sometimes, and inconsequential, and maybe we are, but we are here. We are bodies on this Earth.

NORTHERN HAIRY-NOSED WOMBAT · STRIPED GEKKO · EUROPEAN EEL · ORNATE GROUND SNAKE · GREEK RED DAMSEL · SPRING PYGMY SUNFISH · SOUTHERN BLUEFIN TUNA · GIANT CARP · PERUVIAN YELLOW-TAILED WOOLLY MONKEY · BACTRIAN CAMEL · SAPPHIRE-BELLIED HUMMINGBIRD · ADDAX

On a vast plain near the end of the Cretaceous period, a mother ceratopsian grazes with her child, lowering her frilled and horned head to the ferns and the cycads. The volcanoes have already been rumpling, spewing CO_2 into the air. The wind makes the grasses thrum and whistles through her spines. She tenses, alert, plucking thin leaves with her beak. What is it she's thinking? When she suddenly looks up and sees the meteors fall?

I lean my head against her flank and feel kinship.

BLONDE CAPUCHIN · CAVE GROUND-BEETLE · VIETNAMESE POND TURTLE · ESPAÑOLA GIANT TORTOISE · GIANT MOUNTAIN LOBELIA · SIERRA NEVADA BLUE · GREATER VIRGIN ISLANDS SKINK · WHITE LEMUROID RINGTAIL POSSUM · STAGHORN CORAL · SHENANDOAH SALAMANDER · WHOOPING CRANE · BLACK-FOOTED ALBATROSS · BICKNELL'S THRUSH · AMERICAN PIKA · HAWKSBILL SEA TURTLE · RUSTY PATCHED BUMBLE BEE · MONARCH BUTTERFLY · SOCKEYE SALMON · RED-CROWNED ROOFED TURTLE

A species goes extinct. A civilisation ends. Both are the uncomfortable if constant nature of life. And although I know I need to accept this – that everything dies, and humankind will eventually, too – the part of me that holds my children still needs to carve hope in the future. Hope in sacredness and responsibility and ecological kinship. Hope in bodies and community and connectedness and land.

BRAZILIAN MERGANSER · SUN STRIPE SHRIMP · CADDO CHIMNEY GRAYFISH · APPALACHIAN ELKTOE · ADELIE PENGUIN · CORPULENT HORNSNAIL · ATLANTIC RUBBER FROG · BLACK SOFTSHELL TURTLE · HOODED VULTURE · SLENDER-BILLED CURLEW · COMMON SKATE · SCIMITAR-HORNED ORYX · AFRICAN WILD ASS · SAHARA KILLIFISH · ATLANTIC HUMPBACK DOLPHIN · DAMA GAZELLE

In the backyard, cantaloupe sprout from our compost and I let them sprawl across the lawn. I breathe in air made of atoms that have circulated for eons, atoms also inhaled by crustaceans and brachiopods. I lower my head to the sweaty scalps of my children. Each of us animals on the eve of an extinction. Each of us alive to what we are becoming.

CATE CHAPMAN

Lamping

I dreamed of lamping.
A man whose face I can't remember shot rabbits with an air rifle,
and their small bodies fell in the wet dark grass.
They lay there quite distinctly, warm fur slowly cooling,
wind-trembled and empty of quick breath.
A nameless brown-white dog sniffed and harried with its wide cruel head,
but ultimately let them lie there, unmolested.
I don't know why I dreamed of death.
Perhaps because love is a brutal thing,
holding the tender heart of another, breathless
with extraordinary care, in wet red hands;
offering the precious centre of ourselves up, bravely,
in a terror of trust and joy.

MONIQUE BESTEN

Daydreams for Masanobu Fukuoka

There is no big or small on the earth,
no fast or slow in the blue sky.
– Masanobu Fukuoka

In June 2019 I was invited to spend a month at CACiS, a centre for contemporary art and sustainability in Catalonia, Spain, to research and develop new work inspired by the thinking of natural farmer and philosopher Masanobu Fukuoka.

A week had passed. I hadn't done anything. I sat on the roof of the dry stone wall building with the ancient limestone ovens at its heart, taking in the views. I followed the river. I wandered around in the forest. I discovered where the bees made their honey. I listened to the frogs, at their loudest just after the evening had fallen. I observed insects, watched birds and bats fly, sat inside the old round ovens, all three of them, looking down at the bottom at the plants growing, the stones not moving, the snails sleeping. Looking up, at the sky transformed into a blue circle, clouds passing, casting shadows.

I had come here with a lot of plans but on the first day I let go of them. They would come back if they made sense here. In the next weeks or next year or somewhere in the far future. Like seeds carried in the wind. Landing and sprouting, growing and flowering, or simply vanishing. But even when disappearing, they would still become part of the soil and nurture it.

Doing nothing isn't as easy as it sounds. And it doesn't really mean doing nothing. You only do nothing when you are dead. Until then, at least, you breathe. Your blood flows through your veins. Your hair grows. You shed your skin. You see, you hear, you smell. You think. You dream. You empty your mind and you fill it up again. You make space. And when the space is there, things happen.

Daydreams in my hands, Catalonia, Spain

One of my favourite lines from the book *The One-Straw Revolution* is 'The best planning is no planning.' This doesn't mean to just sit back and refrain from taking any action. It means creating the right conditions for things to come into being. For the world to unfold. Its author, Masanobu Fukuoka, was a farmer who trained as a microbiologist and plant pathologist. He worked at the Agricultural Customs Office in Yokohama, enjoying his laboratory work, until at the age of 25 a life-changing experience made him decide to abandon science and city life. He almost died after being struck with acute pneumonia and when he came out of hospital, still recovering physically and mentally from being face-to-face with death, he wandered aimlessly through the hills. One night, after many hours of rambling, he collapsed at the foot of a tree overlooking the harbour, drifting in and out of sleep as dawn approached. The cry of a night heron woke him up and with the disappearance of the morning mist, his head became clear. He looked around in joyful amazement and thought: 'There is really nothing at all'. Shortly after he returned to his father's farm to work with nature in a different way.

Mr. Fukuoka's way was to let nature decide what was the right thing to do instead of trying to control it and intervene. The first thing he did when he returned to the land where he grew up was to stop pruning the citrus trees. The next year most of the trees died. But instead of seeing this as a failure, he realised he had learned something important. If trees or plants have been controlled by people, you cannot then just abandon them and expect them to thrive. It needed more than he had realised. More time and observation. By coincidence he discovered some rice plants in an old field which had been unused and unploughed for a long time. In between the grasses and weeds he noticed healthy rice seedlings. The 'normal' way to grow rice is to plough the land in early spring, then sow the seeds and flood the fields. It is a great deal of work. Farmers have been growing rice like that for centuries so of course people believed there was no other way of working.

But Mr. Fukuoka decided to stop flooding his rice fields, he planted a specific mix of weeds to keep others down and allow the rice he would sow in autumn – when it would naturally fall to the ground – to grow through. This also made it possible to grow a different crop in autumn. The straw of the winter grain could be left on the fields, where it became perfect mulch for the rice and the rice straw became mulch for the winter grain. It made perfect sense and it was far less labour intensive.

His yields were high. Not in the beginning, when his efforts – or staying away from specific efforts – failed. But once he had learned what not to do they slowly increased. And as time passed, he could compete with even the most productive farms in Japan. Still his neighbours looked at him with suspicion as people always do when you do things differently.

After a week I took action. I started collecting the seeds from as many plants as possible. I tried to identify them as well but sometimes it was hard. I knew that the amount of different plant species on even a square metre could be vast but just sitting down on the ground and looking at all the different plants around my feet, big ones, small ones, tiny ones, overwhelmed me. The reason for wanting to name them, to make a list, was not entirely clear to me: 'Just in case,' I thought. But in case of what? In case I had to prove that I indeed collected 100, 200, 500 different kinds of seeds? To prove the great variety present here? And prove it to whom?

One day I worked on a different plan. It involved walking a shape in the meadow in front of the limestone ovens. It was important that the amount of steps that were needed to walk it again and again was exact, so I took my tape measure and marked the corner points with some big rocks in order to know where I had to turn. When it was all set and I turned around and let my gaze wander over the landscape, Trufa the dog was there suddenly. One of her favourite pastimes was to pick up rocks and carry them around. She had one in her mouth and wanted to play. I looked at the rectangular parcourse I had set up, saw that a stone was missing, cursed, took it from her, measured again, and put it back where it should be, but in the meantime Trufa had taken another one already and this continued for a while until I gave up and took her for a walk, or she took me for a walk. When we reached the river, she dropped the rock. We looked at our shadows in the moving water. At the frogs leaping. The tiny larvae swimming. The dragonflies mating.

Masanabo Fukuoka once wrote:

> I do not particularly like the word 'work'. Human beings are the only animals who have to work. Other animals make their livings by living, but people work like crazy, thinking that they have to in order to stay alive. The bigger the job, the greater the challenge, the

> more wonderful they think it is. It would be good to give up that way of thinking and live an easy, comfortable life with plenty of free time.

Although Natural Farming is also called 'no-till' or 'do-nothing farming', it doesn't mean you can just sit back and relax. It means questioning yourself. It means thinking about what *not* to do. It means staying away from chemicals, fertilisers, even compost. Doing as little as possible with a maximum result, so there is a good supply of healthy food and time to enjoy life. In the Japanese countryside you can still find poems written by farmers on old walls and stone bridges but in modern agriculture there is hardly any time for a farmer to make music or read a book. It is no different in the Western World.

In Mr. Fukuoka's orchards, trees grew alongside vegetables and weeds. He would randomly spread different seeds around, not thinking about what was the best place for each seed to develop into a plant but being convinced that nature would know best what would grow where. To grow plants on a bigger scale, such as rice, barley, vegetables, he made clay seed balls. The seeds were protected by a layer of clay, so that animals wouldn't eat them, and nutrients were added. After successfully reviving this old technique he started dreaming about ways to regreen the desert in the same way. The clay balls should contain seeds of more than one hundred varieties – trees, fruit trees, shrubs, vegetables, grains, useful fungi – and could be broadcast from aeroplanes to revegetate large areas.

After his book *The One-Straw Revolution* became a success he started to travel the world to talk with farmers, policy makers and politicians about sustainable farming methods and fighting desertification. He carried his art supplies everywhere he went during his travels. He sometimes drew to explain his philosophies, always combining them with words and poetry, Japanese symbols that look like drawings in themselves. Usually they depicted anonymous people as representatives of humankind. However once, at an international permaculture conference, he shared a platform with Bill Mollison, co-creator of permaculture, and Wes Jackson, founder of the Land Institute in Kansas, giving a talk that intended to find common ground from three distinctive viewpoints. Lacking the words he drew the three of them: a picture of Don Quixote's donkey with a blind Bill and a deaf Wes riding backwards while he himself was hanging desperately from the donkey's swishing tail. Three Don Quixotes, trying to return to nature, trying to stop the donkey from

rushing wildly toward the brink of disaster. When the audience asked what was going to happen he drew President Reagan sitting comfortably on the donkey's back facing frontward, dangling a carrot in front of the donkey's nose.

The farmer-philosopher didn't believe in religious practices, meditation, yoga, or required reading. He didn't believe in books, not even in his own. 'I think people would be better off without words altogether,' he wrote in one of them. He didn't see any purpose in modern science, apart from showing how small human knowledge really is. His daily farming was his spiritual practice. He considered nature as sacred and impossible to understand. The key was not trying to understand it but just being in it. Being it. Few people are capable of this, he noted. Only those 'who have the heart and mind of a child' and lack the obstructive blocks of desire, philosophy or religion.

In the daytime I kept collecting seeds. I made ink from oak galls and plant parts. At night I watched the stars. Although I had a comfortable apartment, I sometimes slept in one of the restored dry stone wall huts in one of the neighbouring fields. Those huts, still existing everywhere in the Catalan countryside, were built when people started clearing the land in order to use it to grow crops. The big stones in the soil were turned into simple structures, which were used afterwards by farmers and shepherds. These days they're not in use anymore, they are only a reminder of life in past centuries. You get a glimpse of it sometimes when you wake up inside in the middle of the night in complete darkness, embraced by the same old stones that kept those farmers and shepherds safe and dry.

In the stone quarry behind the limestone ovens, where big rocks were once extracted to be turned into calcium, now plants were growing sparsely. The ground was dry. It was one of my favourite places. I felt at home there, sitting on a rock in the middle of the open space or high up on the wall to catch the last rays of sunlight in the early evening. I started walking lines in the middle of the quarry. In squares. The exact ground plan of my apartment in the city where I lived, Barcelona, 75 kilometres away. I walked it again and again, my steps forming lines in the hard soil; I walked it 100 times a day sometimes, not thinking too much. I kept the first principle of Natural Farming in the back of my head: no cultivation, no ploughing or turning of the soil because the earth knows best how to stay in good shape. Plant and tree roots penetrate the soil. Microorganisms and animals work on it in their own ways.

Sometimes I wondered if what I was doing was in line with the first principle. I thought that if I were to walk the same path again and again, the soil would open up and be a less hostile environment for the flower seeds I was planning to sow: *Cosmos bipinnatus* 'Daydream'. I imagined them growing side to side in the lines I had walked, so that in a few months walls made out of flowers would copy the stone walls of my city apartment and you would be able to walk from room to room here in the same way as you could in my other home. But was I disturbing the soil by my actions or was I just an artist doing what an artist does? Like a worm does what a worm does? Was I overthinking after all?

I remembered what Larry Korn observed in his book about Fukuoka's work, *One-Straw Revolutionary:* 'In the West we believe that there is some permanent identity inside of us. This sense of self is most closely associated with our mental process – our rational, analytical faculties. That is summed up in Descartes' celebrated "I think, therefore I am," sometimes translated as "I am thinking, therefore I exist." But it is precisely this assumption that alienates us from the world.' I switched off my thinking and continued in my own way. I walk, therefore I am.

When I finally finished walking and distributed the seeds it was the end of June and temperatures were close to 40 degrees. I waited for a day when an evening storm was forecast so the seeds would have some help. I sowed them in the morning but I hadn't taken the ants into account. When I came back to the corner where I had started dropping the seeds I saw a long line of them, following the lines I had walked, all carrying a seed in their front legs, on their way to their nest that was situated right in the middle of what represented my bedroom.

I stored the seeds I had been collecting from all the different plants growing in the CACiS area in paper boxes so they could dry and be turned into seed balls after the winter, with water from the river and clay from the river banks, and then be spread in vacant lots in cities, every clay ball containing the full potential of the beauty and serenity of the place where I had been daydreaming for a month.

Then I walked home, back to Barcelona, through mountains and villages, 75 kilometres, following winding roads, sleeping under the open sky, leaving a trail of Cosmos Daydream seeds behind me When you walk, time doesn't exist. Not if you don't have to be somewhere at a certain time. First it slows down and then it disappears all together. Mr. Fukuoka believed that time is only what is present, an ever-changing

continuum of the present moment with the past and the future embedded within it. One of the reasons why Natural Farming hasn't been applied more widely is because it is a slow process. It asks for a leap of faith. And since it is hard to do it on a big scale, it can only have a big impact when many people not only believe in it but put it into practice. It seems that the idea to regenerate dry areas by distributing clay seed balls by planes has been embraced, although not to the extent that it makes a big enough difference. In Asia experiments are being done with drones as well. You could question whether this is a proper way to reconnect with nature but it is no different from what Mr. Fukuoka concluded after his fruit trees died when he stopped pruning them. Before you can recreate the proper balance that has been destroyed by human beings, you might have to use the products of their intelligence, the ones that might not be in line with your philosophy but will help to not need them in the long run.

When I came home to the city four days later I wondered if my research had taken me anywhere. If I had produced anything useful. If I had managed to understand Mr. Fukuoka a bit better or if I had just tried to force some of his ways of working into an artistic approach. When November came I thought about retracing my steps to see if any Daydreams had grown and flowered. I was pretty convinced they hadn't.

I had sown them during the one of the hottest weeks of the year and in the months afterwards there had hardly been any rain. I postponed walking back; I told myself I didn't have time and I wouldn't see any results. But one morning, when the days were getting cold and the first Christmas lights appeared in the city, I just packed my bag and headed out.

It is strange to walk back in your own footsteps. When you start encountering your own old self, you also wonder if your old self encountered your future self. If so, they must be on that road continuously, passing each other every moment. I can't be 100% sure that none of the Daydreams flowered because once I started walking my eyes wandered off all the time. I looked at the beautiful yellow of the ginkgo trees, the fake flowers in the enormous cemetery, the deep red of the soil higher up in the mountains, the clouds covering the valley in the morning. I realised one of my dreams had been to walk back and I wouldn't have done that if I hadn't left the trail.

Just as in Natural Farming the ultimate goal isn't the growing of crops 'but the cultivation and perfection of human beings', in making art the goal shouldn't be to produce the best or as many artworks as possible. The goal is the same. You could say though that the benefit of being a farmer is that you have something to eat at the end of the day. That you don't have to break your head over what to produce. But that is too easy.

Many years ago after my wanderings had led me to Sweden where I lived and worked for a while in the forest with some modern pioneers, I found *The One-Straw Revolution* in the house they had built from tree trunks and insulated with moss. I started corresponding with Larry Korn, who lived and worked with Mr. Fukuoka on his farm. He had translated *The One-Straw Revolution* and brought it to America. Sometimes I wrote to him that I was tired of trying to be an artist and dreamed about moving to a piece of land and growing vegetables. But whenever I did that he told me you don't have to farm to be a natural farmer. There are many ways to sow seeds and be a co-conspirator in the one-straw revolution. In the last chapter of his book about Masanobu Fukuoka he writes, 'The one-straw revolution is about remembering who we are so we can live freely, joyously, and responsibly in the world.'

I thought about this on my walk back. I thought about the importance of remembering. When we want to restore, regenerate, repair, return, we have to remember. We have to remember like a child does, like people who are part of nature, like the indigenous people Mr. Fukuoka referred to many times. We have forgotten this. We have even become so separated from nature that more and more people are starting to wonder if there shouldn't be a new word for it. But maybe it is better to try to remember what nature really is. What our nature really is. And that it doesn't really matter what we do, in the sense of what we do professionally. What matters is who we are. When we remember this, when we construct our lives according to this, we will get somewhere. The beginning is also the end. The end is also the beginning. And in the middle you can go in both directions. You don't have to choose. You just have to remember where you came from and where you want to go.

All quotes by Masanobu Fukuoka unless mentioned otherwise.

Sources

Besten, M. *The Middle of Nothing,* blog based on CACiS experience, themiddleofnothing.blogspot.com

CACiS (Centre d'Art Contemporani i Sostenibilitat) website, elforndelacalc.cat

Fukuoka, M. *The One-Straw Revolution,* Rodale Press, 1978, and *Sowing Seeds in the Desert,* ed. Korn, Larry, Chelsea Green, 2012

Korn, L. *One-Straw Revolutionary*, Chelsea Green, 2015

RANAE LENOR HANSON

Listening Circles

A grandfather from North Minneapolis leaned against my door frame, halfway into the office, halfway in the hall. Richard spoke slowly, nodding his head. 'What I don't get,' he paused, 'is who stops the US. There's these laws to protect the Earth. And we're breaking them. I always thought… always thought there was someone in charge.'

After a while, I said, 'There's only you and me and the rest who can try to protect.'

'Yeah,' he said. 'I don't think it's in me.'

Then he pulled away from the wall and stood solidly on his feet. 'I get it though, Miss Ranae,' he said. 'We really are all we got.'

*

Three colleagues and I offered listening sessions on campus for students who might be troubled by impending climate distress. A dozen students gathered for each of the first circles.

Two older students in neat black suits and closely cut hair sat together during the first. They listened as younger people spoke of their fears for the future. Then one of these elders said in quiet English, 'The Somali crisis did not start with a war. First came the drought.'

'Yes,' the other man said. 'And the drought was because the climate had changed. The clouds did not come. The rain stopped. The herds of the cattle tribes had no grass. The fodder available to the camel people became less. There was nothing for the goats. The goat people moved onto the camel people's land; the cattle herders brought their animals, too. There was not enough for the camels. How could they share with these others?'

'What would you do?' asked the first man, looking one by one at the non-Somalis in the room. 'Let your children starve?'

We sat together in silence. 'So there was battle,' they went on.

I had read in the news that the Somali crisis was a matter of tribal war. These elders added context that altered the story.

A few students stayed on for the next listening circle. Among the new people who joined us was a third Somali elder. He sat quietly until halfway through when one of the students asked him, 'The war in Somalia, did it start because of a drought?'

The man furrowed his brow and nodded. 'It did,' he said. 'Many people and animals died.'

'What did you do then?'

'As the animals died, some of us men went to the city, to Mogadishu. We thought we would get work. But there was no work. So we went back to the countryside, and we cut down the trees. We knew if we cut down the trees, we would further dry out the land. If there are no trees, the rain does not come, and when some water falls, it cannot soak in. But we cut them down and we made charcoal, and we took it to the city to sell. We made the drought worse, and we fought among ourselves.'

'You were trying to keep your family alive,' one of my colleagues added sympathetically.

'I was,' he said. 'I was a leader there. Now I am your student.'

*

As a young child, Derartu had lived for several years with her mother's mother in a rural part of what had become Ethiopia.

'My grandma told me about climate change,' Dee said to her classmates in my ecofeminism class. 'She wasn't educated – not in the way of being able to read. But she listened to the land. She could grow anything, and she loved each tree. Oromo people always love trees.

'My grandma told me and my cousins that she could swim,' she went on. 'Swim! We asked her, "How could you swim?" *We* did not know how to swim. There was no water to swim in! Grandma pointed to the valley and told us that it had been a lake, a big lake with hippopotamuses. But now it was gone; already it was gone in my childhood.

'Grandma didn't know why the climate was changing,' Dee said, 'but she linked it to the arrival of cars. She said that the earlier colonisers had done bad things, but that none were as bad as the British, who came with tractors and fertiliser and cars. She would have nothing to do with cars.

'The trees were dying, Grandma said, because the rains were not coming like they used to. The cattle could not get food. The new ways of trying to feed them, she said, were killing them instead.

'It's all on that NASA website about climate change,' Derartu announced, 'all that my grandmother told me.

'When Grandma grew old, she had to move to the city. The land was not fertile anymore. All her children had left the village. She was sad. She grieved for her grandchildren because they would not have the good life she had had.'

*

Martina, a young student from a village in central Mexico, and Amina, an elder student from rural Somalia by way of refugee camps in Kenya, offered to speak at my Quaker meeting. They had not shared their stories before.

'Our trouble began with a drought,' Amina told us.

'Ours, too,' Martina said. 'The rains did not come.'

They looked at one another. 'Also in your part of the world?'

Quickly the stories tumbled out. 'When hunger and fighting came, the men left.'

'Our men, too.'

'And we had to leave, we women and children. We had to go where we could.'

'I also. I hired a coyote to get me across – oh, I am legal now! I am legal, but my uncle is not. And, at first, I hired a coyote.'

'Children died. Women died. Giving birth as we walked.'

'My aunt also.'

'To make fires for cooking, we cut down the trees that were left. We knew that this was wrong.'

'So many trees – my grandfather, too. He cuts the trees. He sells wood in the village.'

As we left the meeting, the women hugged one another. Then they turned to me. 'These people were nice,' one said. 'They listen. It seems like they care.'

Please join me in witnessing. Do not turn away.

*

Ogmani came into my office, bowing slightly to me. 'Hello, Teacher,' he said. I could hear the capital T.

The essay he had written had become a love song to Kabul, his home. 'A beautiful city,' he said, 'no matter what you hear in the news.'

'Were you born there?' I asked.

'Oh no,' he said, 'in a village, even more beautiful. Here, I will show you.' He pulled out his phone to show me a picture of a family – grandparents, younger adults, a couple of children – standing smiling in snow.

'They sent this yesterday because they were happy that snow had come. We don't get snow anymore, hardly ever,' he said. 'That is the problem. Not enough snow for the crops, so most of us have gone to Kabul. That one, the small girl, she is my niece.'

I have heard this too often – no longer enough snow. No runoff in the spring. Where there used to be drifts of white, now there are deep drifts of longing.

I tapped my phone and showed him a video of two of my grandnieces being pulled on a sled behind a car.

'We still get deep snow often in northern Minnesota,' I said, 'though it doesn't stay as long as it did when I was a child. See how happy my grandnieces are!'

Ogmani laughed as he watched the girls.

'Will you go back?' I asked him.

'I must,' he said. 'I can't leave my niece there alone. I am afraid for her. She is a girl... and the Taliban will come. I will go back and become a politician. I will make things better for her. She reads already.' He looked up with pride. 'I want her to go to school.'

'But you could stay here,' I said.

'I could, but I will not,' he said. 'I expect to die. One day there will be a suicide bomb attack and I will die. Just last week a man blew himself up outside the office where my brother works. Each day when my brothers leave the house, my mother blesses them because that may be the last.'

'Could you stay and bring her here instead?' I asked.

'I will go back,' he said. 'Afghanistan is my homeland.'

*

The next semester Ogmani, no longer my student, stopped by my office. 'Hello, Teacher,' he said.

'Ogmani! So glad to see you! But... you've shaved your head.'

He looked away. 'For my brother,' he said. 'Last month there was a bomber. My brother survived the attack – for a day.'

'May you be well, Ogmani,' I said as he turned to go, 'and your niece and your brothers. I will think of you.'

'*Insha'Allah*.' A bow.

Then he was gone.

NICK HUNT

Vault of the Wordmonger

Our father bought words once a week. He was a big man in our town and fresh words gave him status. He paid for them in animal parts from the farm our family owned and sometimes in mineral parts from the mine beyond the hill. He did not own the mine but he had interests there. The animal parts and mineral parts he carried there in his hands and the words he carried back in his mouth. That is the way to carry words. When I say back I mean he carried them back to the house in which we lived. It was a large house with pillars and a garden. When I say there I mean to the wordmonger which is where the words came from. I do not know how it was in your town but that was how it was in mine.

The wordmonger had her shop at the bottom of the hill and we lived at the top. Not at the very top of course but close enough to matter. This meant that our father carried the words back uphill which meant that he was out of breath by the time he reached our house. He could not use the words straight away or they would come out broken. All of us would gather around waiting for him to speak the words. By us I mean myself and my sister and my brother and my other brother. Our father would speak the words and we would wonder at their shapes. Their rounded bits and their curves. Their hard sounds and their edges. Then he would speak them again with a bit more confidence. Sometimes he would shout them. Later that night he would take his words to the place where other big men drank and he would demonstrate their use. A crowd would grow around him. I felt lucky as a child to have a father who could buy fresh words when he felt like it. I hoped to grow up like him.

A lot of time has gone by now and I can hardly remember the way he looked apart from his teeth and his moustache.

If he caught us using his words he would beat us with a shovel.

Occasionally he let me or my brother or my other brother go with him down the hill. He never let my sister. I was proud to walk with our father down the hill and through the streets with all the people watching us. We went past the salvage yards and over the dried river. The wordmonger had her shop on the other side of the wall which some people did not consider to be a part of our town at all but rather some other place. There were other shops down there selling things that I did not understand the uses of or what they were. The people looked different there but I cannot tell you how.

The shop was a building made of bricks that looked as if it had been built for a purpose that was not a shop but which no one remembered now. Its walls were painted green. The sign that hung above the door showed the parted lips of a mouth with lines flowing out of it wriggling here and there. I always liked that sign because it had a meaning. There were other signs in our town whose meanings were unknowable such as two crossed lines or an animal with four legs or a stick with a line through it or other things I did not understand. I do not think that anyone in our town understood them. The door of the shop was closed if the wordmonger was away but normally it was open and our father would walk straight in. The wordmonger would be waiting standing behind the counter.

She was not an old woman but the effect of her was old. Her hands were old and her hair was old but the rest of her was younger. She had a creased yellow face like a piece of picked fruit and a dent above her nose as if someone had pushed it in. Her eyes were small and squinty. There was nothing inside the room but the counter and the booth and a long dark space behind. There were shelves and boxes there which was where she kept things.

Our father would place the animal parts or the mineral parts on the counter and she would take a look at them. She would pick them up and feel the weight of them in her hands and sniff the surfaces of them and look underneath them. Then she would disappear into the long dark space taking the parts with her and we would hear the sound of drawers scraping and doors opening. During this we would have to wait. Sometimes it took a minute and sometimes it took much longer. I suppose the length of time it took depended somehow on the words but I was never able to work out how. Our father would close his eyes as if he was sleeping.

The booth was a sort of wooden box with an entrance on each side. I imagined it was very old but I had no way of knowing. When the wordmonger returned she would go in one side and our father would go in the other side and sit down on a little stool. We were not supposed to look but sometimes we looked sideways. Between them in the wooden wall were lots of small square holes and our father would put his ear to the holes and she would put her mouth to the holes and speak softly into them. This is how the words were exchanged. This is how he received them. When his ear was full of words he would rise to his feet and brush his knees and say thank you to the wordmonger. I never heard him say it to anyone else but he said it to her. Then we would leave the shop and walk back up the hill. We were not allowed to speak to our father on the journey home.

Normally he was pleased and often his lips would be practicing the shapes of the words silently. When he had a difficult word in his mouth he would frown. Occasionally the words he received were ones that he already knew or ones he did not know the uses for and he would be disappointed. But he never attempted to take them back or to complain to the wordmonger no matter how disappointed he was. Our father would argue with anyone but he did not argue with her.

People would stand aside as he walked back up the hill. They knew he was full of words and they did not want to spill them. The only person who was not respectful was the skinny old man who begged outside the salvage yards on his hands and knees. He was from the older time when words were not approved of. When he saw our father coming he would spit at him or make crude signs and our father would react or not depending on his mood. Sometimes he would kick the old man or try to step on his hands but mostly he ignored him. The old man was wordless and not worth the trouble.

Through the years of my childhood and my early adulthood I watched our father grow with words. He swelled and glowed with them. The outside of him did not change except in the usual ways but the inside of him changed in ways no one could see. There were thousands of words in there stored up ready to be used. Even if he did not know their uses they gave him power. Even if he never spoke them but kept them inside himself they still made him powerful. Perhaps even more so that way. Because he had so many words he was admired by everyone apart from the old beggar man who hardly counted as a man. He was admired by the bigger men who lived further up the hill. They came to him for advice and to help them make decisions and to have around them while they drank and played their games.

Our father said that one day his children would receive his words. Before he died he would give them to us dividing them equally. By us I mean myself and my brother and my other brother but not my sister because some words were not considered right for her. In my mind I planned to share them with her anyway. This was a great inheritance but it never came to pass. All we had to do was wait but unfortunately we did not.

It was my other brother who came up with the idea. Not my brother but my other brother who was the youngest one. The idea did not come from nowhere but from the beating he received after our father caught him using one of his words. I do not know which word it was because I did not hear it. All I heard was the sound of the shovel thumping on my brother's legs and on his backside and on his back and his crying afterwards. When he had finished crying he came in search of me.

He did not want to wait for our father to be almost dead before he got his words. He wanted his own words now. His idea was to follow the wordmonger when she left her shop and went into the dead woods which she had been observed to do. He thought that she must know a place where words were just lying around for anyone to pick up. He would help himself. Once he had got words of his own he planned to leave our family home and marry the girl he was in love with lower down the hill. The word he had been beaten for was stolen to impress this girl but it did not mean what he thought it did. She had only laughed at him.

We chose a day when our father was out counting animal parts on the farm and we knew he would not be back until the evening. The two of us went down the hill and over the dried river. The door of the shop was open which meant that the wordmonger was inside. We waited there for several hours but no one left or entered. The day was hot and there was no shade in the area beyond the wall and we were thinking of going home when the wordmonger appeared. She locked the door of her shop and went off down the road.

My other brother followed her and I followed my other brother. We walked past the empty buildings and the rusted old machines and across the charcoal fields until we reached the dead woods. Neither myself nor my other brother had been there more than once or twice and we did not like it there. Everything was black and grey and there was no smell. We followed her along a path that led to another path that led to another path that led to another path. She walked ahead not looking back and we walked behind. At last we came to a place where the dead woods ended at a wall of grey rock. At the bottom of the rock there was a door. It was not normal sized but very tall and wide and it was not made of wood but of rusted metal. Its size did not matter though as it was not completely closed. There was a gap. The wordmonger approached this gap without once looking back to see if she had been followed and slipped into the darkness.

Myself and my other brother waited for a while and when she did not come out we went a little closer. The wall was not made of rock but of something smooth and grey that was as hard as rock. I had seen this stuff before but only in small pieces. On the door was a sign that showed an open mouth like the sign above her shop. But instead of random lines coming from the mouth there were pictures we recognised. There was a human figure with a line going through its body and there were black flames and there was a skull.

Vault. The word was vault. I knew this from our father. We had heard of places like this but only in the stories. We were not supposed to listen but sometimes we listened sideways. When the big men drank too much they talked about the older time when words were not allowed. They were not allowed because of the bad things they had done. Words had caused a great fire or perhaps many fires and words had caused the sea to spill and drown the towns and buildings. Words had caused some men and women to kill other men and women and the other men and women to kill other men and women. Most of the animals had gone and words had caused that too. I did not understand exactly how words had done these things but for years afterwards they were kept away from us. They were hidden in deep holes and doors were closed upon them. These holes were called vaults and this was one of them. The pictures coming from the mouth were threats like our father's shovel.

Perhaps we would have gone inside or perhaps we would have gone away. I do not know because we heard her footsteps coming back. My other brother hopped about breathing very fast and picked up a piece of rock and put it behind his back. I stood beside the door. Something filled the dark gap and we saw the wordmonger. She had not noticed us. Her mouth was moving as if she was working at the shape of a new word. Or perhaps she was out of breath from where she had gone. As she stepped into the light she saw us both standing there. Her small squinty eyes went smaller and more squinty. She opened her mouth to speak but she never spoke because my other brother hit her with the rock.

She fell without a sound and lay there without moving. My other brother threw the rock away but it was done. Perhaps he expected words to spill out so that he could pick them up. But the only thing that spilled out was blood.

We waited for something else to happen and when nothing else happened it was like a sign. We both turned different ways. My other brother took the path back into the dead woods and I went through the rusted door into the vault.

A lot of time has gone by now and I do not remember everything well. There was a hill inside the earth going down to somewhere deeper. At the bottom of the hill there was another rusted door and it was open like the first. Rocks had been pushed into the gap to keep it open. I wondered if the wordmonger had pushed the rocks in there or if it had been someone else. Someone from long ago perhaps. But everything was dusty and there was no way of knowing.

Past the second rusted door was a great pit with smooth walls. It went down to a depth so deep I could not see its bottom. There was a hard confusing sound rising up inside the pit. It sounded as if a storm was trapped inside the earth. But it was not a storm. It was words. They were flying around down there bouncing off the walls and bouncing off each other and smashing into little bits and joining up again. Something had unleashed them from their trap and they were loose. I wondered when they had escaped. Maybe it was years ago. Maybe it was years and years. No one knew that they were there apart from the wordmonger and me. Now the wordmonger was dead it was only me.

I lay down on my front and looked into the pit. I thought that there were stars down there but they were little lights. They went bright and then dark and then bright again. There were also bigger things like pale glowing squares. The glowing squares were in the walls and across the front of them passed spiky lines going up and down and up and down. When the words got louder the lines got spikier like knives. I knew that I was seeing the secret shapes of words.

A great excitement came to me. I never knew that words had shapes. I knew that they had sound shapes but not seeing shapes. If I understood the shapes then I might understand the words.

Then an excitement came that was even greater than before. If I understood the shapes then I might know how words were made. I could make new words. Words that were my own.

With this excitement in my head I walked around the pit. On the other side of it were bars sticking from the wall. The bars went down into the dark. Ladder. The word was ladder. I put my foot below my foot and my hand below my hand and started going down.

But the words did not like me being there. They got angier and louder. I wanted to block them out by putting my hands over my ears but I could not move my hands. If I moved my hands from the bars I would fall.

Sometimes I thought I understood the beginning or the end or the middle of a word but they were only broken parts. As the word parts filled my head I saw bits of things. Not clear pictures but only ugly pieces that went round and round. Smoke and flames and machines and black water from the earth and animal parts and human parts. Things I did not want to see. Things from the older time. Then I saw the dead woods but they were not dead woods then. They were not black and grey but green and green and green.

It was a different kind of green to any green that I had seen. A green from the older time or before the older time. The goodness of it made me hurt. The hurt was worse than any hurt caused by the ugly things.

The green pain filled up my heart as the words filled up my ears. I put my hand above my hand and my foot above my foot and climbed out of the pit and ran back to the light. I ran back to the dead woods hoping that I might see green. But they were only black and grey as they had been before.

The wordmonger was lying with her yellow face against the earth. She looked ugly lying there. I did not want to see her. I took hold of her body and pulled it through the door. Her body weighed almost nothing like an empty bag. I carried on pulling it down the hill inside the earth. I pulled it through the second rusted door and over to the pit. I carried it to the edge and then I pushed it in. It fell into the words and I did not hear it land. The words closed over it and it was gone.

When I got back to our home my other brother was not there. He had returned and packed a bag and said goodbye. He had not gone to the girl he was in love with lower down the hill but to another town or an area between the towns. Our father sent out men to search but they never found him.

The wordmonger's shop stayed closed. Our father went there every week and came back sad and angry. He no longer swelled and glowed. He even stopped beating us. The big men further up the hill did not invite him to their games. From that point on it seemed he started growing smaller.

When at last our father died all of us stood around his bed. By all of us I mean myself and my sister and my brother but not my other brother. We have not seen him again. Our father breathed up and down and we waited for his words. We waited for his words but he did not share them. His face was like a smooth grey wall and his mouth was like a rusted door. When it closed it stayed closed and perhaps that was better.

NEALE INGLENOOK

It's All Still Here

A conversation with Obi Kaufmann

I first encounter him through his book, set on a table among all the others in the local shop. Everything around me is muffled and dry. The millions of leaves of new paper induce synaesthesia: I can taste the rasp of the fibres, smell the rubber soles rubbing the short carpet. The murmuring voices, absorbed by the thirsty pages, are the sound of volumes in alphabetical order. Though the air is perfectly conditioned, I breathe the feeling of dust suspended in sunlight.

Some books emit a particular gravity. In this storehouse of dead ideas, I can't help but pick up this volume, weighty as a Bible. On the cover, the eyes of a mountain lion stare into mine, and a hawk strikes from the sky toward black trees, its feathers painted in blood.

Within, it is as wild as it is organised. Maps of ecological zones and their numbered notes abut portraits of coyote, salmon and salamander, night heron and king snake, blue oak and red fir, condors on the wing. Always this bodily presence of the land, the felt shape of California. The courses of her rivers run through my lungs, her mountains rise from my knurled bones. Eagles wheel below the thunderheads of my thoughts.

Two years later, we meet in a small café, an old brick cube perched on the wall of a stream canyon in the Sierra Nevada. Snow holds in the shadows under Ponderosa pines. Below us, Deer Creek tumbles white around water-worn granite toward its meeting with the Yuba River.

This landscape was the epicentre of the California Gold Rush. After the gold discovery in 1849, after the native people had been killed or pushed off their land, after all the nuggets had been panned from the streams, industrialists turned to excavation and hydraulic mining in order to extract wealth from the mountains. Many of the hydraulic mines, 170 years later, are wastelands of barren rock. In exchange, the bed of the

California Condor by Obi Kaufman *Watercolour.* The California condor is North America's largest land bird. They have been brought back from the brink of extinction by conservation efforts, but are still critically endangered.

Yuba was filled with tailings, rising by 60 feet in some places. The Empire Mine, a hardrock mine and the richest deposit of the era, still leaches heavy metals from its shafts. It is not safe to eat fish from the river – mercury lines the streambeds all the way to San Francisco Bay.

Today, the Yuba cascades through granite gorges that seem untouched by human damage. Remediation ponds, filled with native cattail and the songs of redwing blackbirds, steadily filter the suppuration from Empire Mine. Human structures dot the ridges, among sugar pines and incense cedars, where black bears and cougars, rattlesnakes and ravens make their lives. Wildfires burn the homes and forests indiscriminately, their smoke mixing in the heavy summer air. The mountains hold the harm, of the genocide of native people, of the flaying of the Earth for gold. Wounded, impinged upon, untamed and burning with life.

This is the land beneath us when I meet with Obi Kaufmann. His *California Field Atlas*, an artistic paean to this more-than-human landscape, combines cartography, portraiture and ecological essays. His second book, *The State of Water*, continues the project, tracing the state's watercourses and the human effects upon them.

NEALE INGLENOOK: Could you describe how you came to painting?

OBI KAUFMANN: In the seventies my family moved to northern California; Mt. Diablo to be specific – the great mountain where I cut my teeth as a naturalist, climbing waterfalls and playing with tarantulas, mapping sage mazes. That mountain became my axis mundi. Especially in light of what my father was teaching me as an astrophysicist, with his scientific ways and his wily mathematics. Every afternoon while I was in high school we were doing calculus homework before he set me free to play on the mountain. So that was my training. Of course, for all his efforts, he made a painter.

I went to UC Santa Barbara as a biologist, but I quickly fell in love with the paintings of the Chumash, which covered the Santa Ynez Mountains. I went backpacking every weekend to find these art sites. There are hundreds of them that are off-trail, unmapped and unprotected. You might pull back a bush of ceanothus and find a ten-foot condor painted on the underside of a sandstone wind cave. And that condor might have sort of a lizard tail and maybe a little centipede motif, a human foot. I don't know the story, but the impression on me was that here's the human capacity to engage nature in this mythic landscape, using a very sophisticated visual language that was deeply rooted in tradition and worldview. Now on the cover of *The California Field Atlas* I've got a red hawk, and its wing is cut off in a funny way, for a graphic conceit. But your mind is putting that together because you are of the same culture that I am, this European three-dimensional visual language that we have. Playing with that has always been a core interest to me. Through the art and science, and the visual language, I'm trying to tell this very basic story, giving it all back to the thing that I love most, which is the natural world of California.

NI And you've made contact with that landscape by walking.

OK Walking is very important. It's a mode of learning itself. As if walking and reading are somehow equivalent knowledge sources. As if the day of walking is a narrative unfolding, a beginning, middle, and an end, replete with characters, drama, beauty, epicness, adventure, romance. And a book is not unlike a hike. What are books but trails to understanding thought? You need a book, frankly, to get your head out of your computer, with your 240 characters or whatever. Human stories need to unravel over miles of pages.

NI Interesting that so many would be focusing so intently on these quick developments in the sphere of the internet.

OK It's never not happened quickly. About 100,000 years ago, there was this phenomenon called the cognitive revolution, which was probably even more important than the agricultural revolution, or the industrial revolution, or what I think is coming next which is the ecological revolution. The cognitive revolution was where we invented fiction, where we invented art, which is a completely globe-changing phenomenon. There were many other types of humans on the planet, but we had an advantage in that we were able to capitalise on this opportunity which was the technology of story – this world-breaking technology, this world-making technology. Never before in the history of all zoology has any creature been able to remove their nature from their bodies and pass it to someone. That's what story does; I'm able to give you my nature. And that is a profound power.

So that's what I'm engaged in now. When I'm talking about the world of California nature, I'm talking about me perceiving it, about us perceiving it. So these books are more about me – about us – on some level, than they are actually about nature.

NI At the same time that you're communicating to other humans, I also get the sense – whether it's a portrait of California as a landscape, or a portrait of a coyote or a condor – that you're speaking to that place, that animal, empathising with it and taking from it a sense of its own internal life.

OK I don't think I'm taking anything from it and I don't think I'm speaking to it. What I think I'm doing is just speaking to myself. I let you, as my viewer, build the image in your mind. I can just wash the paint around, and you can say, 'Oh, that's sky,' or 'That's a wing. Those are feathers.' You're building that in your mind because we share all this cultural information.

I really want to resist the metaphysical. I think it's all very much here and now. We have our capacity to crack our hearts open for deeper understanding of our connection to place, and that story that we can collectively tell about our responsibilities towards all of biodiversity. This is the pathway to healing this psychological trauma that we have endured at the hands of industrial capitalism for hundreds of years, where all of nature is commodity, all of nature is only for us to take. That is largely an Abrahamic worldview, that this was all set here for you.

One of my big influences is J.R.R. Tolkien. In fact when I pitched *The California Field Atlas*, I had his hand-painted drawing of Middle-earth, and I said, 'I want to do this for California.' This place of more romance and epic adventure than Middle-earth could ever have. But in the history of the elves, there is this primordial spider, and she was so hungry all the time that she ended up eating herself. And I feel like humanity in our crazy quest for ever-increasing GDP, we never let the forest fire cleanse the forest of our economy at all. We just keep growing, and that's not how anything in nature works.

There's nothing metaphysical in my work. But I do think that there's an aesthetic theory. I think that a guy who got aesthetic theory right for us was James Joyce, in *A Portrait of the Artist as a Young Man,* when he talked about the experience of 'aesthetic arrest', when we are not being sold anything. That's how you know you are in the presence of art, as opposed to advertising. When you are still, when you are the eye of the universe perceiving the thing of the universe, and both are made one.

NI Do you ever experience that same feeling coming in contact with the non-human as well as with art?

OK For sure. In the natural world it's the interpretation or the absorption of the sublime. My books are works of art, they're not works of science. They are not neutral. I'm not making textbooks. Even though they sort of appear like they might want to be.

NI It's a very particular object you've made, in this collision of fine art, cartography, guide-book-like form, and essays ranging from the scientific to the philosophical, all the way over to poetry.

OK I really love the idea of how the story evolves. *The California Field Atlas* was my first book, and it opens with the line, 'This is a love story.' I put in these passionate feelings and invented geographies, everything I knew and felt.

But then I move through to *The State of Water*, my second book, and it kind of reads like a math problem. It's about usage, storage and conveyance of this substance, water, around the state. Trying to get that right in my own mind. Almost a reaction to that divisive rhetoric that we're sold every day. Looking at it from an ecological point of view, what do we need to keep this biodiversity intact? Water is the circulation, water is all the life.

The salmon for example have seen a steep decline over the past 100 years. And we knew that when we built some of these larger dams, that this was the end of the salmon. We were trading salmon for agriculture. They said that explicitly, back when the spring run of the Chinook salmon up the Sacramento River was 600,000 fish, making their way to their headwaters, depositing hundreds of thousands of metric tons of calcium, phosphorus, nitrogen across the watershed. This was how the forests got fed. And now we're starving our forests.

As much math as there is in *The State of Water,* there's also a lot of poetry. Now it's more prose poetry, and it's usually inspired by a particular animal.

NI The one that touched me recently was the one about the tule fog. There's the sensibility of the tule fog itself, and it mourning the lost elk, and that the fog itself is disappearing as warmer temperatures come.

OK There are fewer and fewer days of that breath that fills the Central Valley, through the mouth of the San Francisco Bay, across the body of California. There's something very physiological, humanly figurative about our state. You could almost see Yosemite as a heart. Maybe the incredibly biodiverse mountains of the Klamath are equivalent to some sort of brain.

We've got all of these living networks, this incredibly complex cat's cradle between so many fingers, how all these different living systems work. Now I'm not an ecologist. I'm a naturalist, I'm a painter, I'm a walker, I'm a systems researcher. I'm really interested not in the 'where' of things, which is funny for a thing calling itself an atlas. I'm not telling you how to go anywhere or do anything. What I'm talking to you about is the 'how' of things. How these systems coalesce to present this reality, this most beautiful of all corners of the globe.

NI And your own particular sense of connection and contact.

OK It's got to be that. But all of my books are part of a bigger effort related to the subtitle of *The State of Water* book, which is *Understanding California's Most Precious Resource*. It implies that water is our most precious resource. But I think now, two years on from having written this book, and having toured the state, and having seen the electric passion of the citizenry, that our most precious resource is actually this ability to trust one another with this very powerful technology of story, which will determine our future, more so than water.

In the past 100 years we've really transformed California's waterscape in such a way that it rivals anything humans have ever done with anything anywhere. The infrastructure, the machine of water that we've built, is remarkable. But I say that it is rivalled only by how much it will again transform in the next 100 years. So we've got a lot of decisions to make. We're talking about balancing rights and responsibilities, to one another, to this place.

I'm not here telling you what the answer is. I'm not going to tell a farmer how to farm. I will lose before that argument even begins. I don't ever want to place myself in the pundit's chair, like a talking head on TV that says 'I've got answers!'

All ecological truths, as all political truths, are incredibly nuanced. And you have to be sensitive to traditions, and to people's lives. We're talking about life and death. When you're talking about water in California, you're talking about world-view. What could be more interesting in this life than to talk about the substance that makes us go?

NI And launching from that, you have these questions of restoration, renewal, conservation, all of those words that come up a lot in your work.

OK I love all those words. Preservation. Connectivity. You can't talk about restoration without connectivity, you can't talk about connectivity without conservation. All of these are certainly political postures.

I don't talk a lot about policy. I'm more interested in the ethical story, of what responsibility means living in a free society, who are we responsible to, when do we get to stop being immigrants into this place and start calling this our home. Not something we are dominating, but something we are living in harmony with. Our non-human neighbours provide so many services. Services that we don't even understand yet. We understand the nature of cascading effects within biodiverse ecosystems. How it's this Jenga tower, where you remove these species and you're talking about weakening the foundation of it all.

Our 20th-century conservation policies gave us things like national parks, which were a good start, but we're finding that they are woefully insufficient for the challenges of the 21st and into the 22nd century. We have to get the story right about the importance of biodiversity. This gets into the larger idea of hope: for every point of despair, there's at least one point of hope. Although all of our natural ecosystems are either threatened or endangered, we have a very low extinction rate in this state, less than one per cent. It's all still here. Including the salmon.

Now, there are no laurels to rest on. When it's going to go, it's going to go hard. So it's the time for vigilance and reprioritisation, and that is all about story. I think we have a better story. I think that's how you change things, get in there with your hands into that living soil and change that paradigm. And it's happening fast. It was only 50 years ago that Robert MacArthur and E.O. Wilson wrote *A Theory of Island Biogeography*, which was the first time that Darwinian principles were really applied to ecological theory at all, showing that ecosystems evolved. This is something that people understand intuitively, but they found the scientific language to say 'these systems are living'. So it's actually changing at a breakneck speed. It's like we're pounding against the seawall.

The paradigm is going to change. And if we can't find a way to do it, it's going to be imposed on us anyway. The post-carbon economy is coming, one way or another – let's get on board.

Coyote
by Obi Kaufman
Watercolour

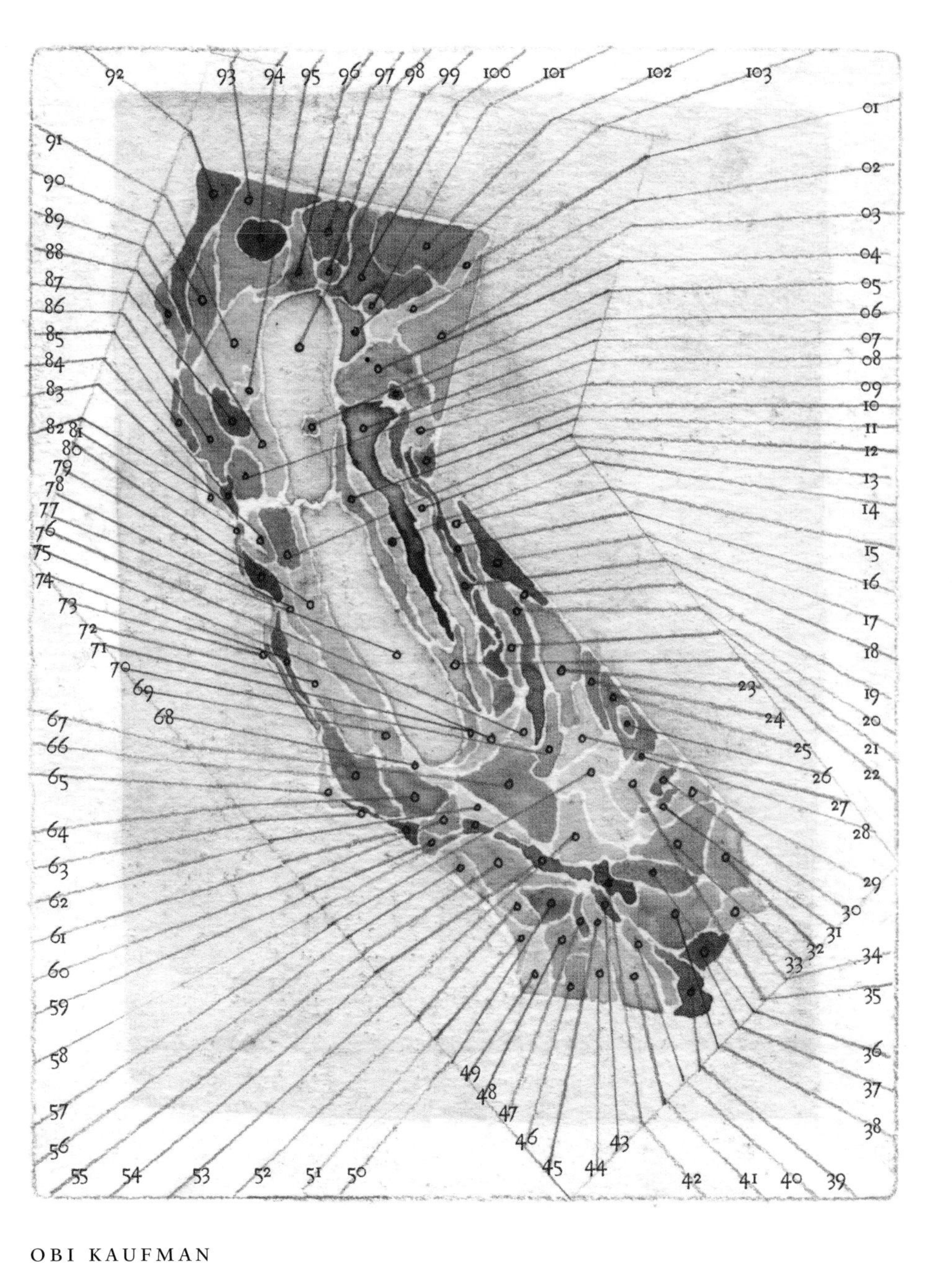

OBI KAUFMAN

Contemporary Ecological Zones of California
(from The Field California Atlas)
Watercolour and ink

An ecological zone may contain several dozen ecosystems defined by a larger geographic feature or region (e.g. '01. Desert conifer and sagebrush forests of the Werner Mountains, 02. Pit River riparian wetlands of Big Valley'). The zones are generalised here, each landscape feature forming a link in the narrative chain that is California's ecology.

ANNE CAMPBELL

Stag

Analogue photograph, hand printed using lith chemicals

They tried to map the soul as we watched the old stag turn,
disappear into the blizzard,
as the mist rolled down, reclaimed the hill.

One of Europe's last wild places, the Flow Country sits at the northern edge of mainland UK. A vital defence against the effects of climate change, this fragile environment often lies under a blanket of snow during winter, making it impossibly treacherous for humans to cross, yet somehow the deer still manage to pick their way through, to the hills and forests beyond.

SUSAN JOWSEY

The Sigh

Cameraless photograph of a chrysanthemum stone

Caught in the endlessly distracting forces of the now; rocks appear inert until they slide or fall into our consciousness. Yet metamorphic bedrock ceaselessly reshapes time – the mantle of Earth pushes up, crumbles and re-forms. In this alchemy of perpetual topographic rebirth, rocks enfold us within the chronological warp and weft of the universe. Re-emerging from the convolutions of an ancient past, our rock ancestors weep, their stories crumbling to dust on the tongue of time.

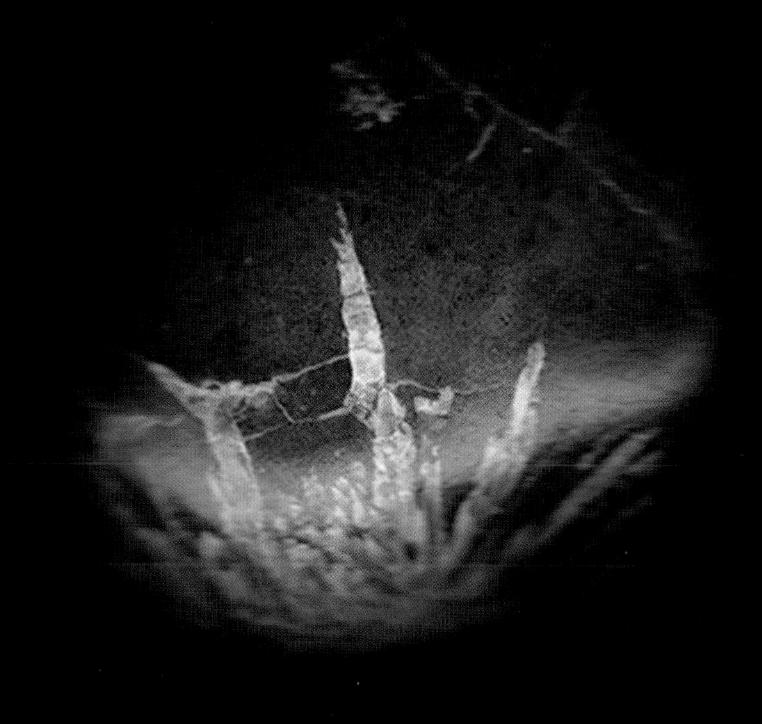

JANE CIPRA
Lazarus Taxa No.1: Coelacanth
Oil on canvas

MIKE CIPRA

Coelacanth Pantoum

You are discovered in the depths
After we presumed extinction
Your tragic, blue and beautiful body
Like Lazarus, if he'd had fins and scales.

After we presumed extinction
You gasp in the hot sun and wonder
Like Lazarus, if he'd had fins and scales
Why you die to be discovered.

You gasp in the hot sun and wonder
Electroperception shows the shape of lovers
Why you die to be discovered
There are species we can recover.

Electroperception shows the shape of lovers
The ocean spits, the ocean speaks
There are species we can recover
And things that are lost forever.

The ocean spits, the ocean speaks
Your tragic, blue and beautiful body
And things that are lost forever
You are discovered in the depths.

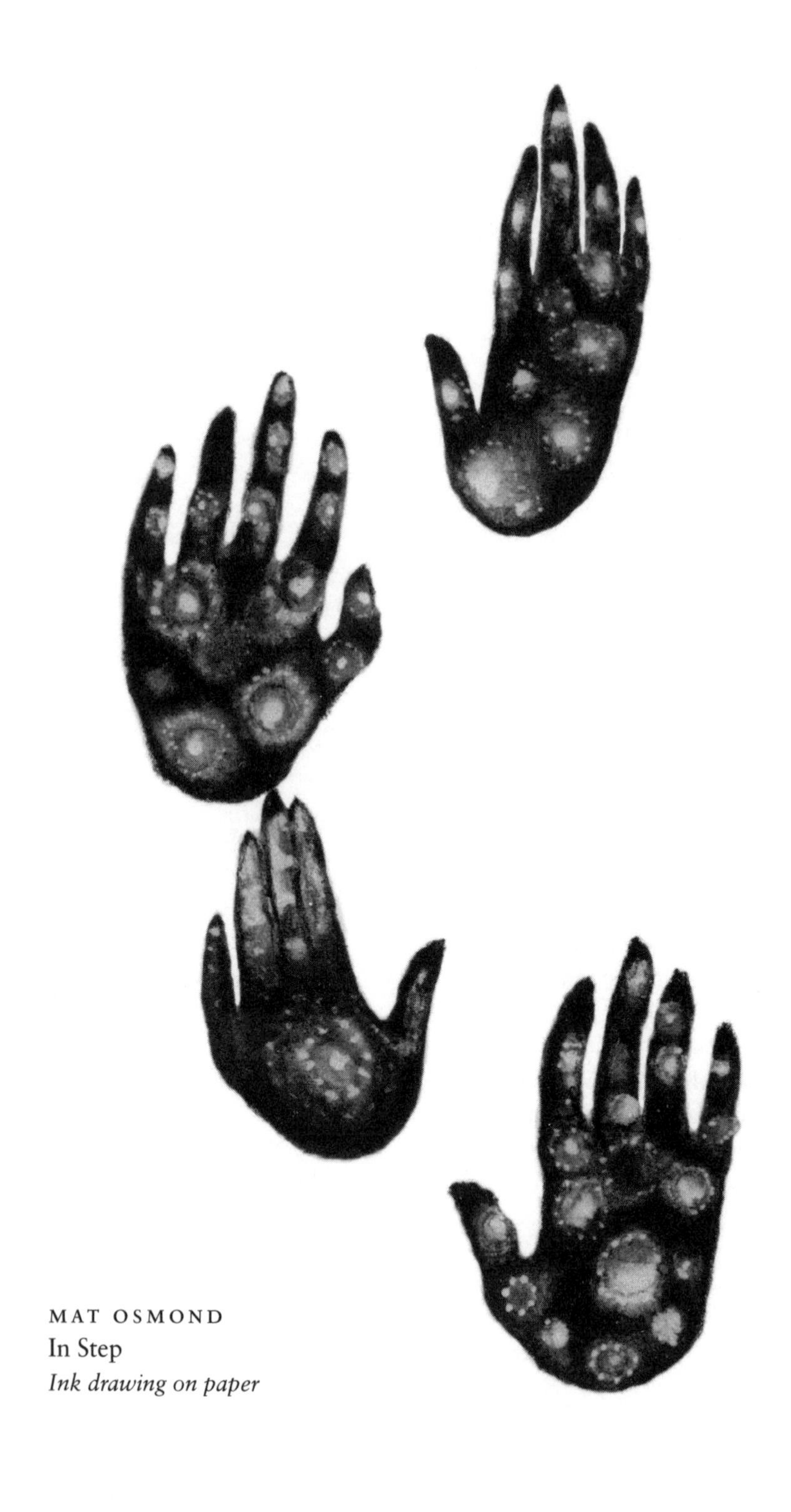

MAT OSMOND
In Step
Ink drawing on paper

MAT OSMOND

Black Light

On mourning, regenerative culture and the tangled roots of the Black Madonna

But the sorrow is radiant, like light shining in the darkness of
a black stone lying over the heart.
– *Lodestone*, Meinrad Craighead

Call and response

In March last year I joined Extinction Rebellion for a five-act Funeral for Extinct Species in the nearby city of Truro. As this sombre, oddly cathartic piece of street theatre began to paralyse the city's traffic, we agreed to cooperate with police requests to relocate its central act: a call-and-response litany of species extinctions since 1930, their names standing in for the countless thousands of unnamed others lost over that period. In this way we found ourselves unintentionally assembled on the steps of Truro Cathedral.

With the front edge of Storm Freya fast approaching, our windswept performance finally got underway: *Santo Stefano lizard, 1965*; *Arabian ostrich, 1966*. As each name was read out then shouted up at the Cathedral's façade by 200-odd voices, the whole scene began to feel like an invocation, or maybe a summons: 'Earth's web of life is dying around us: not metaphorically, but quite literally and with terrifying speed. Our so-called leaders remain incapable of even saying this aloud, let alone doing anything to prevent it. Religion, have you nothing to say?'

There are many replies to this aching need emerging from monotheism's cool stone interiors. Indeed, when a week later the former Archbishop of Canterbury, Dr Rowan Williams repeated his support for Extinction Rebellion's popular uprising in the face of ignored catastrophe, it felt like he might have heard our ragged extinction choir gathered at his front door.

Or perhaps what caught his ear was silence. The silence falling over fields and rivers, over the ever-diminishing wild, as human civilisation progressively wipes Earth clean of her remaining communities of non-human life. Over 98% of American old growth forest has gone since the arrival of European empire. In my own lifetime, over 60% of wild animals have been killed, 75% of the insects gone in one human generation. And then there are the oceans. Crushing new statistics seeming to arrive by the week now. Taken in the round, there's surely no more coherent response to that anthropogenic silence than grief. And if we're to address this situation in positive, measured terms like eco-spirituality and deep adaptation, a foetal-positioned moaning might be the most honest place to begin.

But what, anyway, does *spirituality* mean? For me, that slippery idea's become more or less synonymous with prayer. Not mindfulness, not contemplation or insight, valuable as these may be, but prayer as Alcoholics Anonymous might speak of it: a reaching beyond the self, the admission of a fundamental inability to stand alone or to complete ourselves in this matter of being human. So in speaking of ecological grief and the Black Madonna, what I'm really groping for here is an understanding of prayer itself: of what learning to pray might allow, and what learning to pray might restore.

Extinction Rebellion offers an introductory talk for those new to its take on our collective predicament. Wherever you find it, the title and the basic pitch remain the same: 'Heading for Extinction and What to Do About It'.

What to do about it? Of the replies to biological annihilation which have blown into my life, one has us sitting in traffic declaring rebellion against an ecocidal social order; the other, clutching the dark mother's muttering garland, learning to trust in her help. That *other* is called 'The Way of the Rose', an interfaith rosary fellowship with a subversive mission: to come together in reclaiming this old grassroots mother-devotion from the various weaponised agendas she's been enlisted to. A re-wilding of the rosary.

Perhaps it's a mistake to entangle these two responses to ecocide here. But here I am entangled in both, as 12 years left becomes ten and the wicked graphs continue to spike. Wondering what we'll be doing about all this when the reassuring deadlines have come and gone and here we still are, with no more years to pretend we have left. Wondering if it might be an idea to start jotting notes now, for the story we'll be telling and the response we'll be forming then. And wondering if we might find a role for prayer in that, as we meet what our culture's made of this one wild and precious Earth and decide how best to spend our time here together.

Dark river

An English Buddhist priest once taught me that in learning to pray, we learn to get smaller. To get lower, closer to the ground that supports us. Of the many valuable things which I've received from the hands of Buddhist teachers, that priest's idea of prayer is the one I hold closest: when we get down to it, all that we are and all that we value in this life comes to us as unearned gift, and what we cultivate, in prayer, is a grateful awareness of this condition. Which is one of abundance. Which is also one of permanent, radical dependency.

If we understood prayer as lowering us to Earth, coming back to ourselves not 'as gods' but as the barefoot, teeming mutualists we are – something more like moss, or fungi – the question remains: who, then, do we imagine we're praying to? And what does it mean to address this gravitational, interspecies *who* in personal, singular – rather human – terms? Over the five years since I stepped away from a longstanding involvement in Buddhist practice and picked up the rosary to see where this fusty ancestral bead game might lead me, the Black Madonna has become the figure that, for me, best fathoms questions of this sort.

Her image is not one that entered my life through books. The dark Mother of God haunted my imagination long before I began hearing about or even had a name for her. I met her in my early twenties and thirties, in dreams that preceded by decades any interest in the insipid cliché of my childhood nativities, Mary. I'd hazard a guess that the Black Madonna is the Marian icon most widely associated with spiritual ecology, especially with its eco-feminist thread. Be that as it may, the conversation with her is not one that I started. She did. And the quiet shift in perspective provoked by this conversation has, it seems, allowed me to uncouple from the compulsive, wearying *hope* which I stumbled after across all those intervening years. And right now, that alone will do.

My current understanding of her owes much to the mystical confessions of the artist Meinrad Craighead, who died last April. Other voices have chimed in more recently, mingling their perspectives with hers. The

New York-based academic Neela Bhattacharya Saxena observes that even the many atheists she speaks with are curiously clear about the God they don't believe in being a *male*. In her 2015 book *Absent Mother God of the West: A Kali Lover's Journey into Christianity & Judaism*, she considers what this entrenched cultural bias negates, turning from the word Goddess as she does so, to speak of God the Mother. Saxena's reticence about popular Western notions of the Goddess is rooted, in part, in her Bengali upbringing within a *shakti* tradition of Kali devotion. In place of a monolithic female creator, wide-hipped counterpoint to monotheism's bearded overlord, she offers our dark mother Kali-Ma: the fluid, gynocentric matrix of her own Bengal religious heritage; the primal ground or womb of all spiritual experience.

From this Kalian perspective Saxena maps the eradication of the mother from the Western spiritual imagination – that long matricide which bears heavily on our present failure to be especially bothered about our culture's ongoing extermination of the living world. As many others have done, she frames the Black Madonna as one thread within this generic mother-culture, which she imagines as an instinctual current confined by no religious border. In Saxena's Kali-ma we meet 'the mystic river that connects the world's religious ways', whose dark surface mirrors our present and passing need in a profusion of sacred forms, all of them - as with the many Black Madonnas found at the leaky edges of European monotheism – peculiar, vernacular, *local*.

Crucially, Saxena also presents Western monotheism's millennial quest for a totalising, singular 'truth' as inseparable from its war on this ambiguously plural mother, and likewise, its war on the dark – on darkness: twin campaigns which eventually spawned the ballooning, light-addicted extinction-engine of industrial civilisation.

Our Lady of the Fireflies

Where Saxena grew up surrounded by Kali-ma, the childhood of US psychoanalyst Clarissa Pinkola Estés was steeped in another of the dark mother's local, compound forms: Nuestra Señora, Our Lady of Guadalupe. Drawing on the mingled Nahua-Catholic heritage of her Mexican upbringing, and that of her own immigrant Hungarian family, her 2011 book *Untie the Strong Woman: Blessed Mother's Immaculate Love for the Wild Soul* is a 400-page rambling love letter to Guadalupe, who Estes herself first encountered, much like Meinrad Craighead, as a young girl – through an apparition which saved her from drowning.

For Pinkola Estés the Church's association of Blessed Mother with a docile, obedient purity is simply irrelevant to the visceral compassion that she embodies. Nuestra Señora, as we meet her here, is a ubiquitous presence who arrives at the point of dumb need. The healing that this presence brings is neither a reward for good behaviour nor a thing achieved by skill, or ascetic striving. While invoked personally – as *You*, or *She* – Pinkola Estés recalls that of the great many encounters with Blessed Mother which she has listened to over the years, far fewer are a matter of human-faced, spoken apparition than they are moments of intimate connection with a reciprocal, animate world.

Among the many things I've kept from Pinkola Estés' writings on Blessed Mother is a quite ordinary, un-miraculous childhood memory. In a passage on the Black Madonna, 'Our Lady of the Fireflies', she recalls her old aunt Katerin rummaging in the still-warm ashes of a fire in search of the charcoal-shard madonnas which she'd plant along the edges of her vegetable patch. Presented with one such burnt mother the young Clarissa improvised a bedside shrine for her, illumined by a jam jar that she filled with fireflies at each dusk, releasing them again when she woke.

As someone who gets queasy around most Marian imagery in Western art, I find in this gift from the young Clarissa's elderly Hungarian aunt a provocative and sustaining icon, one that speaks to a generic current of spiritual longing rather than to anything specifically Catholic, or even Christian. Something as ordinary as calling for help when you've no clear idea who or what it is you're calling to. And for Pinkola Estés, it's in this very act of begging for help that Blessed Mother is already at work in our lives with the 'black light' of her compassion, an intimate darkness able 'to heal the soul of a person all the way down to the radical, to bless the cringing spirit with the deep blessing most needed for repair and re-emergence, in ways that carry deepest meaning for the individual.'

The nurse log

Who knows what Extinction Rebellion's revolt against ecocide will amount to? Whatever comes of it, among its ten core principles there's one in particular which I believe will outlive this phase in the cascading process of change now upon us. *We need a regenerative culture.*

Regenerative culture: to my ear it's a more pragmatic, tangible proposition than spiritual ecology. The slow, ground-level process of repair – at once social and ecological – already at work in the vulnerability and intersectional solidarity integral to this understanding of revolt.

What if such re-setting of our broken relationship with the living world turned out to have more to do with adapting to this culture's inevitable collapse than it did with convincing ourselves we can still somehow prevent that, if only we can find and tweak the right eco-spiritual dial? Or even – welcoming all of catastrophism's spectres to the table now – with coming to terms with our own potential 'near-term extinction'?

With no guarantee of where things go from here, perhaps the sheer, radical vulnerability of our present situation has a dark gift for us, after all. As anthropocentric religion's bright dream of the human evaporates in the face of what civilisation's become, what if ecological grief came to be understood as an undertow, drawing that prodigal spiritual culture home? Perhaps the measure of any regenerative spirituality in the years ahead will need to begin with how well it enables civilised humans to inhabit this gathering current of mourning, together. To help each other to meet it, and be realigned by it. That sort of help seems to be a thing that will come about locally or not at all, and at a scale far removed from late stage capitalism's screen-addicted crowd mind.

In his 1947 diatribe against the soul-murdering machine consciousness of British Empire, *The Vision of the Fool*, the artist and writer Cecil Collins suggested, like the good modernist mystic he was, that Western religion lay like so many overturned goblets whose spilled contents were now openly shared, even as the institutions that once held them collapsed beyond recovery. My preferred image for this regenerative collapse feels close to Collins'. Suppose the dying religion I was raised within were understood as a nurse log – a fallen ancestral giant slow-releasing its nutrients, from whose decaying body a tangle of adaptive cultures is even now emerging? Such new, regenerative shoots might turn out to have less to do with belief or exhausted argument than with recovered *behaviours*. Behaviours which allow us to entrust our lives to mystery – to the unearned gift of being here at all. The patterning miracle within which our lives swim, moment to moment, good times and bad. Or as Pinkola Estés might put that, to release our brief human lives into the reciprocal, animate currents of Rio Abajo Rio: the river beneath the river.

If the Black Madonna offers me one makeshift form through which to negotiate that dark river's subtle currents, what I meet in her compound, always more-than-one-thing face isn't complicated, difficult or clever. And the unhurried rhythm of turning to her each day has no more to do with a self-extinguishing path to enlightenment than it does with monotheism's desire-phobic purity. What that rhythm amounts to is a way of carrying on: a game, as her rose-garden devotion has long been known; an unproven experiment, whose step-by-step, wheeling dance requires no particular opinion about who or what we are.

However we choose to address her or not to address her, the dark mother in her myriad local and personal forms is surely synonymous with the ungraspable, all-enfolding river whose eyes we see through, whose lungs breathe us, and whose intricate life-mothering processes are so ancient, from a human perspective, as to be to all intents and purposes eternal. In her presence, be it one we paint on air or carry in our bones, we meet a patience deep enough to swallow the wave of loss gathering around us, an unpredictable and ferocious love already seeding pockets of regenerative culture within this ecocidal civilisation's dying body – tentative, deviant shoots that may yet prove themselves capable of fostering a gradual ecological healing, irrespective of where things go from here.

Cinder Mary

a lovely charred Madonna from my grandmother,
one found in the fire pit after the flames had burned
most everything except this little dark holy woman
made of half-burnt log.

– *Our Lady of the Fireflies*, Clarissa Pinkola Estés

Elsewhere, a cooling cinder
Madonna, pressed into poor soil,
whispers the garden awake.

The tubers hear her
secretive smile, begin to grow.

We know the father may come
to disallow, as fathers sometimes do.
Let's not speak of that.

Charred little sort-of-Mary,
fireflies round her head,

tucked between green shoots,
she breathes her black light
into their swelling roots.

Sources

On a Buddhist understanding of prayer

Brazier, David *Authentic Life: Buddhist Teachings and Stories*, Woodsmoke, 2019

Itsuki, Hiroyuki *Tariki: Embracing Despair, Discovering Peace*, Kodansha, 2001

On the Black Madonna

Estés, Clarissa Pinkola *Untie the Strong Woman: Blessed Mother's Immaculate Love for the Wild Soul,* Sounds True, 2011

Finn, Perdita & Strand, Clark *The Way of the Rose: the Radical Path of the Divine Feminine Hidden in the Rosary*, Spiegel & Grau, 2019

Osmond, Mat, 'Meinrad Craighead and the Animal Face of God', *Dark Mountain: Issue 15*, 2018

Osmond, Mat and Walters, Kate *The Black Madonna's Song*, poems and paintings, Atlantic Press, 2020

Saxena, Neela Battacharya *Absent Mother God of the West: A Kali Lover's Journey into Christianity & Judaism*, LEX, 2015

Strand, Clark *Waking up to the Dark: Ancient Wisdom for a Sleepless Age*, Spiegel & Grau, 2015

On culture and ecocide

Collins, Cecil *The Vision of the Fool and other writings*, Golgonooza, 2002

Powers, Richard *The Overstory*, W.W. Norton 2018

ROBERT LEE THORNTON

Unland

Here behind the purple marsh,
where the Heron is an expanse of wing dark-
ening the low pools, my grandfather
points to the Waterskipper
and the ellipsis of ripples it leaves behind, says nothing.
We drift our rig,
rig our hooks with strange kernels
that glitter like swamp grass slick with oil,
like the puffy eyes of the carp we throw back
into the deep mere. It is as
alien here as the eye of the sunken car it squirms into.
There is a woman in this swamp who was soldered
from a boat rib. I saw her once.
She rides a cattail raft and after
the sun burns the mist from the water she sleeps
with the carp on a bed of lake muck. It was her,
not Bog Oak, I saw lying below, those days before the Heron
– cross shadow, pagan saint –
returned to the land.

LORI MICHELLE WELLS

That Third Thing

Stuffed in the back seat, she is gasping for room, trapped between two small boys, wild animals. Man, she's mad. Smoking hot, like that pile of leaves Daddy burned in the yard yesterday. She's always getting in trouble for what Mommy calls her temper. She's supposed to ignore them. That freckled boy with mean blue eyes and the other one, blond buzz cut, big, with poking fingers and hard feet that never stop kicking the cracked vinyl edge of the car seat. Bump bump. *Whatcha got for lunch.* Bump. *Ya dropped somethin. HA. Made you look.* Screeching giggles. *Saw your underpants.*

One, two, three... She starts to count to ten. Shapes her face into a mask. A mask to show them: *I don't care about stupid boys.*

The boys tumble out of the car but she dawdles, stiffening at the rowdy racket coming from the playground. Blond boy dares her to go in the woods behind the school. *Scaredy cat.* She's been warned. There are bad monsters back there. *You can't make me.* Sharp push. Poking fingers. She runs, ducking between heavy metal chairs. Looks back and trips. Pop. The tiniest sound from her wrist as she stops her fall with her hands. She tastes grass. And tears. Her mask is about to break. Hastily, she takes off for the bathroom.

Alone she sits in the rosy pink stillness. Smells briny pain. *One two three. One two three.* She knows she must not cry in front of those bad boys. *One two three. OK, I'm OK.* Brushes at her grass stained knees. Dutifully she tries to wash the dirt from her palms. *Ow ow ow.* Hides that hand behind her skirt.

She creeps back to her seat and breathes in crayons, glue, and paper. *I'm OK.* She holds her secret hurt, waiting for Mommy to come.

*

I broke that arm when I was five. No one noticed until my mother picked me up, when finally they saw that my arm stuck out at an unnatural angle. My mother was disappointed that I didn't speak up. She didn't understand the cost of crying, of showing weakness to those boys. Fear of the woods, fear of the different, fear of looking weak were all born in that instant.

We live in a world built on commerce, competition, colonisation and conflict. Visible, loud and persistent – like those boys. If I allow myself intense moments of freedom and brilliance, blazing in the company of Perseid meteor showers and barred owl duets right after sunset, they must be followed by a strict lockdown while at work. Must pay the bills after all. This system, this civilisation has taken on a life of its own and I am deeply embedded and in debt. Hoarding, depriving, selling out, and then numbing myself to the pain of all this loss becomes my life. But I used to know that I was simply a small but essential piece of it all. Before the fears took hold, the maps of our interconnectedness were plain to see.

*

She is just four years old, outside in the backyard, in the dirt. Her gentle pink dress is full, buoyed by eyelet-trimmed petticoats and she is squatting on the lawn, her knees stained green, her hands and bare feet filthy dirty. Mesmerised by the swaying blades of grass, she sinks down to watch the roly polies. The grass is exhaling a tuneless whistle. If she had the words, she would tell you all about it. That midnight sky is right down there and it is filled with glittering stars. Pointing, she would tell you, *I belong right here*. Already the night is calling her name.

*

Recently, I found myself drawing dancers whose arms fly out like raptors singing for the breeze and whose feet can hear the truth rising up from the ground. They were tossing their heads like beach balls, smiles on their lips. Later, in a dream, I finally figure out how to unscrew my own head, and just let it drop off. It hits the lawn with a wonderful thud. My brown eyes stare down into the earth, past beetle grubs and moldering leaf litter. But my body floats into the sky. Without my skull's weighty anchor, I am floating into space, into dusky night and the embrace of Cassiopeia and the Great Bears of the heavens. Who untied that discarded box of secrets that I stowed away at age 13 and let the stars loose once again?

Out with my sister stars; I fly on home to the Night Mistress, Shadow

Walker, Protector of Wildness, the Devourer. I tremble. Will I survive becoming visible to the Night? I had utterly forgotten that this is where I belong. She demands that I release all of my unworthy inhibitions. *But aren't my voracious hungers better left alone?*

Why do I need this fearsome bitch of a goddess anyway? Maybe I would prefer to calmly sit in my tiny remote corner, keeping to myself and reciting a compassionate prayer with the lovely Kuan Yin or the pliant Aphrodite. *Pray for peace. Pray for beauty.* I have carved away my spiky hair, painted my carmine fingernails a lovely shade of shell pink, *oh, so natural*, and draped myself in muted swaths of softest yarn so that even the meekest will approach me. *Don't think about it. Just send out love and kindness.* I have finished it all off with an enigmatic Mona Lisa smile and a bemused chuckle, and carefully packed away my wildest instincts along with my ceremonial dagger and cauldron. *Everyone will like you better this way.* But now I have lost my way.

*

She slips into the room, breathless, and slowly removes her disguise. So much padding, so much shielding to unravel. *Oh no, everyone else is so young and perfect and brave.* The sounds coming from the speakers, shrill and staccato, scrape at her nerves. *Oh, let me out. Let me go.* The Night Mistress catches her wrist and blocks her escape. Invisible no more. The instructions are clear. Shake yourself everywhere. Especially those places that never get moved any more. Shake up against your fellow dancers. No symmetry. No pattern. No grace. She starts to come undone. *Ah, please let me out.*

You must let us in.

*

Ankoku Butoh – the Dance of Utter Darkness. Because it arose in the aftermath of the atomic bombing of Hiroshima and Nagasaki, it is tempting to think of this dance form as one of grief and despair. It is that. But Kazuo Ohno, one of the early dancers, reminds us to look beyond our Western ways of thinking about the dark: *Darkness in butoh refers to our unconscious, to that which is hidden from our awareness.*

*

At age 57 I showed up to dance with people half my age. We danced seed to sprout to maturity to blousy overripe to stench to decay to compost to seed. Sinking through the floor, I finally hear my own body, your body, our collective bodies. *Please,* they are chanting, *you must keep us in the dark. Let us germinate in our own times, each to their own rhythm. Do not rush us with fertiliser or hydroponic trickery. Give us our hibernation, our incubation, our time to decay and crumble into dust motes and cinder.*

Inside this dance, nothing is certain. Inside this dance, each move arises out of nothing. As I decay, there is no guarantee of rebirth or resurrection and I am not certain that my despair will transmute. My head would tell me, *Breathe out pain, sorrow, anger, breathe in light, joy, peace.* But remember, my animal body has left my head to rest out on that lawn, that marker of civilised order and dominance. I may pick it up. Later.

*

Her mother is calling her in for breakfast. *Lori Michelle!* she calls again, impatient. But Lori Michelle is not there. Invisible she reaches out to the invisible.

*

The dance grows disjointed, jerky. I move amongst the fragments, outtakes, bits of old film that I gather from the floor and put back together with cellophane tape that has grown yellow and brittle with age. My grandfather growling, *What do you think you are, a fucking elf?* There are long sequences of garbage-strewn beaches and the lonely wail of an orphaned seal. Snippets of endless freeway traffic going nowhere. And later, my ex-husband, with a pitying look on his face, whispers, *It must be hard, not being one of the pretty ones.* I think, *What if I* am *wilder than those small scary boys after all?*

*

She is snatched from the dirt, her mother hissing, *That's not ladylike, what did I tell you about not getting dirty?*

*

Spit back onto the reel, these frames flicker in my internal movie house and reignite my anger, despair and quiet grief. I stay in motion. The sacred threads of my wings are being re-stitched where they were rent by past battles. The untamed language of the red-tailed hawk returns to my mouth. Predatory, praying, I plummet toward sunrise. Love whispers. My body creates a shape I have never before even imagined. I resist the impulse to hoard it away. And on I dance. My love grows large, laden with an unwieldy aroma, the scent of grapes heading toward wine, seeping out and grasping with sticky fingers and suddenly desire overtakes, overcomes, overwhelms. I grasp for reason. Like a wall of jasmine warming in the late summer heat, my desire will not be contained or ignored. I cannot mask this musky, sultry sweet odor with a monologue on the virtues of non-attachment. I smash away shame and surrender. I am surrounded. I give up.

I never used to dare to show my teeth when I smiled or you would have caught a glimpse of my hunger and my ecstasy. And now, you might put me out with Queen Maeve, the Goddess of Intoxication, with her unashamed appetites.

Back out in the world, I straighten my clothing, my back, and screw my head back in place. A mature woman nearing sixty should not be this wild, this sensual. Modulated, regulated, balanced. I should be planning my invisible demise, retiring into quiet contemplation of a life already harvested of its ripeness. *Please pass the sugar, and yes, the cream to lighten this biting, bitter blackness*, I would whisper with one hand clenching the starched white napkin in my lap. I should be learning to gracefully fold into my brittle cronehood, relinquishing the stage to younger actors.

But instead I am devoured by night and stung by starlight and I pulse with the strength of the ebony panther pacing, pacing, pacing in the jungle. *Settle down,* I entreat my heart. She bursts through her amber cage of rib bone and safety nets. *You are going to have to admit that you are getting old,* advises a friend and still I dance. I check myself for delusions, for lies I have whispered in my own ears, for evidence that I am railing against the swift current of time that sweeps us all away. *I am just getting started,* I scream, *and I call on Kali, Black Madonna and Hecate to destroy my doubts, my hesitations, and any bad advice that slips past this fierce protector I have prayed for and received.*

*

Let me put it to you straight. I have been rummaging around in my very own basement, down there, in my deep pelvic bowl. Retrieving trunk-loads of discarded old maps and sacred vows written to the land and to the wild. I am reaching for that third thing, that synthesis just beyond the polarity of the invisible and the visible. *How can I have been so careless with my word?* Dancing, I use the savage sensual intensity of my own Dark Goddess to move muscles turned to granite by the poisoned stare of disapproval and tendons frozen in fear and silence. *Why is being civilised so inviting and yet so painful?*

A precious soul fragment – one that got trapped when I clenched my teeth and stopped my tongue – now flies out like a golden arrow. Out breaks my desire, yes, sexual and sensual, along with both my wisdom and my holy ignorance. I am returned to the dark. I am restored to my proper place. Community becomes visible and so do the invisible cords of communion and communication with stones, sky, raven, skunk and beetle, feral boys and wild woods – turns out I might have tried looking to them for clues for belonging all along.

DAN PORTER
Near Long Lane
Kent, England

NEALE INGLENOOK

Inauguration Day

for John Berger

Remember the fire. Remember it spreading down the hill in the floor of the pinewoods eating through the groves. The bodies fed to burning light. The trees silent dark marks.

Remember we walked through the smoke with our pots and jugs and pails over ground turned to ash. We sought out the gouts of flame poured the water in a boil of grey steam and the burnt gauze of the dead.

Remember how pails empty we returned to the stream. Our skin was painted in cremation streaked with charcoal. We soaked our feet in the cold flow the soles blistered. The water was the colour of bloodless flesh.

Remember the flames laddering up the bark of the cedars. We scraped them away with sticks they sprang back after each stroke. Our thin sandals pressed into the soft ash the floor of the world gone rotten. On the ridgeline a pine consumed in a crackling blaze a single great torch.

Smoke rose from the soil where the tree roots smoldered. We passed through the haze to fill our pots from the silted stream lay down in it the current brushing fingers through our hair. The sky was bad milk.

Remember the day before the plane flew over. The next day the fire. Some of us thought it's our fault we didn't look. Some thought fuck you fuck you fuck you. Others were in grief like a baby bird fallen into their chests flapping unformed wings.

The light left suddenly at dusk. We made our way back to camp in the dark feeling with our burnt feet the familiar paths. Willow thicket meadow dry needles of mountain hemlock. Remember the green scent of herbs – wild onion trillium lovage waterleaf. Muted birdcalls over the shushing stream.

There was the small fire at the heart of the camp in a grove of firs. We had to keep it burning if we were going to eat. Remember the vague glow against the still trunks. The coals settling sparks skating the darkness.

Remember the moist wind off the meadows. The mating frogs giving their cries. Another tree erupting in ravenous light.

We ate roasted roots and boiled grain and looked into the fire. Food blank on our tongues. Images in the decaying coals. Stories. Remember someone spoke them as now. Remember someone looked out into the dark full of living trees.

No starlight nor moon. We lifted our pots from the black earth. An owl spoke in the throat of the valley. The woods on the ridge were gutshot with flame.

Last night I dreamed a crow landed on my hand and looked into my eyes. I still feel its claws.

LUCY ANN SMETHURST

Earthbound

Part III – Rubbernecker

I can see as far as Frith Hall today, no further; Storm Diana has smudged out the distant horizon. Curtains of grey rain sweep the valley sideways. Ulpha Pike is a moving mass of leaf-empty trees and shrouding mist.

He looks less dead today than three days earlier. His tongue is swollen, pale pink and prune-puckered. His left eyelid moistened open by relentless overnight rain, the slit eyeball a blue-black bloom of death. I don't like that his ear is facing skywards, collecting rain in his skull. His coat is water-logged and the blood is washed from his teeth and neck. A small fell stream flows beneath his headstone and bubbles out near his dead head. The sound of the flowing water is more insistent than usual.

Cars drive south, out of the valley towards the coast, headlights on. I wonder if they see me sat up here on the north slab, and if they think I'm a crazy person. I don't really care, but it's a moment of self-consciousness. I stroke his full wet fur and touch his tongue. Have I become a voyeur of death? A slow rubbernecker of decomposition? I feel compelled to spend time with him most days now. Perhaps I hold necromantic hopes of reanimating him just by paying attention to his deadness.

The rain has trickled down my too-short-to-sit-down-in waterproof trousers, my greedy woollen socks have sucked up the droplets. Pools of rain gather in the elbow creases of my waterproof jacket. I stand and walk back to the track. I look for the wood pigeon wing feather stuck in the ground; it has been spun around and soaked by the storm. The pile of dog shit that marks the turning off the tarmac track is beginning to lose its definition.

*

Part II – Untameable Mind

I run up the tarmac track towards Low Birks Wood and turn sharp south into the bracken at the mouldering dog turd. There is a sketchy track, made by the ubiquitous Herdwick sheep that blotch the fells. I used to call these tracks *sheep tramples* when I was a kid. The wood pigeon's wing feather points out of the gently frozen ground, marking the way. I sit down on the flat north slab. The protruding east slab is his headstone. I get up to touch his dark pink tongue; it still yields to the poke of my curious finger. His nose is less squishy, firming with death. His coat and paw pads are fine-frosted, bright wet blood lingers on his neck. I stroke him and the frost melts; moist finger tracks in his fur. I sit back down.

Tuna, I need to add tuna to the Tesco home delivery order before midnight tonight, and some other type of meat…maybe sausages. No, too processed, something healthier. We should be eating more protein. I drag my mind back to now. Thankfully this mind is untameable but right now thinking of our protein intake is irrelevant and irreverent.

I cry a little. I've visited the fox a couple of times since I rested him here. A mix of morbid curiosity about how his body will decompose, a continued honouring of his continued death, and a childlike denial that he is dead. One morning I'll come to him and his meat jerky tongue will be back in his head, his right foreleg re-membered, he'll trot towards me and knowingly nuzzle my right hand as I sit on the north slab. This image is vivid, real in my mind. My untameable mind.

Goodbye fox. I jog back to the track, forgetting to acknowledge the dog turd marker as I leave behind the bracken and bog. I run further up the steepening hill, past the house that isn't a home. A bird feeder half full of peanuts dangles mournfully; it is unattended, like the house. Through the gate the uniformity of asphalt gives way to a stony uneven track descending through recently felled larch and birch, a place for surreptitious firewood foraging. At the other side of the de-forest the track winds back up the fell. I pass by an old Quaker burial ground, a small, square dry stone wall enclosure with three tall Scots pines as sentinels. I wonder whether I should have brought the fox here instead. *No*, he says, *not enclosed*. He is where he needs to be, on the open fell.

*

Part I – Go North

I pull on my wellies and fingerless gloves, two shiny pound coins in my hand. I stride over the stream through the sog of bog mosses and juncus reed and onto the road. I'm going to get eggs. The air is clear, bright, cold. My head down, I walk fast. A couple of cars pass me heading into the valley. The Dunnerdale fells flank my left side, the fast-flowing Duddon river to my right.

Blood and red fur flash into my eyes like an assault. Into focus comes a dead fox lying, no, placed on the low dry stone wall of the bridge. I stand quietly, taking it in, shock giving way to curiosity. Its right foreleg is missing. In its place, torn pink skin and sinew, blood and white jagged bone. Thick dark red blood is congealed at its mouth and is drip-dried on the lichen-covered stone. It's a male fox, that much I can tell by the furry gonads lodged between its stiff back legs. He has a healthy-looking coat and sturdy body, a fine creature, aside from the deadness.

I walk onward up the hill to the farm that sells eggs. Before I cross the cattle grid I can see there are no eggs, just an empty space and a white plastic honesty box. *Shit. No eggs. No omelettes.* Maybe I wasn't meant to get eggs today; I've got both hands free to take care of the fox now.

I walk back down the road and I sit down next to him. I touch his ear and as I curl it gently forward it boings back to pointless alertness. With two fingers I stroke up the bridge of his muzzle from his soft squish of a black nose to between his ears, like I used to do with my lurcher when she was sleeping. I decide to carry him onto the fell. I lift him carefully and find that his foreleg is not missing but folded underneath him. He is stiff and heavy with death, day-old death, I think. His tail sticks out almost comically as I hold him in my arms.

I walk up the fell through broken bracken the colour of fox. I can smell his unmistakable musk. Ahead there is a grassy spot surrounded by rocky outcrops and spiny whin bushes. I rest him down near a stone slab, his wounded side facing upwards. I replace his torn limb in its rightful position then I turn him over so that his wounded side is earthbound. His dead tongue is crushed between his dead teeth. I touch it and it is soft. Long strokes down his back and tail. *Uh, it might have fleas* my mum protests in my head. *I don't give a shit*, I answer.

I sit near him on the north slab and cry pulsing snotty sobs. A part of me believes he'll come back to life, he will start breathing again, the warmth will return and his fur will bristle under my hand. I say to him that I'm sorry, on behalf of the humans. I say he should run north, to the woods and mountains; *go north, the direction your body lies. Go north.*

PAUL FEATHER

Eternal Return

I am a merchant of death.

In a society where we insulate ourselves at all costs from the violence that is necessary for survival, there's an economic opportunity for those of us who will carry it out. I'll admit that I don't generally think of it all in such starkly economic terms, but there it is. I'll kill your food for you. There's blood on my shirt and mud caked to my knees. Your new porch needs killing too. So, there's sawdust in the cuffs of my pants; my hands smell of bar oil and are sticky with the blood of trees.

I am not one to think much about appearances.

I don't intentionally wear bloody clothing in public, but then I don't always remember to change my shirt before I go out either. Last week, I stopped in at a coffee shop to kill time waiting for someone. I hadn't taken stock of my appearance until the wave of air conditioning hit my face in the doorway. My shirt is torn, and even though the bloodstains are not fresh, I suspect I'm as out of place here as would be the *campesinos* who grow the coffee that everyone's drinking. There's a lady in the corner wearing scrubs, but her I-just-got-off-work look fits right in.

I want to know what you do for a living.

There was a time when that old bar-stool introduction seemed shallow, at odds with the sense that I had to get at something deeper – to know *who you really are*. Maybe because the economics of wage slavery force most of us to work at something we don't really believe in; because our jobs only peripherally express our innermost being. But now, I think that's bullshit. I don't care about your religion or your hobbies or your wildest dreams anymore. I want to know what your survival depends on.

Wear it out in the open.

*

Before I killed food for a living, I taught music for a while. My expertise was in West African drumming, and although I can claim no special gift with music, I had studied enough to teach beginners and children. This music is unambiguously polyrhythmic. Each rhythm incorporates several parts that are nested together in interlocking and recurring patterns. Sometimes one part is longer than another so that shorter patterns recur a few times within a single iteration of the longer part. The rhythm as a whole is a structure of recurring patterns with varying frequency.

This is also how the world is made. Even now my work is polyrhythmic, because agriculture is musical in every way. The familiar return of seasonal themes is marked with the unexpected and intricate improvisations of weather, species and variety. The rhythmic movements in the threshing of beans only occur as part of a polyrhythmic structure that includes the familiar and longer motions of saving that seed, planting again, eating them fresh, gathering the swollen pods as the vines die, staving off the moths whose worms would eat the seeds. Even the dying of a chicken vibrates with the frantic beating of a heart, the lightning flashing through the nerves, the slow release of tension in the muscles eased out by the tension in my own hands. They're all in rhythms. Every part of every whole.

*

The basis of meaning is recurrence.

Everything, every event and every experience derives its meaning from recurrence. In order for something to exist – to have meaning – it is not sufficient for that thing to *occur*, for in this single instance there is no thing. There is only noise. In order for something to exist, it must *recur*. There must be a pattern, a rhythm. It must be, and then be again – a self-affirmation. It isn't nouns but verbs that hold their own against the tides of entropy.

Everything does something for a living.

*

Just now, I am contemplating the health of my soil, whose vitality supports my own existence. I have let the weeds grow up, which is a helpful thing to do. But sometimes neglect is not sufficient, and I suspect I'm shirking. I have taken a lot from the garden this season, and I have yet to put anything back. I feel indebted.

I decide to haul some woodchips into the garden. I have a pile of them that I made several years ago when I hired a machine and pulverised all of the cutoffs from the sawmill. The pigs ran over the pile for most of the spring, so it is well mixed with their manure and with compost and scraps we've been tossing over the fence to feed them. In some way, I consider that these woodchips and manure will even my debt with the soil, but I'm reluctant to model this exchange upon all-too-human economics. This is not simply an exchange of goods; it won't do to imagine that I'm trading manure for this season's harvest of potatoes. The debt that I owe here is rhythmic. If this is an exchange, it is of the sort that dancers make.

The meaning of my exchange with the soil is to resolve a tension that has developed in my rhythmic interaction with the garden. The interplay of my activity with the plants and the soil develops an improvisational melody, and as with any melody there are expected notes – tensions that build into logical conclusions. We may avoid these concluding notes and even create especially interesting melodies in doing so, but we also risk dissonance. Dissonance has a place, but I don't think it's a livelihood.

The economics of my existence – the debt I owe to the soil – is to resolve these tensions in the interwoven and recurring stories of my being. Plodding now back and forth across the field with the wheelbarrow creates a note or a chord of a particular frequency. At approximately ten minutes to load and empty the cart, this note is played at about 0.0017 Hertz. (The soil plays a slower tune than we are used to.) There are other concordant notes that I am playing with this movement: my breath, my heartbeat, the rhythmic pacing of my legs, the scooping of the shovel; and this single chord is only the grace note upon even longer tones set by the rhythms of my digestion and sleep. My physical body *is* this set of rhythms; they are not separable at all.

Then too, this chord is set amongst notes that others play. The feeding and defecation of the pigs echoes in my going to and fro with the cart, for this is part of the meaning in these actions. The trees' slow notes add ring after ring of growth. Even the uber-fast revolution of the machines that turned these trees to chips echoes in this chorus. We can say this movement is economic; it is an acknowledgement of reciprocity and participation, although it can't be reduced to an exchange of *things*. It is sufficient to say that when I dug the potatoes, a chord was played, and this chord follows that one.

Truly, all these notes together are the meaning of me. Who we are is in the polyrhythms that form the basis of our existence, both those that reside in our own bodies and those created by our interactions with other beings and Earth's own biorhythms. The beginnings of language may have been in the mimicry of these rhythms in particular animals, making the whole basis of language a symbolic representation of these polyrhythms. In his essay in *Dark Mountain 12*, Rob Percival suggests that, through mimicry, early humans

> became cognisant of the rhythms of the animal world ... of the migration of herds moving across the savannah ... They became cognisant of the ... repetitious, rhythmic stability of each species. They caught a glimpse of the rhythms that extended beyond, intimations of the Earth's rotation through space, in the turning of the seasons, in the spinning of the stars.[1]

The polyrhythmic composition of our being extends into a cosmology in which we find our place within a rhythmic universe. The rhythms of our modern livelihoods, however, are no longer defined by the changing of seasons or the run of salmon, much less by complex improvisations upon unfathomable variations in those rhythms. On the contrary, our routines have become so prescribed and mechanical as to be algorithmic. Yuval Noah Harari has pointed out that Google and Facebook algorithms already show signs of predicting our behavior more accurately than our family and friends and that the capitalist machine which can predict us will replace us.[2] It appears that the death knell of liberal humanism rings in the monotonous dirge of our modern nine-to-five; by uprooting ourselves from the complex dance of a polyrhythmic cosmos we're becoming disposable automatons.

*

When do you jump ship?

As our lives become more and more mechanised and the capitalist machine threatens to grind us into cog-like anonymity, is there a moment when we must proclaim our humanity and flee? And what does that look like? While it's true that humankind won't collectively abandon the capitalist machine, I think it's also true that more and more people are being called away from our machines and toward something else. I believe there is a song that calls us all back into rhythmic exchange with the soil, and that more people are beginning to hear this song.

I can at least say that I hear a song, and that I've been hearing it since

I jumped ship myself 18 years ago. I hear it in the soil, in the stars, and lately in the wind, and that's all very romantic; and for most of my life this romanticism made it hard to talk about this music I hear, except that now I think other people can hear it too. If for almost two decades I've become a person that stands out a bit in the coffee shop, then I think it's because I've been hearing something that most other folks didn't. And now I think that other people can hear it after all. Maybe it's getting louder.

My personal experience is that now more than ever before, people seem to be having trouble resolving the dissonance between the rhythms of their lives and livelihoods and some other melody – some other possible way of being. I have never before seen so many of my peers in crisis – wrestling with who they are and especially with their relationship to the capitalist economy: my neighbour feels complicit in the crime of saddling families with healthcare expenses that will not save their dying loved ones; a friend who works in education believes that she is indoctrinating children into the hyper-rational worldview that she herself is trying to shed; there is a ex-gangster from L.A. staying on my farm, trying to figure out if living off the land is even a real thing. Some of my friends' livelihoods are called into question by divorce or business failure, but underneath it all I detect something else – a questioning of more basic values and rhythms that once validated our lives. These kinds of questions are a curse of privilege, and they are truly terrible. They cast everything into doubt.

Beyond these anecdotes, there also appears to be a mounting global movement in response to the ongoing murder of our planet that conveys an urgency in response to ecocide that environmentalists have seemed unable to muster until now. The test of this movement will be whether its traffic blockades, student strikes, marches and other actions remain largely symbolic or actually succeed in disrupting the rhythmic motions of people's livelihoods.

There are two parts to this rebellion. It is an uprising against legitimately unjust systems of exploitation, but – if genuine – I suspect that it also entails the rejection of our own rhythmic identities that are cast in the mold of those systems. It must be a response to the rising song that calls us back to the soil.

*

The ex-gangster who lives on my farm is in love with the cowboy era.

'Those were the days,' he says, 'when people were free. You were responsible for yourself. There wasn't big government turning everybody into fucking babies.'

'I guess it took a pretty big government to commit the genocide of millions of people living here before the colonisers came,' I say.

'True that. But if you were just a regular person and you could farm a piece of land, you could have it. And if you had a problem with somebody you settled it. You were free.'

'A regular person? You mean a white person. You mean a fucking white man, and that's not the same thing.'

'Ok, ok, so they got fucked, but it's over. What do you want to do about it?'

'No man, it's not fucking over. It's not.'

When we jump from this ship of progress, we are restored to cyclical time. It is a return to returning.

Ahnishinahbæó^{t}*jibway* author, Wub-e-ke-niew, denotes his people's recurrent time with an underlined letter 't' in order to differentiate it from linear time, in which 'Western Europeans become detached from their continuity in time and thus seemingly insulated from their history.' He warns Western Europeans that they 'cannot run away from the consequences of their past, because it is inextricably part of their present...'[3]

To the extent that cyclical time is acknowledged at all in Western thought, it remains oddly linear – a repeating series of events that nonetheless retains some orderliness and a sense of beginning and end – as in Nietzsche's description of eternal return where

> This life as you now live it and have lived it, you will have to live once more and innumerable times more; and there will be nothing new in it, but every pain and every joy and every thought and sigh and everything immeasurably small or great in your life must return to you – all in the same succession and sequence... and even this moment.[4]

It may be meaningful to consider that although every *thing* may not return in the 'same succession and sequence', the rhythmic chords of past actions still define those themes that must return and be resolved within the structure of our symphonic state of being. We have heard the overture. We know which themes must return.

My friend would believe that the cowboy era and its attendant genocide are lost in the annals of history. But perhaps our modern society returns now to the awareness that time is not so linear – that the victims of our genocide possessed a basis of perception that we will need in order to survive. It seems to me that our reparations with these people must start with the acknowledgement that this genocide eternally returns. I believe that as inheritors of Western civilisation, we must humble ourselves enough to return to these atrocities in search of some piece of humanity that was lost there. For without this missing piece, we will not survive.

In effect, that search itself must become what we do for a living – that search for a lost chord that imparts meaning to those of us who can no longer find ourselves in this strictly mechanical economics of things. And while it is true that many of us may very well merge with our machines to eat coal, others of us will not do this, and at whatever moment we jump ship we'll have to extract our identity from the story of the capitalist machine and find a refuge in these other stories of the soil, of falling leaves, rotting wood, of blood, bone and bacteria; these stories that we've lost and found so many times.

*

I've now piled several loads of oak leaves from the ancient tree in my neighbour's yard alongside the woodchips in my garden. There are enough acorns mixed in that I'm wishing I'd raked it all up while I still had pigs to feed them to. Also buried here are the entrails of two pigs.

It is clear to me that these pigs do not end here. I can't tell you what happens in the soil, but I can tell you about the steam that rises in the cold air from these piles of rotting wood. I can tell you about the heat of this decay that sings of life and rebirth, and I can ask how our linearised notions of time – even our cyclical time falling short of omnipresent time – might cloud our perception of death? What will be reborn from this decay under my feet? I will be, for one, and my family and friends.

It is only through this exchange with the soil that I exist. In this polyrhythmic cosmology, we each exist only as that set of rhythms that keeps us alive – our breath and heartbeat, yes; but also those recurring themes defined by our livelihood. Some of us may experience dissonance as our rhythmic interaction with the soil is intercepted by our participation with the capitalist machine; and as the voice of the Earth rises, we may find need to pause. To strike. And if we do, our rhythms will change. We will entrain ourselves with this rising rhythm of the Earth.

References

1. Percival, Rob, 'Pig Rhythm', in *Dark Mountain 12: Sanctum*, Dark Mountain Project, 2017.
2. Harari, Yuval Noah *Homo Deus: A Brief History of Tomorrow*, Harper Collins, 2017.
3. Wub-e-ke-niew *We Have the Right To Exist: A Translation of Aboriginal Indigenous Thought: The first book ever published from an Ahnishinahbæó'jibway Perspective*, Black Thistle Press, 1995.
4. Nietzsche, Friedrich *The Gay Science*, 1882, transl. Kaufmann, Walter in *The Portable Nietzsche*, Penguin, 1954.

SIANA FITZJOHN

Sleepover with a Pig

This piece is dedicated to someone I admire very much, who has never wavered in her wisdom and kindness through the loss of two children and the unthinkable persecution of her family.

> ***Code of Welfare: Commercial Slaughter*** *(October 2018, Ministry for Primary Industries, New Zealand Government)*
> *The welfare of terrestrial animals is covered from the time at which they are unloaded at slaughter premises to the time at which they are slaughtered. To ensure that the welfare of animals is maintained during stunning and bleeding out and that the process operates at maximum effectiveness, the system of stunning and bleeding out is required to be included in a quality management programme.*
>
> *Facilities factors to be considered include:*
> - *prevention of means of escape*
> - *the slope of ramps*
> - *design, maintenance and condition of the floor and wall surfaces*
> - *washing facilities*
> - *lighting*
> - *races (including those leading to point of slaughter)*
> - *noise*

The vet stood up. 'A nasty case of pneumonia.'

'Is there anything you can do for her?'

The vet's name was Errol. Kind eyes. 'Do you want me to wave my magic wand?'

I nodded. 'Yes please.'

'Well I can give her an anti-inflam, and a shot of antibiotics in case there's any bacterial infection, but her lungs are struggling, she's not eating. She's a very sick pig.'

'So in your opinion…'

'It's not good. Given her age… if she doesn't improve you need to think about options. We can either inject her heart from each side with an overdose of anesthetic…or there's a humane destroyer.'

'In the…'

'In the head, yes.'

'Faster…'

'Yes.'

We looked over at Splodge, lying listless on the grass in the sun. On my 14th birthday I had walked into the shed to find a compact black kunekune piglet. My joyful shout sent her dashing for cover, but we soon won her round with cheese and biscuits. She was a dream come true. And her name Splodge, well, that just made sense.

'I feel for you,' Errol began. 'If someone hasn't had a pig they wouldn't understand. We had one when I was at vet school, called Jackson. He'd come up onto the deck and drink beer with us. He was great, old Jackson. We had intended to eat him, but in the end we couldn't.'

I smiled.

He continued, 'Another flat down the road couldn't eat their pig either. Got too attached. So we swapped pigs.'

'Oh.'

Horror and amusement. Rural New Zealand is something, really.

I looked back at Splodge. Long black wiry hair, tongue just poking out of her mouth. Shit.

'Should I try to tempt her back into her hut?'

Errol smiled. 'No, she's master of her own destiny. Call me tomorrow.'

'Thanks Errol.'

In the kitchen I put my hands on the bench, bent over, and sighed.

Then screamed.

Minimum Standard No.3 – Facilities for Large Mammals

- *The maximum slope of ramps should not exceed 20°*
- *The presence and absence of cladding on gates and barriers*

should be arranged to encourage movement of animals in the required direction and to minimise the likelihood of gate or barrier charging by animals that are attempting to escape.
- *Sufficient fixed or portable lighting must be available so that animals can be inspected in their pens at any hour of the day and night.*
- *Floors should have non-slip surfaces.*

That evening, Splodge nosed dispiritedly at the straw in her hut, arranging it into place before lying down. Routine is very important to pigs. She wheezed heavily. I had asthma attacks when I was a kid. Lungs suck when they don't suck properly.

Grunt.

It wasn't a grumpy grunt that says 'I hurt, do something', but one that said 'I don't know if I'm going to get better.' Inside, I ate dinner and said goodnight to Mum and Dad. Then grabbed a big jacket. Thermals, torch, socks. More socks. Sleeping bag, blanket, and walked out into the winter night.

Across the paddock. Moon was up.

Grunt.

'I came to have a sleepover.'

Grunt.

'Thought you might like the company.'

Pause.

Grunt.

I crawled into the hut, spread my sleeping bag out on the straw and lay down next to her, pulling the blanket over us both.

Grunt.

'It's pretty cosy in here Splodge. Love what you've done with it.'

It was a ramshackle wee hut, with a low roof and haphazard wooden sides, and a tarp over the top and weighted down against the wind that tried to creep through the cracks. Deep straw, and a few spider webs overhead. Homely.

'I wish we'd had a sleepover before now… this is lovely.'

Grunt.

'Well I never thought of it before.'

Her breaths dragged. Tears pricked.

'If you need to go, I understand. You have been such, such an amazing friend to me. I love you. So much.'

Grunt.

'I could give you a couple of years of my life... I'd do that. To spend that time with you.'

Grunt. She wouldn't have them.

My heart tore. Running outside one winter night 14 years ago after a row with Mum and Dad, I'd flung myself in the straw. A much littler Splodge came and snuggled beside me, listening and grunting, her solid black presence a comfort to teenage woes. Her smell took me back to that time, when we were smaller and woes were simpler. When death was further away.

She shuffled over so I could rub her belly. Get right in there, under the legs. *All* the belly. OK.

'What's your favourite colour?'

Black.

'What?'

Grunt. Black.

My eyes lit up in the dark. It wasn't the colour I would have guessed, but of course black. She's a black pig.

'Cool.'

Grunt grunt.

I put my arm around her.

'You're here tonight Splodge, we're here. Alive. And I love you.'

The moon held tides of Earth's grief at bay for a moment. The crash of ecosystems muffled and distant beyond our rustle and breath. Splodge sighed. I buried into the straw. I was a piglet. Her piglet. Things were nicer, here. More of me was here. Safe in the smell of straw, warm in the warmth with the winter outside. Up against her big black body, grunting soft magic. Some moments just feel more real.

This was one of those.

Minimum Standard No. 4 – Handling of Large Mammals

- *Cattle, sheep, goats, pigs, deer, equines and camelids must not be held in lairage for longer than 48 hours before slaughter.*
- *All swim washing and high-pressure or high-volume spray washing must be closely monitored at all times to ensure the welfare of the animals.*
- *Any animals that go under or swim in the wrong direction during swim washing must be assisted immediately.*
- *Animals must not be washed more than twice.*
- *Electric prodders must not be used on animals, except on –*
  - *i) cattle that weigh over 150 kg; or*
  - *ii) during loading or unloading for transport, on pigs that weigh over 150 kg;*
  - *iii) during loading of a stunning pen at any slaughter premises, on pigs that weigh over 150 kg*

'Remember when the vet came to get a barley grass seed out from behind your eye? You lay quietly and let him do it without any sedation. He said none of the other vets would ever believe him. That's how phenomenal you are.'

Snug in the straw, we listened to the breeze move around the hut. An occasional bird fluttered on its pine tree roost above us.

'I don't know what to say, I'm so sorry about George.'

Grunt.

Splodge had two litters of five babies. Before farrowing, she spent days organising her nest. When her piglets came, she talked to them constantly. The smallest of her first litter, a friendly little black one with dark eyes, died of an infection. Everyone cried. The cat and I lay in the straw and watched Splodge give birth to her second litter. The piglets came out frontwards, backwards, didn't seem to matter. One even tried pushing his way back in. We found homes for all except Georgie Porgie. We kept him to keep Splodge company. Black and white, greedy and gorgeous.

Grunt.

Pigs have very inflexible spines. George had rolled over in the paddock four years ago and fractured his back. We had tried. But…

Grunt.
It was awful.

Splodge never stopped picking up stones in the paddock and rolling them around on her tongue. She started doing it when she was a piglet. I think she was lonely.

'I'm sorry Splodge. I didn't know. I wish I'd come to say good night to you every night.'

Grunt.

Death comes close to show us how deep our emotions and relationships are. Or could have been. If only we'd known then what we know now.

Grunt.

'Yeah. Stuck in my head, you're right. But it's hard not to blame myself and feel guilty, I wish I'd...'

Grunt.

'I've just made so many mistakes in relationships. When things go wrong, well... I think it's my fault. Then kinda hate myself for fucking life up...'

Pause.

Grunt!

I laughed through tears. 'Maybe not all human brains. But that's how my brain goes. Ridiculous. I know.'

Grunt grunt.

I oinked back.

Grunt grunt grunt.

Oink oink?

Grunt grunt.

...oink.

Grunt...

Tears and snot.

Oink oinkoinkoink. Don't die, please don't die Splodge.

Gruuunt grunt grunt grunt grunt...

Softer noises now. Gentle. My voice cracked.

'I want to have a baby.' God, where did that come from?

'Maybe. In the next few years...I want you to meet my piglet like I met yours. If you could just hang on for a little while longer...that would be the best thing.'

I was bargaining. Trying to.
Grunt grunt.
Oink oink.

Minimum Standard No. 5 – Restraint for Stunning of Large Mammals

- *A restraining device must be used if the natural behaviour of the animal and the system of handling do not allow the accurate application of the stunning equipment.*
- *Where a restraining conveyor is used for sheep, goats, calves and pigs in which individuals are separated:*
  i) the width and angle of conveyors must suit lines of animals that are being processed; and
  ii) conveyors must be designed and operated to prevent animals from climbing on the backs of animals in front of them.
- *Animals must not be left in any restraining device during regular work breaks.*
- *During a breakdown or if the processing line stops, animals must be removed from the restraining device if they become distressed.*
- *Electrical stunning of free-standing pigs is acceptable, provided that, when selecting and positioning a pig for stunning, stress is minimised for that animal and other pigs in the pen and provided that the application of the electrodes is accurate.*

Splodge sighed. I wriggled through the straw, snuggling against her back. Black bristly hair. The kink in her tail. Solid. Warm. Familiar smell. Then something happened.

A force, an energy – something I could feel, or see – encountered me. There it was, sudden and clear at my front. Strange, unexpected, trusted. A dark black colourful unseeable thing. A deeply physical … something. Love? Perhaps. Love long shut off.

It was alive.

Drink with a thirsty heart. It travelled into me, pouring into my head, throat, chest, stomach. It came from her. My heart returned in kind, my stomach roaring reverence, echoing the soul sound of grief for her losses, my loss of her – the silent and deafening sound of kindred friendship. Utter admiration. For her understanding. Her wisdom. And the deeper, less touched reserve of respect. For her. And I pushed from every cell of my body the force of nature to keep itself alive.

Grunt.

Oink.

Then we slept.

- *Severance of major arteries supplying the brain and heart is an acceptable method of slaughter, provided that the animal has been first rendered insensible to pain by stunning.*
- *Large mammals must be unconscious before being shackled.*

Morning came. Glinting off the grass and dew, stirring me in the straw. Splodge was already up. To everyone's disbelief, she ran away from Errol when he came to give her another injection. She recovered. And for the first time in 12 years, I stopped self-harming.

She recovered. With the deepest appreciation, I share this with you.

I still cannot fucking believe it.

Minimum Standard No. 10 – Stunning to Bleeding Out of Large Mammals

- *The time interval between stunning and bleeding out is particularly important when methods of stunning are employed which are only temporary in nature.*
- *If during the bleeding out process any animal shows signs of regaining sensibility, the stunning and slaughter of other animals must stop immediately and the animal that is showing signs of regaining sensibility must be rendered insensible.*

Dare to ask – how many? Many. The inconceivable many. And of the many, most mothers were unable to build nests, unable to turn around, unable to show their babies the world, or the world their babies. Pigs in their millions denied their talents and motivation – to explore their Earth. To love and care for their children. To be cared for by their mother. Many experience their freest of movements en route to the slaughter floor.

- *A thoracic (chest) stick, severs the large blood vessels that give rise to the jugular veins and carotid arteries. This method of slaughter is achieved by running a knife down one jugular furrow of the neck and then into the opening of the chest between the first pair of ribs. A successful incision is denoted by an obvious gush of blood, both venous and arterial.*

Before the curtain falls on humankind and we take our bows, let us be asked, Why did you do that?

And let us stand there in the bright lights of the stage in dismay, as all our answers fall out of our mouths and scatter around our feet. Let the spotlight follow us as we file off the stage down a ramp, incline no more than 20°, on a non-slip surfaced floor.

- *In the case of heavily pregnant animals being slaughtered, the foetus must not be removed from the uterus sooner than 5 minutes after the maternal neck cut or thoracic stick.*

When I see her trot across the grass, I imagine her every step a tribute to steps denied. When I whisper goodnight, her deep sigh is my prayer for breaths stolen. But those prayers are for us. Splodge is for Splodge.

- *Any living foetus removed from the uterus must be killed or prevented from inflating its lungs with air and breathing.*

Her life is her own.

JANE LOVELL

Fox Map

Over time
you become landscape:

something sinking away
to create valleys and lowlands.

I imagine a clear stream
descending in troughs
and eddies

resisted by your fur
                        to pool
            in brilliant
hemispheres.

Your eye,
clear as glass, green/gold of sorrel
or birch, backlit and evening

is gone
           – sewn in
                        – blind:
a scar on a long hill.

Over time
you become stranger:

paths peter out, lost
in contours raised by bone,

a quiet tectonic shift
redefining earth,

the stone and soil
          and frost

that built you.

CHRIS BOOTH
Let Go
Ink on paper

A medieval cataclysm echoing through to today: Rye, in England, burned long ago but this piece highlights the glacial pace of social change and hierarchies in affluent rural England. What must it take to force genuine change when total destruction simply renews what came before?

SAMUEL OSBORN

Thinking with Bog Mummies

Eschatologies for troubling times

Thinking involves not only the flow of thoughts, but their arrest as well. Where thinking suddenly stops in a configuration pregnant with tensions, it gives that configuration a shock, by which it crystalizes into a monad. A historical materialist approaches a historical subject only where he encounters a monad.

– Walter Benjamin

I.

Human beings are lasting things; we last in each other's memories, in the items we care for, and in the ecosystems we consume. Talking about eternity and finality is talking about eschatology, and so it is religious, it is theological. To engage with eschatology is to talk about end time, apocalypse and eschaton, but to have that conversation one must also discuss the immediate fate of the dead. To understand something of the Ragnarók is also to know something about Valhalla, and vice versa. So, apocalypse is a conversation about individual death, and long-term location of the dead as much as it is about final world-ending. In an intimate way, eschatology is a discussion about what parts of a human last, for how long, and in what way; and that is a conversation I want to have using bog bodies, and the death rituals of the ancient Celts.

There are pleasant ways for a human to linger; there are familiar ways, strange ways, and haunting ways. There are inconsequential ways of lasting: the cup half full on the table is too small for religion. There are dirty ways: the bloated body in the grass on a river bank is too disturbing for modernity. There are readable ways: deciphered by archaeologists. There are meaningful ways: mediated by priests. There are ways that stifle and destroy: trash clotted drainages, infertile fields, strip mines and overfished seas. There are ways that sustain and enable: the fallen redwood supports micro-ecosystems. All of these ways are answers to that most eschatological question: what happens to the dead leading up to the end of all things? Death is not a happy thing to think about. But, we are wise and exhausted people, living in sad times with hard-to-find hope, and it does some good to pick up the old, odd objects that theologians call eschatologies. More importantly, we need to re-locate ourselves in a wide and deep pile of traditions that has all sorts of answers and questions about dying.

II.

The spiritual man should be quite at home
in a world made to be used.
– George Santayana

The Western industrial flourishing was lit by the bright sun of an immediate holy salvation, a post-Reformation sensibility that oscillated between apocalyptic imminence and eternal repose in paradise. In both cases the Earth was nothing more than a temporary abode in a journey to either eternal salvation or damnation. There are certainly many factors that allow Western capitalists to conceive of the world as a resource to be plundered – theologic, scientific and moral – but the one I am interested in calling forward is the factor connected to finality and eternity: the eschatological factor.

It is less that the Christian eternity forgave irresponsibility, and more that they failed to teach us the importance of custodianship and sustainability. Real sustainability is absolutely an eschatological concern; we can engage in sustainabilities that are confined to our lifetimes, but those are very different from impersonal sustainability that permeates into the distant future. In all of the ways that Western theology was interested in eternity, it has not recently been interested in eternal earthly responsibility. To the modernists, responsibility was a transcendental consideration, and our true and eternal place was not on a damaged and dying planet, but at the side of the Lord in kingdom come.

The secular present has inherited this modern Christian theory of death but evacuated all of the dogma and enchantment. Not a few postmodernists wander through nihilist spaces of earthly brevity without a spiritual, philosophical or moral connection to eternity. In the era of disposable everything, our lives hold little value beyond their consumerist role in an economic machine. According to capitalism, once we stop having productive value, we matter little, and this is even more true after death. The postmodern idea of eternity is non-biodegradability; it's idea of longevity is the post-death nothingness of atheistic science mixed with vestigial spiritualisms.

Our postmodern understanding of death has left us blind to what we leave behind and what we take with us when we die. Jumbled blends of mild spiritualism, scientific clarity and end-of-life financial predation have turned dying into a consumerist exercise of terror, suffering and polite unthinkability. No one culture or ideology is at fault here. A braided path, with terminals and shortcuts, has taken us to a philosophical place that finds the Christian world unprepared to understand Earth as our eternal home. We have lost sight of ourselves as fragile, rotting things that will cling to our cosmic graveyard for eternity. We have forgotten the responsibility that comes with dying and lasting in the same place where our children will continue to live.

III.

Staying with the trouble, yearning toward resurgence,
requires inheriting hard histories, for everybody,
but not equally and not in the same ways.
– Donna Harraway

There are fields in Flanders substantiated with the corpses of a generation of dead men from around the colonial world. Iona is so fertilised with the corpses of kings and saints that the island itself is holy and wholly meat. Place and death are interfused exactly because a dying person becomes their death-place. This happens chemically and ecologically, but it also happens socially, culturally and religiously. Instead of an eschatology of removal, repose and comfort, I am very interested in traditions of eternity that focus on endurance, placement, discomfort and responsibility. To get through the mess we are in, the living need to start feeling immediately responsible for the places they will die in. The place where we will reunite with ancestry cannot be a heavenly otherworld, but instead needs to be the damaged earthly places of the immediate and distant future. When death consecrates landscape, the dead enjoy an ownership over it, and the living have a duty toward stewardship. Places made sacred by our dead neighbours and ancestors are easier to connect to, easier to care for and more humbling to inhabit. As death turns into a legacy of location, poetic things start to happen in the space of life-after-death. Literally or metaphorically, depending on your interest in trophic cascades, the dead *become* the place. The two quickly tangle and interfuse so the stakes of responsibility are doubled. To care for the land is to respect the sustainability practiced by ancestors and neighbours. To care for the dead is to honour the landscape as the eternal home of dead friends.

Understanding the potential of a well-formed relationship with death and the dead, the mission now is to explore ways to bolster ours. To that end, we will closely examine the practice and intentionality of the ancient Celts around death, if only to create a model for how to approach the act of salvaging old relationships to death. One of the most alluring things about pagan religious practice in northern Europe is that we know very little about it; it has been a vacuum space onto which romantics and nationalists alike have problematically projected their ideologies. Less dangerously, northern European Iron Age religion is one of those rare spaces where archaeology and cautiously read classical commentary can help us understand what people *did* with their religion, but hardly at all what they *thought*. That is to say, we can, in a limited way, speak to the praxis of their religions, but will never be able to answer the *why* questions, the theological questions. It is a shadow mythology, with few solid deities and concepts and even fewer detailed liturgies. Much of the nuance and texture was preserved orally and then lost to us as these areas first Latinised and then Christianised.

IV.

> We cannot know exactly what was behind bog body burials, but we can be fairly certain that the perpetrators wished these bodies to be placed in spiritually charged, dangerous places, where they would never decay.
>
> – Miranda Aldhouse-Green

The ancient Celts especially seem to have lived in tune with ideas of liminality. Ecologically marginal places are typical of both ritual deposition and domestic dwellings. A classic Celtic motif is the offerings of weapons and human sacrifice into watery places: the River Thames, Llyn Cerrig Bach, the Lindow Marsh all evidence this practice. In Scotland and Ireland, the crannogs homes in lochs were a constant dialogue between shoreland, water and sky. At the same time, the Germanic peoples would move, think and worship where Earth touched atmosphere: hilltops and cliffs. In both Germanic and Celtic traditions, it seems temples and shrines were open to the sky, ramparted onto hilltops or hidden away in groves. The dead were just as involved in marginal places as the living. Burials at or under doorways were common. More famously, bog mummies are known to us precisely because they were deposited in peaty marshland (itself a conversation between earth and water) during or shortly after death. Marginal positions in life and death reflect an intentionality around where things go. Symbolism, utilitarianism, or likely a combination of the two led to a celebration, consecration and ancestral revisitation of places in ecologically fragile spaces such as riparian, marsh and moor. The nature of this sacralisation included patterns of deposition of the dead, and so the reverence of marginal places seems to be built into their understanding of the after-life. Since the Neolithic, the British dead have been buried under doors, thresholds and gates; a practice that continued into Roman Britain. Architectural liminality is just as in play as ecological, and so the message is clear: the home of the dead is a nexus. A place that is between inside and outside, solid land and liquid water. Locating such a place is, equally, an ecological, architectural and theological exercise.

Victims of human sacrifice that ended up in bogs did not decompose. The corpse of the theatrically slain Lindow Man, Graubelle Man, or Yde Girl would have stared up out of their tannic windows into the blue-grey sky for months, if not years. The preservative properties of bogs were known to the ancient world: Irish communities kept butter fresh in them, and the neolithic peoples at Calladh Hallan seem to have displayed two intentionally mummified bog bodies in open air, before burying them under door lintels.

The principle issue at play with human sacrifice into a state of bog mummification was control. To avail a human to sacrifice is to have appropriated all of their living agency. Even if the rare bog mummy went willingly to the peat, which could be suggested from occasional blows of mercy before more ritualised killings began (counter to this romanticism, many bog corpses show clear defensive wounds or bindings), the victim had surrendered or lost control to the killer(s). More than this, the bog mummies demonstrate the living exerting intentional control over the end of life and deathly rest. The deaths of all bog people were long and dramatic affairs, certainly designed to be witnessed by others. Strangulations were the fastest but most endured multi-death overkills involving mutilations, dismemberments or multiple lethal injuries, often all enacted suddenly across the final moments of life. This morbidly demonstrates a performant control of the life-death threshold and a dramatic hanging or tension between two mutually exclusive states.

There is also the control of rot. During the time that most Celtic and Germanic bog people were killed, burial was uncommon. It is a general mystery what the Iron Age people did with their dead, but the lack of inhumation compared to earlier and later times suggests it was likely some form of exposed decomposition or unburied cremation. The typical death ritual of the time was one of release, so that the dead *became* the landscape. The two major exceptions are princely burials, complete with equipment and food for the otherworld, and the bog mummies, who stayed unintegrated into the landscape until their discovery. There is an absolutely beautiful halo of dialectics around the bog mummy. They are preserved and seemingly unintegrated: extractable from the ground as if they were sleeping. Yet, the mode of their preservation is total integration. Steeped in sphagnum and tannins, penetrated everywhere by muds and mosses, and root-ingrown, they are closer than anyone to the landscape that keeps them. It is impossible to say what the religious purpose of the bog mummy was. What can be known is the praxis of that religion: a sympoiesis between a corpse and its landscape, an understanding of preservation, a preservation of understanding, a liturgy of control, and a bloody performance of ending and lasting that is encased in place.

Watery and boggy sacrifice is typical of Celts. Indeed, the La Tène archaeological site that named the second of two phases of Iron Age Celtic culture was a sacrificial lake hoard. That part of the Celtic process of wealth accumulation included sacrificial relinquishment is both archaeologically visible and historically attested. Most famously, the semi-mythologised sacking of Delphi by Brennus brought back so much gold it glutted sacrificial lakes in Gaul. After conquest, we have records of Roman governors dredging these sacrificial hordes out of Gallic lakes and reclaiming the stolen wealth of Delphi. How much of this is true is debatable, but lake sacrifice of treasure, weapons and animal and human victims is both part of the historical zeitgeist and archaeological record. There is no doubt that the Gallic tribes at their height had access to extraordinary material wealth, and that is known to us through patterns of relinquishment. Princely graves in both Germanic and Celtic traditions speak not only to diligently accumulated wealth, but also a desire to retain it, unshared, in the afterlife. This is countered by the sacrificial hordes in vertical shaft holes and watery places, which show us that wealth accumulation and retention was balanced with sacrifice and relinquishment. Wealth was not understood as a completely heritable or appropriable object, but rather a byproduct of ambition and heroism. Something to entomb in death with the accumulator. The bog bodies make the case that human life was considered in the same way: something to be held lightly, given back liberally to the world, literally, and the gods, symbolically. In wealth entombment/sacrifice we have a crystal of dialectic, a religious praxis, an archaeological moment and a theological practice that informs and encourages relinquishment. It is certainly fair to say that relinquishment of wealth and comfort are not strongly reenforced girders in Western society, either theologically or otherwise. Therefore it is important to take stock of how a widely practiced, but now lost, religion carried the tools that are again relevant in troubled times.

The final dialectic to notice is between dismemberment and rememberment. Dismemberment has played a role in British and Germanic death service since the Mesolithic. Decapitation was the most common, but the period between the Stone Age and Roman Britain saw a morbid assortment of ritual treatments including defenestration, arm and foot amputation, and corporeal rearrangements and reassemblies. Irish bog mummies include those with peri-mortem dismemberments. The Cladh Hallan mummies are noteworthy for being assembled from six different individuals. Roman Britain is full of exotic grave sites, and its inhabitants seemed particularly interested in head-foot inversions. A pattern emerges: some dead, for reasons unknown, were taken apart as or after they died.

If remembrance is the recollection of an impression, then the process is much more immediate if the impression was a vivid one. Trauma is entangled with remembrance, and there is much that any of us would rather forget, but for its vivid impression on our memories. It has already been explored how the final moments of the bog people were performed and controlled. Part of that, no doubt, was to control the memories of their deaths in the minds of the witness. A powerful quality of the impact of any liturgy is its ability to be recalled or remembered as a way of re-manifesting an important symbolic package. Understanding that we can't fully revitalise the symbolic packages of human sacrifice and bog mummification, we can at least nod to the fact that remembrance, through trauma and preservation, was part of that process. By balancing the material facts about eschatological dismembering and re-membering we can begin to see the world as our prehistoric neighbours might have seen it. Dismembering might have been impactful in unknowable theological ways, but it also would have had the direct impact of making the process of death, and its aftermath, memorable to those who went on living.

V.

Would that we could find "new theologians" like Nietzsche's
"new philosophers" in Beyond Good and Evil, who could
think with us part and whole, pan-sacred and pan-profane,
in a pan-agential world.

– Philip Clayton and Elizabeth Singleton

Death ritual is fundamentally appropriative: it is culture's way of transmuting the certainty of death, with all its grief and violence, into a conversation with the future and sustainability. In order to find healing in a present and future fraught with ecological and communal grief, this kind of theology is an essential tool. More than that, individual death ritual is the way by which we understand and mythologise the future fate of the world. The consequences of catastrophic climate change are no excuse to settle into an eschatology of relief, irresponsibility, nihilism or violence. The ancient Celts, and others, can show us how to think about lasting and dying in a way that trucks with the uncanny, the performative and the biological. Iron Age people lived a harsh religion, made even more vicious with human sacrifice. We can and should spare ourselves this internal violence, however the unfortunate truth is that late capitalism and ecocide force us to consider a future with more suffering than the immediate past. Borrowing meaning-making tools from this more violent period can help us appropriate the unwanted violence we might endure. There, in the peat, is a dialectic for locating horrific death in a landscape and for sacralising both the dead and place. As scavengers and survivors, we should take the parts that fit and help, and then learn from that excavation how to do it elsewhere. We will know then how to hold eschatologies in our hands, how to turn them over, and how to see through their refracting crystals of dialectic. Positioned correctly these theological objects could guide us toward something that looks like restoration.

JEMMA BORG

Creation Myth

We must speak of stars: those lucid dreamers,
those old advocates   with their simple philosophies.
Every gram of them is lit   with a clear truth-telling –
loops and flares, searing atom-stacks,   bursts of rare gold.
At first, there was no word   in any language
for light – an aeon of birthing in the dark.
Once there was form,   there could be illumination.
Once there were bodies,   there could be memories.
So made was the bright stone   that feeds the green world.

TIM FOX

Children of a Salmon Star

I am the salmon in the deep pool.
– Amergin (The Song of Amergin, 1530 BC)

Liquid winter sun casts long morning shadows across Horse Creek on a cloudless January day in the old-growth forest of the western Oregon Cascades. I make my way upstream toward a broad side channel where as many as 30 spring Chinook salmon spawned about four months ago. Near the outlet of the channel, a rapid spills through a tangled logjam into a mirror-smooth pool where no trace of current can be seen: a paradox of moving stillness. The water curves over a pair of boulders at the pool's mouth. The sparest hint of flow bands their contours giving them the look of upturned pottery, glazed gold.

Born as a ripple between the boulders, the growing wake of a nose wedges into the pool. I freeze. The play of light on slicked fur and the sinuous weaving and rolling of the form are so fluid that the river otter looks like an animated sculpture made of water itself.

After a moment of splashing and twirling within the logjam, the otter clambers out of the channel, lopes up the far bank to the top of a snowdrift, and belly-slides back down. It pours itself into the pool and appears to transform wholly into an expanding set of shimmering rings. They fade like a fleeting thought that came for a moment into the mind of the creek, a mind that thinks otters in light and water.

Stillness returns and I push on, heart lightened. Gentle eddies swirl over river-bottom salmon nests, or redds, that were flurried with fins and glossy bowed backs the last time I was here. The comparison of memory with the present registers their absence. I miss the salmon.

I have to remind myself that they are still here, in a different form. The hope that I might glimpse Chinook fry is what has drawn me to the water's edge. I have no idea if it will be possible to spot the tiny fish flitting holographically among redd rocks, but the timing suggests a chance.

I approach one swathe of bankside stones that was particularly busy during the warmer months. It is located just upstream of a fallen Douglas fir giant, which served as my blind in September. That day, peering over the prone trunk, I watched half a dozen two-to-three-foot-long fish staked out above this pad of submerged gravel. How many eggs did the females bury here? How did those thousands of fragile worlds fare during the swell of snowmelt and rain that came when they were less than two months among the stones?

I clamber over the log, move slowly to the waterline, and crouch as low as I can to scan the current.

It's plausible that a whole school of little swimmers is hovering just under my nose. The cryptic sheen of fish flesh is one of the more astounding adaptations I know of. Trying to spot fingerlings in moving water, with all its distortions and false-positive illusions, could take hours. If the tiny fry are here at all.

There is a fairly broad window of time over which salmon eggs hatch. Emergence in one nest might take place a month or more before or after it takes place in another in the same creek. And the hatchlings, known as alevin, remain tucked in the seams of negative space between redd stones for about two weeks. They survive during that time by feeding on reserves stored in their distended yolk sac bellies. Then, when the last of these nutrients are used up, they ascend as fry into open water where they feed and grow until their second spring when they become smolt, the oceanward travellers.

The fry here may have already risen and dispersed into quiet sheltered spaces among root masses, logjams or other places less exposed than their birth redds. I could be looking for them in the wrong spot. Or the eggs might not have hatched yet.

I wait.

First my mind, then my eyes, wander. A few feet downstream, a curve of white, just a little too pale to be a beaver-peeled stick, arches up out of the creek bottom, rising from one smudge of algae and setting in another. It is a fraying rope of vertebrae, a salmon spine with loose needle ribs swaying in the current. Ghostly threads of sinew barely hold them together. The softer meat has long been transformed into microbe, insect exoskeleton, dipper song, river otter, and many other lives via the incomprehensible energy pathways from mouth to mouth to mouth that all eventually trace back to the sun.

*

For some four and a half billion years, the sun has been pouring out a river of energy. Those umbilical rays feed the whole vast menagerie of earthly life, even deep-sea organisms, like the famous hydrothermal vent tubeworms, who receive none of the energy directly. The push and pull of solar and lunar gravity against Earth gravity quickens the molten depths far underground, generating tectonic heat that wells up along fault lines on the ocean floor. Lava extrusions provide the warmth that fuels, and the structure that supports, the isolated pockets of life in this otherwise frigid, black and inhospitable marine cosmos.

So different is vent-dependent life that, unlike all other known forms, the omnipresent sulphur, rather than the locally rare carbon, serves as its most basic chemical component. It is literally a different expression of aliveness, one in which clouds, rain, rivers and sun are beyond detection.

Yet tubeworm and salmon share a certain kinship: salmon exist in time the way the organisms of the abyssal seams exist in space. The touch between adult salmon and their young, like the touch between tubeworm and sun, is indirect. They never meet. But there is a vital connection.

For the salmon, the intermediaries are mountains, water and light. These are their surrogate parents, these so-called non-living, inanimate forms which feed and rear the fish from egg, to alevin, to fry, to smolt. The mountains shelter them. The water feeds them. The sun moves them all.

*

Every September, the healthiest run of spring Chinook salmon in the Willamette River basin begins to spawn. By that time, the great fish have been in the river since May and have not eaten in months. While this follows a logic of energy conservation, on a deeper level they are serving as a net energy source for the river, bringing with them the bounty of the ocean stored in their very flesh. In other words, they come to feed the mountains rather than feed *from* the mountains. In so doing, their young are born into a world ecologically wealthier and healthier than it would otherwise be. In turn, to the multitude of eggs they tuck into a stony womb, the landscape itself becomes the nurturing parent.

For salmon, mountains flow like water. Each fish is well adapted to riding the currents even though no parent has shown them the way and they accumulate only about five years of life experience before heading inland to spawn and die. Salmon wisdom is of a different order than ours, learned and remembered in a different mind.

Could it be that the brains within salmon skulls are slight because mountains, rivers, and forests serve not only as their wombs, but also as their grey matter? If so, it might be more accurate to say their bodies swim around inside their minds, not vice-versa as animal physiology textbooks, which equate mind with brain, would have us believe.

The knowing-how-to-be-in-the-world that most modern humans – who may live 15 times longer than a Chinook – only glimpse is what salmon are born into.

As I settle in by the quiet channel on this January morning under the stretched light of winter, I feel that humans are also born into it, as are all forms of life from tubeworms to river otters. The key for us humans is to open ourselves to the level of memory where knowing-how-to-be-in-the-world is stored. And that means opening to the world itself.

*

In the world by the channel, here, now, there is only this string of wet bones in the flow and no fry that I can see, but the place sings salmon in every other way. Salmon are written in every feature. And I too am in the mind of salmon, a thought that came into the consciousness of the creek.

To have this sense, I have to redefine aliveness in broader terms than I have before. It starts with water.

Water is essential for life. I've often heard these words, especially in reference to the search for life on other planets. Yet, I've rarely heard the next sensible thought: that water is alive.

Before life as we currently recognise it was born, there was a process underway that displayed the primary qualities we associate with aliveness: dynamism, activity far from equilibrium, self-direction and self-replication. We call it the hydrologic cycle, the wheel of water.

Organic organisms are its offspring. We are born from, and are included in, its ceaseless circulation. The water that composes 80% of a person is simply water flowing through a different kind of channel than that which buoys thrashing salmon and feeds oxygen to eggs hidden in the gravel bed. Water makes up most of the lifeblood that courses through veins not only of flesh, but also of bedrock, cobbles, pebbles and sand, the vessels of our shared body of Earth.

Our aliveness derives from the aliveness of water. We are water in human form. Chinook are water in salmonid form.

Paradoxically, salmon display their attunement to this sense of aliveness most clearly at the time of their death. Salmon spawn, then dissolve like twilight, melting back into their liquid world and the substrates of the creek. They feed the greater ongoing life of the land with the bulk of their exhausted bodies knowing, in their way of knowing, that salmon perpetuation depends on it.

Much of the energy that the creek uses to 'think' fry comes from the energy released in its 'forgetting' the adults. This maintains the broader continuum of salmon, a continuum that, with the recognition of the aliveness of water, is so expansive and inclusive it can be traced beyond the age of the Earth. The lifeway of salmon is a lifeway that predates the planet. Even the sun.

*

Some five billion years ago, a giant star went supernova and dissolved into the river of time. Her strewn bulk coalesced into a smaller star and thousands of other celestial bodies: eight planets, dozens of moons, countless asteroids, comets, rings and particles of dust. Like salmon, the parent star gave all of herself to her offspring, offspring that would not meet her because they *are* her, transformed.

Her material elements – many essential for life yet nonexistent before her death – were not all she passed on to her children. She passed on her way of being as well. It is recalled in the cycle of salmon.

Through salmon we can see that it is a cycle that emphasises life; death is embedded within the context of a greater process of life. Salmon display a profound determination for presence – a moving stillness, a drive that goes beyond the goal-focused notion of purpose. To perpetuate in the manner of stars. Theirs is a life that embodies patterns billions of years old and wisdom written with a cosmic sweep more durable than planets.

*

There are many stories about how we, humans, salmon, all the living, came to be. The creation myth into which I was born, a myth of exceptionalism, superiority, and separation from the rest of the community of life, has been building on itself for some six to ten millennia.

Here, by the creek, in the forested mountains, everything around me speaks not of creation, but of procreation and birth. Births represent profound transformations that can be called beginnings, but avoid the tricky philosophical conundrums associated with the idea of creation – the willful conjuring of something from nothing by an outside source.

Our primary instruments of creativity – our hands – evolved for the arboreal existence of our prehuman ancestors. That we used them to make things once we left the trees does not mean we ourselves were made by some outside hand. That belief reduces our bodies to mere dead mechanisms, requiring an explanation for the animating quality – the soul – the ghost in the machine.

What if we were to allow that the universe is self-born – like an ocean in a cosmic water cycle, an ocean beyond which we cannot see any more than the life of the abyssal vents can see the stars? What if we understood that the level of transformation that represents the birth of the universe is such that no direct evidence of the parent remains because, in the way of sun and salmon, the parent literally gave its all to its offspring?

How might such a view alter our sense of who we are? And how might it inspire us to comport ourselves in the world?

*

Even though I fail to find any fry flitting among the stones of the channel, the enveloping presence of salmon that I have found calms the urgency I felt when I arrived. I stand and begin shadowing the waterline back downstream. At the mouth of the channel, the root ball of a western red cedar hangs suspended in the air, levered free of the earth by its toppled trunk. A deep opaque pool fills the bowl of earth where the tree once stood.

Contouring the curve of one of the cedar's wide roots is another string of salmon vertebrae. They are arranged as if still threaded onto spinal cord, but there is only air between each round bone. A cushion of moss holds them as if they were still integrated within the body of the fish.

Further down the trunk, a moldy mound of otter scat hints at who, in October, may have hauled the still-meaty carcass from the water to this perch to feast. Even while the otter fed, other smaller mouths were digging in, stripping the carcass down to the white puzzle I see now, a puzzle that could not have been more carefully pieced together, even by a master artisan's hand.

MIEK ZWAMBORN
Palmaria palmata
Bistre on paper

MIEK ZWAMBORN

Submerged

We are large and ubiquitous, we sway and untangle, we are never made up of an I, we are *Laminaria*, not a flock, a herd or a school, we are always legion, numerous and innumerable, a myriad spread, we stretch together, deeply entangled or waving separately in clumps of fleshy fingers.

We stand upright in the current, remain free of leaves without branch or trunk, beneath mirrors of water we wave, not sparse but amassed, sequins sprout from our main blades.

Our foliage is corrugated, our borders ruched. We are gelatinous. We are brown, in dim light we look black and on land, shellacked, sugared with purple.

We are gymnastically inclined, arise from stems, rapidly bear leaves that finger and fork. We crosshatch the sea, are latticed beings, we tolerate and close up and in, we are mild towards those that know us and leave us unharmed.

Dampen us, we have floats, we are accommodating by nature, we watch things happen, don't intervene, we let be, we adapt, we can develop, this time is our time, this water our water. We follow the waves, are opportunists, we endure silt, penetrating rays of light, acidification and the air that dehydrates us at low tide.

We anchor ourselves to rocks, mark the coast, regulate the impact of the waves, swirling we advance unhurried, we unfurl, grow in breadth so that our crowns bathe in light. We propel the sea, releasing green weeds like salad leaves and hushing the red weeds that are afraid of the sun. We are a salty universe, an inverted wood.

We are perennials. We multiply, can count and measure, jellyfish
planulae and polyps depend on us, we help reduce weight now that
people are heavier, we keep airways free, we remove dental plaque
and the remains of tumours.

Yet greedy ships beleaguer us, nets tangle up in us, people pulverise,
crush and bite into us, but electric rays still seek their prey in us, flying
fish and abalone shelter in us and clownfish live in us.

Let our seas flow calm and cool, we grow brittle on land or become
submerged, we want to sway, are unperturbable, we are legion.

Translated by Michele Hutchison

[opposite]

MIEK ZWAMBORN
Laminaria digitata and *Saccharina latissima*
Bistre on paper

After beachcombing I see the silhouettes of the algae spread on the sand projected on the inside of my eyelids at night before I fall asleep: green and red, brighter than in reality. The seaweed floats freely inside my head, tumbling like bright costumed acrobats in brain fluid.

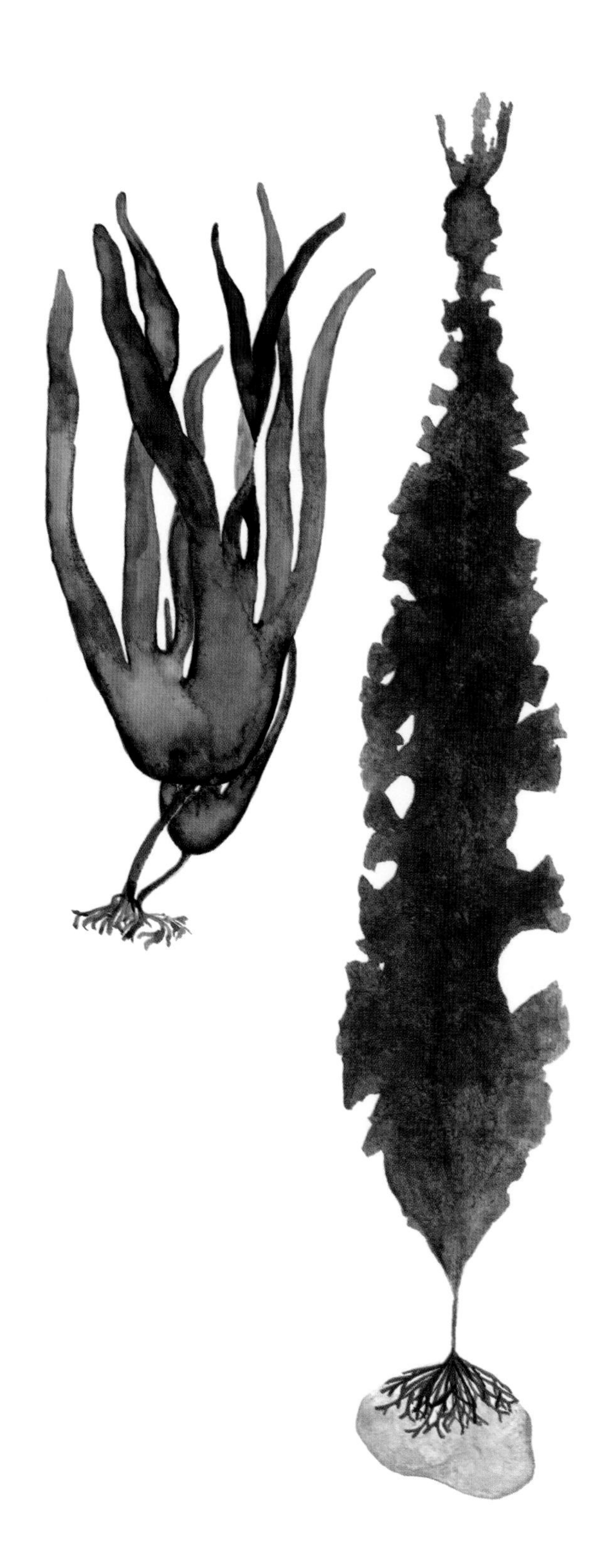

ANNA MAYO

Añaquiwi Moth

Handmade watercolour (from rocks) and Indian ink

To paint this moth's portrait I made watercolours from the rocks of the land where it was born – the Añaquiwi river on the western edge of the Peruvian Amazon. Crushed smooth the rocks' hazy colours reminded me of this delicate moth I found one morning, washed up after the raucous jungle night. I wanted to capture the moth's beauty in death before its elements were returned again to the same earth at Añaquiwi.

MARI FALLET MOSAND

Storm I

Earth pigments, linseed oil paint, charcoal and ink on canvas

'Storm' is part of a series on the 'life-death-life' cycle, an attempt at understanding death on different levels – the death of my own mother, but also death in nature. I learned that death is also life; death lies embedded in life itself, and is a prerequisite for further life. Among the rotting leaves of autumn lie the hopeful seeds that will sprout in spring, drawing their nourishment from the decomposing matter.

MERIDEL RUBENSTEIN
Adam and Eve in the Southern Iraq Marshes
Near the possible historic site of the Garden of Eden
UV-cured acrylic ink on linen

This photograph is from *Eden in Iraq*, a water remediation wastewater garden project and photoworks that explore environmental devastation and renewal in the Mesopotamian marshes of Southern Iraq.

RICHARD METZ
Night Creatures 2
Gouache and ink on paper

For the last ten years I've been filling up sketchbooks and using my imagination to see characters that I can recognise in the shapes of plants and seed heads. I've been searching for a kind of magic where you can just imagine what that buzzing and whirring in the forest at night might be. That feeling of the great mystery that so many artists and writers have tried to envision. I want to see it, and if I can't exactly, I paint those dreams and fantasies of what could be out there. So my paintings are attempts to dream, to imagine the 'genius loci', a spirit of place, to ask: if places really have spirits, what would they look like?

KATE WALTERS

Till Dawn Break Through the Branches

Watercolour on Saunders Waterford paper

This painting, one of a sequence, came after some years working as artist in residence at Tremenheere Sculpture Gardens. I've been spending time tuning into the slow and mighty spirit of trees, and becoming more and more aware of 'interbeing'. Many indigenous cultures see the tree as one of the shaman's instruments for attaining sky consciousness ('I climb my sky tree'). One of the illustrations for the pamphlet, *The Black Madonna's Song*, with poems by Mat Osmond (see *Black Light* p.59).

EMILY JOY

Untethered (Growing in Stone)

Ink on postcard

A nostalgic image of the Swiss Alps is transformed through erasure, the isolation of elements creating a new narrative with unexpected possibilities: a mountain reduced to a rock, a rock split to reveal the endolithic growth. It is part of a series of altered postcards retracing an Alpine journey made 50 years ago, a journey of personal and environmental mourning.

EMILY JOY

Stopping Distances

'We did not know it, but we felt it; in the taut balance, the taking,
the shift of energy extracted and the contraction of ice; in the fracturing
and vertigo of over-description, the untethering of mountains and
blocking of passage; in the unrooted lichens and stone-moved mosses.'

Like a daydream before an actual journey, I found myself making a virtual journey, wandering from website to website along an uncertain route through the Alps. After meandering for a while, I began to search for an image of a specific view familiar only from a 35 mm slide.

The view of the mountains and path around the Morteratsch glacier is one of around 20 locations recorded on blue-plastic mounted slides from a journey through the Swiss Alps made in the 1970s. The slide image – when seen in a viewer – is so clear, so startlingly crisp, the view so perfectly framed and composed, the striations and shadows of the rock so deep, that it feels possible to step onto the curving path. Viewing this image is like a plunge into a cold lake, a bright immersion in another place and time. The mountains are as sharp as the deeply shadowed, brightly lit foreground; it was a sunny day in August, the unknown figure walking the path on the right is lightly clothed. The person looking through the viewfinder, finger on the shutter release, was my father.

The visible figure is facing away towards the mountains, relaxed and mid-stride. Although a small element, the person stands out as a luminous speck against dark rocks. The figure, like the *Rückenfigur* of a Casper David Friedrich painting, is wandering (walking) or wondering (gazing) out and away into the landscape. Having long since rounded the corner of the outcrop and disappeared into the mountains, they stand as a marker of what is past, of the unknown other which is both figure and wilderness. They leave us behind, forever unable to catch up, watching a departure whilst we share the perpetual view from behind the camera lens of someone also departed. We are both long gone and left behind.

That late evening internet journey led me to the hiking route from Morteratsch to the glacier, and there, abruptly, was what was both expected and almost unimaginable; a recent photograph which showed the same view, taken from the same location as my slide. A hurried reach for the slide viewer for comparison revealed transformations; the glacier has shrunk; the trees have grown.

The images misregister, and time folds backward and forward. There is a sensation of doubling up and halving, a throwing out and reeling in; projection and evidence. Beneath these observations, things shift. The glacier is in unstoppable melt with no way to arrest it. We can only watch, placing signs to mark the loss of each year.

That nostalgic man in the nostalgia of a nostalgic walk in the nostalgic Alps – all vernacular architecture and dreams of unspoilt nature – was both walking out and walking in. Walking away from the behemoth of progress that takes too long to slow to a halt and continues to destroy whatever got caught in its cogs; a freight train of climatic change so vast its brakes need more miles of track than we have to slow its speed. The trees have doubled, the images are doubled. The glacier has halved accordingly as if there is only so much matter to go around.

The glacial tongues of the mountains are withdrawing, the mountains crumble into stones. Unstoppable movement around which stopping distances become an irrelevance.

ALEX FREILICH

Broken and Whole

I live on the edge of what some would call a wasteland. It's a forgotten place, tucked away from the world, sacrificed to industry and abandoned. Those who live on its periphery and who share a strong, strange love for this Place call it the Quarry. In past lives it has been old-growth forest, cattle pasture, gravel mine, and industrial waste dump. Here, on the outskirts of town, in the epilogue of this long, sordid tale, all that is wild and weird coalesces amid the ruins of what once was. Here the seeds of hardy plants take root in barren soil. Here the winter sun shines brightest, as the towering forest is long gone. Here young radicals practice in the weeds with slingshots and bows. Here coyotes play their tricks in the night, and lovers walk thorny paths in moonlight.

In its ungainly beauty, in its sickly vitality, the Quarry is a strange, singular entity; a place of many facets and many contradictions. It is a place worth knowing, an unlikely yet consistent source of inspiration and wisdom. It is my home, a part of my being. May these words ring true as a testament to this Place; broken and whole, wounded and healing, showing the way.

I was once shown a photograph taken of the Quarry in the mid-20th century. Grainy black-and-white film showed a landscape that, more than anything recognisably terrestrial, resembled Mars, or Mordor. Industrious men with an arsenal of machinery, stripping the Earth down, down, down, until all that remained was rock too coarse and sand too fine for gravel export. Years of illegal industrial waste dumping has also left its insidious legacy. This piece of land has been pushed over the edge, becoming a blank slate of lifelessness. But from this seeming point of no return a new world has been born – and in quiet, subtle ways, I watch it unfold.

For six and a half years I have walked the trails and thickets of the Quarry, watching, listening and wondering at the miracle of this Wild reclamation. It is a strange thing to seek the *genius loci* of a place so utterly transformed by human greed and negligence. Six and half years – a laughably short amount of time on the grander ecological scale, but enough to begin to see the shape of what could be. Enough to see the myriad ways the land begins to heal, without a guiding human hand or 'permission' from the authorities. Call it Earth magic or ecological succession, but there is something happening here; something slow, patient, unstoppable.

From nothingness, innumerable Wild ones have come to inhabit this Quarry. Scotch broom and Himalayan blackberry are the plant rulers of the realm; two tenacious opportunists brought to North America by colonisation and, ironically, or perhaps auspiciously, the first to start reclaiming ravaged earth after the machines have done their work. Here, these plants are free to thrive and spread, defying the controlling desires of humans. Some of the oldest broom plants take on tree-like proportions, growing over eight feet tall, gnarled branches covered in lichen. In late summer the blackberry reaches its glorious, thorny peak. Dense walls of canes and thorns hide seedy, sweet fruits; gashes and punctures await heedless interlopers. The coyotes rejoice, feasting on the abundance and leaving berry-laden scat on every trail. They make their dens in hidden places, cunning and evasive as ever. On some nights a frenzied howling chorus rings out, echoing in the still air.

Birds flock to the Quarry in numbers and diversity unsurpassed for miles around – with more species appearing every year. Killdeer hide their nests of pebble-mimicking eggs amongst the remnants of machine excavations. Swallows loop and dive after insects on warm, clear evenings. Waterbirds of all sorts spend winter days paddling around ponds of accumulated rainwater.

Pacific tree frogs use these same pools for their early spring mating ritual, filling the night with a thrumming, cacophonous celebration of life and the promise of warmth to come. There is also water that dwells deep in the ground here: a grove of towering black cottonwoods, obscured at their base by thorn and thicket, is the tell-tale sign. Ever the water-lovers, their roots drink from the aquifer where it has almost found its way to the surface. This same deep water creates Green Cove Creek, which flows out to the Salish Sea, also providing drinking water for numerous human residents of the area.

This fragile and hopeful Place deserves to respected and left at peace, but the machines and the men who worship them have not finished with their destructive plans. For more than 15 years, a real estate developer has put forward plans to bulldoze the Quarry, cover up the abuses of the past, and build dozens and dozens of identical houses, densely packed with tiny turf lawns – a demented vision of wealth and prosperity. Only fierce neighbourhood resistance, pointing emphatically at the fragile and poisoned nature of the Quarry, and the seeming lack of ecological oversight on the part of the local government, has stymied them again and again. A kind of limbo-state endures.

But with every round of bureaucratic absurdity that we fight, it seems the inevitable approval of their plans draws nearer, and we who love this feral Place are left asking the same questions time after time: who can afford to buy this sprawling wasteland, and just let it 'sit'? What can be done for a place that has no 'value', no endangered species or old-growth trees, no profitable resources left to extract? The Quarry's defenders have no illusions that passionate tales of coyotes and amphibian choruses are enough to turn back the tide of development. Cold capitalist logic collides with a deeper ecological sensibility; this story is an old one, and our battle is a tiny microcosm of an ancient struggle.

But in walking these trails and thickets, abstractions and equivocations fade. Allowing oneself to be enveloped in the living world, in this Place, a different kind of truth is shown. I have seen a life-force here, a *will to live*, that shows itself clearer than in any 'untouched' wilderness. The speed at which the Quarry transforms itself, seasonally and cyclically, never ceases to amaze me. Perhaps there is some hidden plan, some distant inkling of a future state of health and balance that the land is quietly working towards. The invasive species, the opportunists, the scavengers; everyone has a place here, and a role to play in this hidden scheme.

Observing the patterns and cycles of these plants and creatures over the years, I struggle to describe it as anything but miraculous. At some point, all of these Wild ones found something in this ruined land that called to them – an invitation of some sort; to make a home, and begin again. The destruction of this place is both tragedy and blessing. The power and intelligence of Life is plainly shown here in all its supple resilience. Bearing witness to this renewal is really a form of schooling – the land's lessons are potent for those willing to be humble and receptive. By its wilful recovery from near-death, the Quarry has taught me much about how to live.

All of these miracles have not revealed themselves in a day, or a month, or a year. Patience, above all else, is the essence of communing with this Place. Ever-accelerating modernity has robbed most of us of this skill, and even those who mean well are forced to compensate for destructive forces that can work at lightning speed. So much can be destroyed so quickly, and the processes of returning and reclaiming work so slowly, even with the aid of human hands.

I dare to imagine a future Quarry, left wild and strange, where the saplings have become proud trees, where creatures of all sorts thrive and multiply, and where humans still return to reflect and wonder. Visions such as these are a necessary first step towards action, that which looks beyond the self and the span of a single human lifetime. I walk the Quarry year after year, dreaming romantic notions of wildness and resilience, and see those dreams embodied and enacted at every turn. Vast, immensely complex relationships and interconnections have worked their ancient powers to bring life back to this Place. Yet, on the surface, the Quarry remains just another post-industrial wasteland, a tiny piece of the larger fragmented landscape. And so it goes about its mysterious, sacred work; gently, dispassionately, clearly. Healing is nothing more.

KATHLEEN PALTI

Haunted Spaces

How cities connect people with nature

On a clear night, when I lie in bed I can see the stars of Orion perfectly positioned in the skylight window above us. We live in a fifth-floor city apartment, and streetlights bleach most of the stars, but these ones are bright enough.

In October and early November I catch the train home from work two days a week at dusk, at just the right time to see many rooks, a hundred or more, gather before their roost on a large crane that overlooks the station platform. They flock in together, settle on the yellow bars and call out to one another. A few are restless and cannot find a spot that suits them. They share their news noisily. They are full of being.

Then, closer to the solstice, it is already dark by the time I reach the station, and the rooks are nowhere to be seen.

On the other days I pick up my children from school and while we wait for our underground train home we sometimes see a little pale mouse run out from behind a billboard, dart under the platform benches, gather crumbs and dash back. The boys are excited to see their friend. To them, it is one mouse, though I suppose there could be many. My younger son feeds her nuts from his lunchbox. If he has already eaten all his nuts he's filled with regret. The mouse is okay, I reassure him.

Eventually the station staff will poison the mouse, but he does not know that.

Before spring arrives the clusters of hazels that grow on the slope above the playground sprout hard catkins and tiny pink-red flowers like sticky stars emerging from green buds. There is still snow on the ground, but the hazel branches are golden brown, the colour of my children's skin in summer.

My children have never seen the Milky Way, nor heard a frog croak, nor seen a hedgehog. They were born and have grown up in cities, far from the countries where their parents were born. We have no car, so the countryside is difficult to access. It is not impossible. We have been camping during summer holidays, and we go outside together whenever we have time off school and work. The city has many parks, and in the summer they bloom and buzz with living creatures.

Nevertheless, I feel that the children have come to know non-human nature in scraps and fragments. What we find, like the rooks and the mouse, makes our daily urban world a little more alive. Contact with that which isn't human creates a shift in perspective. It can help us to enter the present moment of the breathing world. But what if all we find of non-human life feels fragile and sparse?

In part this is a consequence of choosing to live in a city. It's easy to become disconnected from nature when your feet never step off concrete and artificial floors all day long. However, wildlife is threatened everywhere, and people in the countryside have also noticed the thinning.

In the summer the children chase butterflies and are excited to find another small white. I remember many more butterflies in the garden when I was a child. In my lifetime insect populations where we live, in Germany, have plummeted. There are fewer insects and wild mammals like hedgehogs; there is less birdsong. The scarcity of wildlife feels normal to children and starts to feel normal to adults like me. We forget what we once knew and anyway, we never encountered the wild abundance familiar to previous generations. Our experience of the natural world is distorted by shifting baseline syndrome, so that broken and depleted ecosystems start to feel like the best we can hope for.

At times the creatures we see in the city, rooks, the bold mouse, a single butterfly, feel like a kind of haunting. Many creatures once lived here and have been exterminated, and these animals are what remain. Perhaps the city is already haunted by its future: a world without wildlife; the greater nature that nurtures us, broken. We humans have already covered the Earth with ghosts. We can't seem to stop.

But the boys stop on the way to kindergarten to throw some of their bread to the pigeons and laugh at the way the birds peck among the crumbs.

At the zoo they watch ring-tailed lemurs from Madagascar leap perfectly from bare branch to bare branch. They love these vibrant animals, who ought not to be here.

Urban children have their experiences of nature, and it helps no one to declare what they know inadequate. More than half of humans today live in cities. Cultural ideas of connection with nature that value our experiences are essential.

It is true that learning to love nature can be a challenge when you live in an ecologically-depleted environment. Time in wilder places is a gift and strengthens our love for the natural world. There's great value in a rich, diverse ecosystem with many species living together. However, I do not want to teach my children that time 'in nature' means being somewhere other than where we live.

Wherever we are, we experience real connections with the wild Earth all the time, because it is everywhere and within us.

Experiences in our compromised urban ecosystems are often vivid. Urban nature encourages us to search, become alert, and see how the non-human is constantly negotiating the human. There are animals who thrive in the city. Many do not, as the life of the city is tangled with death. When we pay attention to the wounds in nature we learn more about our related lives and how we might take responsibility for our own part in our ecosystems.

Urban nature, even the faded night sky, builds connections between people and the living Earth, and I would argue they are the kinds of connections we urgently need today.

Historically, the city in Western culture was often imagined as a walled fortress against the wild threat of nature outside. Parks and zoos allowed contained, controlled fragments of the wild to be consumed as a kind of spectacle, cages that confirmed urban civilisation's benevolent order.

The paradigm has crumbled. Cities always had their own human wildness, and now they spill out across the Earth, through networks of agriculture and industry, an energy-hungry machine that eats remorselessly into forest, river, sky and ocean.

In place of free-living wild animals, we have bred greater and greater numbers of caged animals. An estimated 70 billion farm animals are produced each year, the majority on factory farms where they will never experience sunlight or freedom to move. They live in suffering; that's what humans have decided to do with the living creatures who share our world. Agriculture intensifies to feed these animals, destroying more forests, insects, and the soil itself.

The endangered species trapped in zoos are refugees from something like a genocide.

A mile from where we live, I watched an orangutan put her hand on the glass in front of us, and my son put his small hand up to hers, palm to palm, separated only by the glass. We were looking at an individual who should not live in a cage, and whose kind may be extinct within our lifetime for no reason but human stupidity and greed.

Escalating extinctions, habitat loss and climate breakdown issue a moral imperative: we have to learn more about the unravelling of our ecology, and find ways of acting at every level (personally, politically, locally and globally) to create healthier, life-sustaining relationships with the wider natural world. Interactions with urban nature help me to see the crisis and the possibilities.

In a city we see scarcity. We sense how the Earth is haunted by the losses human actions have caused and will cause. And we can start learning to establish more reciprocal relationships.

What do those reciprocal relationships look like?

They are diverse. They do not have to follow the most celebrated patterns. Some people want to live off-grid; others do not, and there are other ways in which they can have intimacy with the living Earth. Becoming a settler or a wilderness explorer ought not to be valorised as the only or even best ways to know nature.

If my family travels to a place with richer wildlife than can be found where we live, we also create pollution and put that wildlife at risk. If we chose to live in the countryside, we would take up more space, and we would probably have to buy a car and drive it to get around. Yes, we might hear a dawn chorus in the morning, but would it be a choice that teaches my kids to love nature?

It might be. I can't say for certain. I have no wish to pit urban against rural, or tamed against wild, but rather to notice that problems arise when the longing many of us feel for wild, species-rich ecosystems makes it difficult to value nature as we actually experience it.

It is also problematic when cultural concepts of what being 'close to nature' look like are inaccessible or feel irrelevant. This worsens a sense of disconnection from greater nature at a time when it's crucial to strengthen interconnection with the natural world.

Actions that support life include choices not to cause harm, for example making the decision not to buy meat or not to fly to visit a wilder place than the one where we live. Such choices might not look like much. They are, after all, just omissions. Yet they can help to restore connection with nature, because they practice care for the natural world. Furthermore, they do so in a way that could be experienced and celebrated by large numbers of people.

It would not be viable for all the people in my crowded neighbourhood to run organic homesteads. We are too many. On the other hand, my street has no garages, so very few people here own cars. We can think of this as in itself an act of caring for nature, and recognise how our simplicity is a kind of ecological practice.

We have no gardens or balconies on this street, but there is a park close by. We can go to the park and notice trees and birds there, and feel that our *not owning* those living beings is in itself valuable. We don't need to own a piece of non-human nature to be a part of it.

In other words, let's encourage cultural ideas of connecting to nature that are open to ways of living that do not require a wilderness or a plot of land, and have meaning for us as humans within our radically interconnected living world. Deep receptiveness to our living world is not only to be achieved in wild places or rural communities. Nature's many voices can be heard in cities, including cities where you don't belong by birth or nationality.

Sometimes I have had the impression from people who write about nature that my urban rootlessness and wandering across cultures must cut me off from the natural world. That the restoration of my nature-connection should take place on a patch of land where my ancestors belonged (although I don't know of such a place). It isn't so. A connection with nature can happen anywhere.

I am not German. I have no roots here and mangle the language daily. Also, we're Jewish. I doubt we could ever feel entirely at home in Bavaria. And when my children and I step barefoot into the river Isar on a sunny day and scatter tiny fish downstream, our foreignness does not cease to matter. Rather, it is part of the fullness of how we experience radical connection with this world.

Restoration must flow through our cities if it is to touch most people. So let's be inclusive about what a nature connection looks like and how it is lived.

If we feel connected with nature, perhaps we care for it more and develop diverse restorative ways of living.

And in fact, there is more potential for wildlife in urban spaces than is currently realised. Last April in our local park gardeners planted a wild-flower strip, and by July bees, butterflies and flies filled the air above a rainbow of flowers.

The meadow strip makes up a tiny fraction of the park. In mid-summer it was an island of life surrounded by a desert of mown grass, bleached brown by hot weather, and almost silent.

Imagine if that were reversed, if flowers were allowed to bloom across the park, and communities of insects and birds were welcomed back to live alongside us. There is near-dead space along verges, on rooftops and between buildings. If we value these places and change our treatment of them, stop spraying and hacking at them, even in the city we could live in ecosystems bursting with life.

What's more, the city is good for organising people and building a regenerative culture. My kids and I go to the climate protests, which have grown and grown. During street activism I've spoken with people from all over the world about the animal agriculture industry and veganism. Last spring there were daily queues of people at the city hall as 1.75 million Bavarian citizens lined up to sign a petition for greater protection of insects. In 2017 the city voted to close its remaining coal-fired power station early and switch entirely to renewable energy generation. These actions are an essential part of connecting with nature today.

Experiencing a wild ecosystem, tending a garden, switching to a plant-based diet, and nurturing your own animal body, the animal bodies of others and our wild minds, can all be healing actions towards a restorative connection with nature. And there is a crucial role for learning how human actions are damaging nature. Where possible we may yet see how we could restore it. We can then act to support life. We can create refuges.

In the summer months swifts dive and shriek above our street. They circle into the courtyard behind our building and back up into the sky. Perhaps swifts came here long before the city existed, and they continue to return as long as there are places to build nests and insects to eat. Their pleasure in flight and wild calls speak to many of us. The city without them would be a lonelier place.

At times I ask myself how many used to come, and if they will keep coming each year from across the deserts. At those times the birds seem already to be ghosts.

But they do still come. The city is still more-than-human. In paying attention to nature here, I can come, as many have done also elsewhere, to the heart of our interbeing, our deep and radical connection with other living beings, in this time when great damage is being done by humans to the breathing Earth and her children.

Maybe there is a chance at restoration. Many people are working for it. But regardless of the choices others make, our connection with nature can be restored wherever we find ourselves. The living world calls to all who listen, and we are always and everywhere a part of it.

JANE LOVELL

Exhibit, '*Song of Lost Species*'

(ONCA, Brighton 2016)

Bell jar, in a row of bell jars
holding only silence
and a memory of birdsong:

thin wisps of birds, half-remembered
dreams of birds, airborne waifs
pared from wind and reeds

balanced on tines of wire
in gallery light,
their calls the grief of dwindling.

This one labelled Bewick's wren,
others names we do not recognise.

With their final breath they sing to us:

Scoop me up, my bones lighter
than stalks, feathers that fracture
in your fingers; remember.

On the screen, we see forests
of birds, trees teeming with life,
peep and shriek and trill.

We take home a flutter of wings,
the thinnest piping,
a future emerging from banks of mist.

We tell our children: *Watch this.*
Remember...

CHRISTY RODGERS

Memories of Some Times in the Open

One October day, my husband and I drove out of San Francisco to take a walk in the South Bay hills. It was the final day of Fleet Week, when the Navy comes to town each year to attract new recruits, culminating in an airshow by bomber jets called Blue Angels. People flock to see them, crowding the sandy strip of the bay shoreline for miles. The pilots perform stunts of great virtuosity, flying in tight formation, dropping from astounding heights to roar just over the spectators' heads. The jets scream across the sky, producing a sound so loud and elemental it is as if the sky itself is in pain.

I always looked for excuses to leave the city when these displays were happening. I could not imagine the people who came to see the Blue Angels had ever had any personal experience of what the planes could do in war.

There has never been a single day in my life when a war was not raging somewhere on Earth, but those wars were almost invisible to me (and, it seemed, to everyone around me) until I went to live in El Salvador, in Central America, in the late 1980s. At that time, more than one-fifth of its five million people had been displaced, exiled or killed in a decade-long civil war.

In El Salvador, the bomber planes were called *push-and-pulls*. The US government had paid for them. They were used by the Salvadoran military to fight leftist insurgents who had established strongholds in remote areas and were trying to take power.

In November 1989, the rebels attacked the capital city, San Salvador. They stormed into the slums, where they had many supporters, and the government was unable to dislodge them by sending in foot soldiers. So it used the planes to bomb homes and streets in its own capital. Many residents fled up the forested slopes of the sleeping volcano that towered over the city.

I was living in a quiet suburban cul-de-sac on the mountainside. My next-door neighbours were fundamentalist Christians, expatriates from neighbouring Nicaragua, which was then socialist. They stood on the roof of their house and cheered each explosion, each distant building collapsing into dust and sooty flames. The boys wore the starched white shirts and dark trousers of the evangelical church; their mother clutched a bible and prayed, eyes closed, rocking on her heels.

The planes climbed higher and higher, with a weird droning sound, then dropped into a breathtaking dive. At the bottom of the dive, a sudden silence. Then a cloud of black smoke would go up from the streets below.

Ultimately, the bombings achieved their objective. The insurgents failed to take the capital, and the civil war returned to stalemate for another two years, until a negotiated settlement was reached. These turned out to be the final years of the Cold War. El Salvador, a 'hot' war, was one of its last fronts.

Past the city's ragged suburban edge, we drove through a corridor of second-growth redwoods along the ridge-top road, until the land opened into grassy, treeless hills. From one side of the road you could see the south end of San Francisco Bay, hemmed in by chalk-coloured squares of housing, industrial areas, airfields. Salt ponds marked off by white dikes enclosed their odd colours, from red and purple to turquoise. On the other side of the road, the hills fell back into thickly wooded land, declining toward the coast, with a glinting promise of sea beyond.

At the trailhead where we parked, broad tracks followed the open hilltops and footpaths led down into forested ravines. The sun was warm and bright, and the breeze was gentle. It was the time of greatest dryness, toward the end of the annual six months of drought. The grass covering the hills was white-gold, making them look like sand dunes against a desert sky. Above the blinding white ridge, a perfect blue.

Years before the Salvadoran war, I found my way to a Berber tent in the Sahara. There was a sandstorm; I was stranded with a couple of other travellers. A fine grit covered our bodies as we lay on rough rugs of goatskin and wool. The sand seemed to enter every crevice of my skin, sifting under my eyelids, inside my mouth. At first I didn't really feel as if I was present at all; I'd sent my mind far away. But the place ultimately captivated me. Two red dunes, one star above at twilight, a stone well.

When the storm died down I went outside and poured water from the well over my face and neck. I felt I was experiencing some culmination, even if it was just for the moment I stood with the sweet clear water dripping from my hands.

The Sahara made all other places seem like they existed at some lesser degree of necessity. The desert said it would win over time; it would remain when all other landscapes were lost. When we left after the storm abated, I felt for a moment as if I'd stayed behind and was watching a ghostly version of myself disappear down the almost invisible road through the dunes.

The desiccation of the South Bay landscape was so perfect that every detail of the plant life was preserved, even as all colour other than a uniform pale brown had been drained out. The drying seemed like freezing in this way, fixing all the elements of the landscape in place, preserving them completely in death.

The dead grasses on the hills looked exquisite, although most were not native. Later I found a website mounted by a local man who had dedicated himself to cataloguing the decline of the native grasses in precisely that area, and the advance of the aggressive European species – Harding grass, wild oats, yellow starthistle, snake grass, dog's tail grass – that were replacing them. The website included a sequence of letters he had written to the county Open Space Preserve, petitioning them to take responsibility for a series of controlled burns that had had exactly the opposite of their intended effect, to allow the native grasses a chance to re-establish themselves. Here is his list of the damages done as of the previous summer:

> The exotic weeds that were measurably helped and spread by the five illegal fires were 808,000 Italian thistle plants, 527,622 Harding grass plants, 152,000 yellow starthistle plants, and two million wild oats plants, for example. Those were the taller weeds that spread, plus uncounted shorter annual grass weeds and exotic clovers, also spread and took advantage of the damage to the wildflower fields and native grasslands by the fires.
>
> The fire-killed environmental resources that existed before the fires and need to be restored include 200,000 *Sitanion* grass plants,

> 156,000 *Nassella pulchra* plants that were lost in the fires, 32,000 *Melica* grasses, 20,000 *Festuca* grasses, 20,000 *Koeleria* grasses, 500,000 annual tarweeds, 500,000 owl's clover plants, 400,000 *Layia* wildflowers, 224,000 white yarrow plants, 160,000 *Amsinckia* plants, 52,000 lupines, 40,000 native *Plantago*, 40,000 miner's lettuce, 40,000 coyote mint plants, 40,000 California poppy plants, 40,000 blue-eyed grasses, 12,000 popcorn flowers, 12,000 buttercups, and 10,000 farewell to springs.

I was impressed and moved by the rigour of this chronicle of loss. But as we were walking, I had no knowledge of it, and without that history, I was merely delighted by the heat of the sun, the sweep of sky, and the silence, with only the occasional rustle of a fence lizard or garter snake in the dead grass.

I would often amuse myself, on walks in open country like this, by imagining that my husband and I were among the last people left on Earth. I once tried to explain to him: I start walking and I just walk into the future in my mind. I cross a threshold somewhere, and a thousand years have gone by, or maybe ten thousand. I can *feel* it's another time… He was tolerant, but I could see he was baffled, so I didn't mention it again.

As the years passed this displacement seemed to be occurring more frequently.

A dirt road led down the sere hill to a ranch gate. There we found a little stream, its banks crowded with blackberry bushes and shaded with pungent laurel, like a shout of laughter in a cemetery. We leaned against the rusting gate, eating the ripe blackberries dangling over it, marvelling at their sweetness. For an instant I was swept again into my imagined future.

I felt that neither the future nor the past – nor the present with the Blue Angels hanging over the upturned faces of the city's inhabitants, ready to descend – was as full of menace as it usually seemed. The clouds looked painted on the sky: regal, elegant, and antique as the plumes in a dragoon's helmet.

It was perhaps the profound stillness that reminded me of a visit we'd made to the Sierra Nevada some years before. At night, we sat on a snow-covered porch, our breath hanging in clouds in the dark air, arc lamps glittering on the blue-white snow crystals on the ground. And my mind was again far away, casting itself out into the emptiness of white stars in a blue-black, frozen sky from which the snow was not falling and could never fall, and pushing away the cold that seemed to enter an emptiness just as vast inside my body, which had become the thinnest membrane around that hollow place.

Another winter had come back to me that night. On the winter solstice, the tenth anniversary of the El Mozote massacre, I stood knee-deep in the tall brown grass of a field where there had once been a town of that name. As many as a thousand people had died there, over the course of three days. The whole town had been rounded up, the men tortured and shot, the women and young girls raped and shot, and the children's throats slit and their bodies set on fire. A woman who escaped hid crouching in the bushes until nightfall, listening to her children crying for her in terror from inside the church where they'd been locked up while the adults were killed. When darkness came, she fled. The woman, who stayed silent and in hiding for years from fear and shame, had finally come forward.

'There is no way to live with these things,' she said. 'If we remember too much, it kills us. If we forget, we may stay alive, but inside we are dead. We live among ghosts in any case; we are always surrounded by the shadows of the dead.'

As the wind whispered in the dry grass, I attempted to translate the woman's words to a group of visitors who had come to learn about the war. She did not pause for breath as she told her story. The story lived inside her and expressed itself all at once when it had to be told. So I had to stop thinking about the words I heard, and to speak them as if I were receiving them directly from the other woman's mind, as if her ghosts were entering my body.

The soldiers burned the empty town to the ground when they left. Only ten years later, the grass had covered everything, and there was no sign that any building, any street had ever been there. The remnants of the thousand bodies – bones, ash, shreds of clothes – were nowhere to be seen. Forensic teams had to come and dig for them to prove that so many people had died in that place. For years the army said it never happened.

I believe there is something about forgetting that is necessary to inflicting suffering on any scale, from the pain of one person to the murder of thousands, to the assault on the whole web of life. It is necessary to power. You can only wield power over others effectively if they forget something essential about themselves in the present, and also about the possibilities that existed in the past. You can only destroy the web of life by forgetting you are part of it.

But that was where the ghosts came in; they were insubstantial, belied by the solidity of the physical world from which they had been expunged, and yet they persisted; they were everything that refused to be forgotten completely.

Ghosts – of plants, animals, landscapes, people – may be restored to a contingent life by giving them expression in the mouths of the living. And the living may be rescued from death-in-life by giving their ghosts a voice, unforgetting them. Such witness – not true restoration, which the nature of time makes impossible, but possibly a step towards redress or renewal – is necessary work after great dying, and thus an inevitable task for us now, and still more for those who will come after us.

My husband and I walked the dry hills under the perfect blue sky until we knew the screaming of the jets would have stopped. Then we drove back to the city, joining a gathering flood of machines rolling through the twilight along the grey roads.

References

Dremann, C. 'Inventing Ecological Restoration and Successful Weed Management Technologies', *Craig's Juicy Native Grass Gossip & Research Internet Newsletter*, Number 20, 2011, ecoseeds.com/juicy.gossip.twenty.html.

MICHAEL LEUNG

Little Yoshida Garden

It began on Sunday 13th May 2018 when, without warning, Kyoto University removed students' signs from around the campus and disposed of them off-site. They claimed the signs, made from wood and lying flat against the wall, breached a city ordinance. The signs, with their many messages opposing the outsourcing of security guards and requesting more common spaces, are our collective voice: to other students; to the public; and to those we have yet to meet. Supporters of free speech, we installed a few new signs on the busy intersection of Higashioji-dori and Imadegawa-dori.

A couple of weeks later, we were told by *obaachan* Haruka, an insomniac grandma who walks her red Shiba Inu at night, that the university's security guards brought torches and wire cutters to quietly extract the few remaining signs on the intersection. The following morning over 5,000 students occupied the intersection, bringing traffic to a complete standstill. We only let the emergency services past – ambulances and fire engines only. No police.

After exactly 24 hours, we amplified our simple demand for free speech using a 'human microphone'. We learned this technique in 2011, when Ai travelled to New York on a government-supported grant. She spent most of her free time at Zuccotti Park, reading from the outdoor library and talking to strangers who later became friends there. The human microphone would start with someone shouting 'Mic check! Mic check!'; those around them would repeat it louder, and then a message would repeat and ripple through many voices, resonating outwards from the park to the edge of the crowd. Even the food truck drivers would join in.

Our demand echoed from the centre of the intersection and then we all dispersed, with the potential to reassemble if necessary. Other demands were occasionally added, and we were told by some research assistant friends that this had made the university authorities increasingly nervous. Soon after, they retracted the signage policy and even wrote a formal

apology on their website homepage – though, perhaps to save face, they only displayed it for one day.

Further down the road, the university is now putting pressure on the Yoshida Dormitory to stop accepting future residing students. The 105-year-old wooden building is the last bastion of student rights and full autonomy in the neoliberal university – a model of education that can be seen failing around the world. It is also probably the most affordable student residence in the world!

All this campaigning, alongside studying – I'm in my final year of my Food and Environmental Economics course – has left me exhausted, but I know that I have to keep going. My friend Atsuko once told me that *the future belongs to the determined.*

My long bus journeys between Omiya Kusayama and the university have further drained me. When I heard that there was a sharing from Hong Kong activists at Yoshida Dormitory, I visited and stayed at the end for the give-what-you-think dinner that was cooked by members of a vegetarian cooperative. They shared the ongoing three-year struggle led by villagers living in Wang Chau village in Hong Kong, where the government intends to displace 500 villagers to build public housing high-rises and decimate a greenbelt, home to many species such as the *Oculogryphus chenghoiyanae* fireflies. I drank too much of the Wang Chau jackfruit mead and fell asleep in a room that was filled with manga novels and zines from all over the world.

When I woke up, a French *Zone à Défendre* poster eclipsed the strong sunlight coming in through the open textured-glass window (I later learned that some Japanese students will visit the 1,650-hectare occupation this summer, following the French government's cancellation of the airport plans and subsequent violent partial-eviction of many ZAD collectives).

Looking around, I saw two students in the room with me, whispering as they edited the updated Japanese and English versions of the dormitory's manifesto. It was Akiko and Shintaro – a friend that I met during orientation camp. Akiko recognised me first from the intersection and asked me how I'd been recently. I was slightly hungover and, as I struggled to respond, one of the chickens outside answered for me with a loud clucking. We all laughed together.

After a pot of black coffee, Shintaro told me that he has finally tidied up his room and that, if I wanted to, I could share with him for free. He remembered that I lived far away with my parents and could see the bags forming under my eyes and my scruffy hair (though, as it happens, the latter is a personal choice!).

I took him up on his offer and moved in the following day. Shintaro's room, now our room, is on the second storey of the dormitory. I was amazed by how spacious, clean and well-curated the objects in the room were. The atmosphere reminded me of the adaptation of Murakami's *Norwegian Wood* by Vietnamese-born director Trần Anh Hùng. (I read somewhere that Murakami recently said something in support of the Hong Kong anti-extradition bill movement along the lines of, '*If there is a hard, high wall and an egg that breaks against it, no matter how right the wall or how wrong the egg, I will stand on the side of the egg.*' I'll have to share this with my friends in Hong Kong).

After a week, I was invited by the vegetarian cooperative to farm on the unused green space next to the ducks and chickens. Akiko must have told them that I was studying agriculture and was a '*FarmerX*'. This is a term

2018年 吉田寮 春季入寮募集宣言

(**Manifesto of Yoshida dormitory's recruites 2018 spr. : Check QRcode below**)

2018年2月22日
吉田寮自治会

2017年12月19日、京都大学は『吉田寮の安全確保についての基本方針』を公表しました。この方針には、京都大学が2018年1月以降の吉田寮への新規入寮を認めないことなどが記されています。

Last December Kyoto University published *Basic Policy of safety of Yoshida-dorm*.In this policy, Kyoto University prohibits the dorm from accepting new students, effective as of January 2018.

しかし私たち吉田寮自治会は、学生の福利厚生施設・セーフティーネットとしての寮であるために、またその自治・自主管理を続けていくために、今まで通り新規入寮者を受け入れることが欠かせないと考えています。ですから、私たちは2018年度春期も入寮募集を実施します。

However, we, yoshida-dorm committee, will not follow this policy. Yoshida-dorm has been a welfare facility as well as a safety net, securing basic human rights of students. This has been achieved through sovereignty and autonomy of dorm independence from Kyoto University. In order to keep it that way, we believe it is necessary to continue exercising our rights. We will be accepting new dorm applications for spring 2018.

吉田寮は京都大学の福利厚生施設です。すなわち、何らかの理由で京都大学に通う必要がある・通いたい学生のための施設です。吉田寮はここ約30年にわたって入寮資格を自主的に拡大し、年齢・性別・国籍を問わず京都大学の学籍を有する者に住居を提供してきました。

Yoshida-dorm is a walfare facility in Koyoto University for people who need to go to kyoto University.Yoshida-dorm has been expanding in eligibility qualifications independently from the University over the course of 30 years, and now, anyone can apply, regardless of student status, sex, or nationality.

もしいま吉田寮が入寮募集をやめたら、大学側が提供している経済・住居支援は代わりとなるでしょうか。

If Yoshida-dorm stop accepting new dorm applications ,Will Kyoto University financial and housing support be alternatives for yoshida-dorm?

——答えは**No**です。京大の授業料免除・奨学金制度には問題があります。異なる保障もまた必要です。

The answer is **No**.Kyoto University finantial supports has many problems.

——答えは**No**です。研究生・留学生等が安く簡単に住める寮がありません。大学管理寮は不十分です。

The answer is **No**.There is no other dorm that is affordable and that can be enrolled relatively easily by foreign students

——答えは**No**です。大学管理寮の入居上限は1年で、セーフティーネットとして機能していません。

The answer is **No**.You can live for only one year in other dorms maneged by Kyoto university.

吉田寮は大学で学ぶ人・学びたい人のセーフティーネットであり続けてきましたし、そして今後もそうあり続けたいと考えています。不断の努力によってこそ、このような福利厚生施設およびその基盤である自治・自主管理は存続できます。

Yoshida-dorm has been a welfare facility as well as a safety net, securing basic human rights of students.And we think that we would like to continue as it is in the future. With constant efforts, and autonomy as well as self management at its foundation, welfare facilities can survive.

また、吉田寮では物事を考える上で当事者と対話し、合意形成を図るということを何よりも大切にしてきました。この当事者との対話を尊重するのであれば、入寮募集を行なった上で、その希望者に対し真摯に今の状況を説明していくべきであると私たちは考えます。私たちはこの場所を求める人たちをある日突然追いだしたり、話し合いを打ち切ったりすることは決してしません。「窓」はいつも開かれています。 !

Yoshida Dormitory cherishes the importance of forming consensus by talking with the parties in considering things.So,we think Yoshida-dorm Should not stop accepting new applications and that We should explain the current situation seriously to the applicants. We will never force out people who ask for this place suddenly one day or stop discussing. "Window" is always open.

今や京都大学では、自由と対話ではなく管理と命令が行われようとしています。しかし、私たちはあくまでこれまで通りに自治を主張し、当事者らと大学との話し合いによる老朽化対策の取り扱いを求めます。私たちは約40年にわたり話し合いで老朽化対策を前進させてきました。いま前進を妨げているのは、過去を軽んじて現状を誤認し、未来を命令する京都大学です。「窓」を閉ざしているのは京都大学です。したがって、これまで結んできた確約に則る話し合いをせず一方的に入寮募集を停止させる京都大学に抗議します。

We have been thinking and making progress in finding a solution for the deterioration through discussion with the university for 40 years.So,We insist on self-governing of Yoshida-dorm as before and seek handling of solution for deterioration by discussion between parties and Koyoto university.Now,Kyoto University misunderstands the current situation by mistaking discussion in the past and Interfere with the progress.Therefore, We are protesting against Kyoto university because they have forced us to stop accepting applications one-sidedly without discussion.

私たちは2018年度春期も入寮募集を実施します。来たれ、入寮希望者。

We will be accepting new dorm applications for spring 2018.We welcome your application.

吉田寮公式サイト
（応募書類はこちら）

English Page
(application papers)

在寮期限問題
特設サイト

WEB 署名
「吉田寮を取り壊さないで！」

お問い合わせ

tel. 075-753-2537 / 2538

e-mail. yoshidaryo.jichikai@gmail.com

conceived in the '90s by Naoki Shiomi, a native of Ayabe in the north of Kyoto Prefecture, who proposed that people devote time to cultivating land to be self-sustainable and to reconnect with nature and their senses. The 'X' can be a person pursuing any meaningful task in life – an independent journalist, socially engaged artist, bookbinder, etc. I wonder what 'X' I will be after university…

At Tuesday night's meeting, I brought my entire seed collection to share with the vegetarian cooperative. Hisano, who feeds the ducks and chickens fruit and vegetable peels every day, was particularly interested in *Pippin's fish pepper, Jinju-daepyeong radish* and *Glass Gem corn*. She showed us a hand-painted growing calendar that her friend from Hong Kong sent her that incorporates the traditional 24 solar terms of the year. We had the idea of doing our own version but with Japan's 72 microseasons, running from *Risshun* ('beginning of spring') to *Daikan* ('greater cold').

At the next weekly dormitory meeting, in the secret room of the building, we decided to call the farming area 'Little Yoshida Garden' in reference to friends who have been growing food outside Miyashita Park in Tokyo since January 2017: 'Little Miyashita Garden' is tended by members and supporters of the homeless community, who were displaced by the park's part-privatisation and night-time curfew imposed by the Shibuya City Office and Nike in 2010. Since 2014, the park has been closed entirely for a second re-development as part of the Tokyo 2020 Olympics – that expensive and devastating spectacle that keeps stomping its way around the planet like Mechagodzilla.

The idea is spreading, like a message through the Human Microphone. Our friends in Hong Kong have recently started 'Little Hamilton Garden' on a one-way street in Yau Ma Tei, modestly occupying half a carpark space. Whenever we at Little Yoshida Garden see small harvests from our sibling gardens on Telegram, it reminds us that, when we are organised and united, the future belongs to us – *a shared destiny*.

Gambate!

SYLVIE DECAUX

The Gonesse Triangle, a Story of Place

I want to write about Gonesse. The Gonesse Triangle is a wedge of prime agricultural land 15km north of Paris between Charles de Gaulle airport and Le Bourget airport, where the Paris climate agreement was signed. A great view over the city, with the Sacré Coeur, the Eiffel Tower and La Défense all visible in the haze of air pollution. It is sandwiched between two motorways, with planes flying overhead. Yet, apart from the soundtrack, it is bucolic: there is an old country lane lined with elderberry, dogwood and wild roses, leading up to the plot of vegetables – onions, pumpkins, potatoes – that we activists have been growing. Two endangered species of birds have been spotted, the common linnet and the stone curlew, as well as wild orchids.

Nearly 2,000 acres of cornfields rife with pesticides. Farmers no longer own the land, so they don't really care. Most of it was bought by the State (its public land agency), and by a multinational insurance company, in the hope that it would be urbanised. A megalomaniac project was devised, answering to the barbaric name of Europa City. You can look it up online. I don't want to waste too many words describing it. A *retail-tainment* megamall with an indoor ski slope and shops and offices. Some 2,700 hotel rooms to host the hoped for 30 million visits a year (mostly Chinese tourists), an estimated cost of 3.1 billion euros, plus 1 billion euros of public money to pay for the construction of a train station. It was the brainchild of the French retail group Auchan, with funding from Chinese real estate giant Dalian Wanda. Then they added an urban farm and some lakes to make it look better. The kind of project with great infographics and promises of thousands of jobs – people now know better. Activists have been on the case since 2011, and the protest has kept growing, both on the ground, in the courts and in the media. It was like a roar getting louder and louder. A two-day march was organised last October from Gonesse to Matignon, where the Prime Minister's office is. We had an alternative project to present, called CARMA, involving organic farming to feed the local population through school and hospital canteens and farmers' markets, allotments and community gardens, orchards, livestock, canneries and breweries, horticulture, local tourism, footpaths for runners and hikers, research and education in the future-oriented sectors of urban agriculture, eco-construction, recycling, thermal renovation of buildings and sustainable mobility. Public opinion was won over.

And yet preliminary works for the construction of the railway station went ahead. Activists began to camp there at weekends to be ready to stop it. Then on 7th November 2019, the government abruptly announced that Europa City was cancelled. So we had won, after eight years of constant struggle that demanded courage, patience, dedication, numbers, imagination and time. We stopped the behemoth. The reason I care about sharing this with the Dark Mountain community is to say how tangible fights, over something as basic as soil, from which we urban dwellers have been so disconnected, bring deep meaning. It is as if there is a collective realisation that this disfigured damaged hinterland of Paris is our land, and we want a better use for it. We were reclaiming it. The struggle has brought together a motley crowd, with ever new arrivals: journalists, writers, anthropologists, teachers, grassroots activists, carpenters, builders, cooks, people who own vans, photographers, gardeners, urban planners, agronomists, economists, jewellery makers, pensioners, students, graphic designers, musicians, the list continues. It catalysed around one man, Bernard Loup, the 'Wolf', who started it all and has a genius for bringing people together and empowering them, and who is always there, working away. What made it happen was to connect to place, and to present an alternative world to capture the imagination.

The first time I went to Gonesse was in January 2017. I had heard about it from an activist friend, been to information meetings and signed petitions. It was time to go and see for myself. I joined a tour organised by the CPTG, Collectif pour le Triangle de Gonesse, whose characters would gradually become familiar to me. I met them for the first time: Bernard Loup, Jean-Yves, Blaise, Dominique. It was very sunny but very cold, one of those winter days when everything seems suspended. After going through the commercial wasteland of Paris Nord 2, our small group crossed the footbridge over the A1 motorway and found ourselves in a field. Walking in the winter landscape, with its frozen furrows and remnants of crops, was the cause of an unexpected emotion. Our guides explained where the shopping mall would be, what would be destroyed, who the land belonged to, what was at stake, answered questions. I was more interested in understanding the situation than in letting myself be introduced to the place. Yet it was from that moment that the land began to inhabit me. It took me a long time to understand its geography. I started looking at maps and at the history.

The soil is incredibly rich, they don't need to water the corn, even in a heatwave. It used to belong to the kings of France, and the yield from 'la grange de Gonesse', as it was called, helped build two abbeys: l'abbaye de Saint Denis and l'abbaye de Royaumont. The Triangle is bang in the middle. From the 16th century, a powerful caste of peasant bakers sold their bread in Paris with royal privilege – the bread of Gonesse was famous, known for being very white and delicious. It was so lucrative that the bakers wouldn't travel home on their own, for fear of being attacked by highway bandits. There were also periods of distress, disaster and devastation: the Hundred Years' War, the 17th-century floods, famines, epidemics and civil war. Plenty of blood – difficult to know whether it was a fertiliser. In August 1783, the Montgolfier brothers launched one of their first hot air balloons from the Champ de Mars in Paris, it crashed in Gonesse, and the upset peasants, believing it was some kind of monster come to attack them, assaulted the punctured balloon with stones, pitchforks and flails, tied it to a horse's tail and dragged it for more than 6,000 feet across fields. During World War I, there was a project to build a fake Paris out of cardboard and with fairy lights to fool the German air force. And one of the sites for this fake Paris was the Gonesse triangle, right by Morlu's elm (no one remembers who Morlu is). The Concorde crashed there in July 2000 and 113 people died. And during World War I, a Gotha G.V was shot down. So many stories – these, which are documented, and plenty more. I spent many hours in the Bibliothèque Nationale and the Bibliothèque Mazarine looking at old pictures and old books, taking notes, feeding my imagination. Since the Neolithic period, 200 generations have been shaping the land. I realised that the airports and the motorways were built during my lifetime and that things can change rapidly.

Sitting in the field where the soil has been dug up as a result of archeological excavations. They have found the remains of a Celtic woman, a chief/landowner with her jewellery, surrounded by six men, and of massive Neolithic grain silos using conservation techniques similar to those used today in the High Moroccan Atlas. I saw the Earth dug open, its entrails exposed, the geology. One Sunday, with my friend Marine who is a geo-biologist, we lay on the ground, soaking it in, dreaming. We feel we need to listen to the Earth. A poem by Devi A. (formerly Waiata) Telfer, an Australian poet and playwright, comes to mind:

> If you sit on the land long enough
> It will speak to you
> If you listen you will hear it murmur
> If you sit still,
> if you stop moving
> If you open your ears
> You will begin to hear a foreign language – an ancient tongue
> And if you
> If you can be silent
> You can hear it move
> And if that silence is maintained
> You will hear a faint pulse
> And within that pulse begin to feel the fibre of that old song
> And it will touch every part of your being
> And start to tell you the story of the old spirit that rests in this country.

As much as this deep connection to land is conceivable in the wild and grandiose nature of the Australian continent, is it possible to experience the same thing in a post-industrial environment between two motorways and two airports? Maybe worth trying, this experience of place, the place that is our heritage. I'm not the only one to have that experience. Several people have told me that their relationship with the Triangle is sensory. Even the word *triangle* is evocative. One friend tells me about the time he slept on the land when he was part of the organising team for one of the big celebrations held there. He had the feeling of connecting deeply and of giving the land a chance to exist again. It was also being part of the collective; the next day was a huge success, and hundreds of people came.

Three celebrations in May 2017, 2018 and 2019 that drew hundreds of visitors were organised with concerts and workshops and bread baking, speeches, roundtables and beer, barbecues and banner painting and slogan making, demonstrations led by children with wheelbarrows full of vegetables, demanding *veggies not shopping trolleys*. Early on, the collective managed to get a plot from a local farmer to grow pumpkins, tomatoes and rye. Every other Sunday, *cultiv-activists* get together to sow, weed, hoe, water, harvest, and also picnic, talk and walk around. We get to know a local naturalist, hunters, and the police. Being on the land made it special – connection was built. It was different from signing petitions, leafleting or sitting in committees. I wondered if we could bond with the Triangle in the spirit of indigenous peoples. There is something soothing about walking the land – even when it is scorching hot and there is no shade, or cold and wet and muddy. Lack of comfort is oddly comforting. I saw that people had spent one Sunday drawing plants. There is something slow and focused in botanical drawing, in close observation. Things were built: a wooden tower nicknamed the giraffe, a goddess of fertility, signs with inventive slogans on boards nailed onto sticks, a train station on wheels upholding leeks, beetroot, lettuce and a giant pumpkin. The materiality of it, the construction, the making together gave the struggle its warmth and its strength.

I'm also astonished at the level of expertise – in terms of legal matters, economics and sociology, agronomy, land ownership, environmental issues (water, botany, soil composition). The press review is meticulously kept up to date. A compilation of all the resources and organisations that could be helpful and of potential partners has been drawn up. An anthropologist is writing a book, journalists and photographers are documenting, a fictional film is being made, at least three or four master's theses have been written, a map of all contested land in the Île-de-France region has been printed thanks to crowdfunding.

Of course, the fight is not over, it has just begun. Reclaiming the land. Our opponents, the lovers of concrete, the local politicians, are angry, more than angry – in a rage. They feel abandoned, the victims of an unfair and harsh decision, despised and scorned. As for the government, it is not to be trusted. Few from our collective come from Gonesse, we have managed to create some links with local inhabitants and we would like more. At the march, I leafleted in the town about the CARMA project, mostly talking with women. When you say farming and affordable organic food for their kids, of course they are interested. We don't know what will happen. Another chapter opens. Next Sunday we will make magic on the Triangle, a big bonfire to burn our demons, and we will plant decorated sticks to show our determination, and bulbs, flowers for the spring.

References

The poem by Devi A. (formerly Waiata) Telfer is an extract from her one-woman-show *Song, the Story of a Girl, a Bird and a Teapot.*

Oui aux terres de Gonesse website, ouiauxterresdegonesse.fr

CARMA Pays de France website, carmapaysdefrance.com

ANNA M. WARROCK

Remind Me

Guttural, it rumbles, thunder from a far-off storm, then booms louder and ever deeper into an overhead roar I feel in my bones. A silver dragon soars above the neighbourhood, the bank of jet engines lifting tonnes of steel and human bodies.

We sit in the summer garden. Our conversation drowns in the noise. We wait. Four, five, six seconds. Seven. As the plane grows smaller until it disappears into the blue, our awareness shifts to birdsong and breezes sifting leaves. And then a distant rumble, and a dragon approaches again.

The planes of Boston's Logan International Airport have no choice but to fly over the neighbourhoods surrounding the city. The airport began as a military site in 1923, opened to commercial flights in 1927, and expanded by filling in surrounding marshes. It now has six jet runways. Although days can go by in relative peace, when the wind shifts, requiring a different runway, the behemoths go over our house every five minutes, day or night. Days, we see the brand colours on the glinting metal. Evenings, in the living room the planes are louder than television ads. In bed, we doze in the repeating roar as flights dwindle toward 11.30pm; then one last, late-night flight – likely a freight shipment – loudest of all, rattles windows at 12.30am.

I describe the experience as accurately as I can because I do not mind the noise. It reminds me, as much as anything can, of my role in the Anthropocene.

My neighbours do mind. They organise against the airplane noise, researching flight paths, runways, airport expansions, and regulations. One group posts the Logan Airport Noise Complaint phone number and urges us to track and time incursions. One evening my spouse Robert counted 45 planes overhead in two and a half hours. He called the Logan office and left a recorded message. The next day he called our town mayor's office and spoke with an eagerly sympathetic assistant. The city government puts pressure on the airport bureaucracy.

I embrace the engines' sound. For a moment it feels marvellous – we can fly. The echoes tell me not to forget the motivations behind my actions. Should we fly less? Then Robert and I might not have travelled for a romantic December week in Amsterdam. My childhood friend in California would not have regularly visited the last of her deceased parents' siblings and cousins on the East Coast; and I would see her less. Convenience, speed. We should fly less. But we will we?

The noise reminds me. I hear it and think, there goes my letter, and here comes my Swedish sweater. There go New England lobsters; here comes French cheese. I hear it and remember the oil wells on the Dakota plains, the refineries on the Gulf of Mexico, the pipelines that keep New England heated in winter and that fuel planes. I hear the mines digging deeper into the Earth and the ocean, and the steelworks burning coal, and the plastic factories churning out technically specified materials for engines, seats, overhead bins for our luggage. Look, says the plane, this sound holds only a fraction of what must change.

A transcontinental and international connector like Logan could never be built today within a city. The airport has faced sound issues since 1975. Massport, a state agency, runs several airports in the state. Its website describes the Federal Aviation Administration's technical specifications on what planes can fly when, regulations that change as airliner specs change – different engines, different plane weights. The airport's soundproofing programme has spent a reported $170 million on over 11,000 'dwelling units' and 36 schools. We adapt, we adjust.

I've called the noise complaint office myself. They reply with a letter that writes out your recorded message and addresses the specific complaint. That's how I found out that a very loud, low-flying helicopter was an emergency medivac flight to a Boston hospital, which of course must fly under established flight paths. One August night I stood on our back porch at 10.30pm, a work weeknight, trying to record the continuing roar as background to my words. The official letter came the following January. The five-month delay is understandable. The airport website lists, for July 2019, over 19,400 complaints from 61 communities.

We are many. We use our vacations to see new places and people, to recharge by getting away. We eat Brie and visit relatives, or relatives come to stay with us. Many industries, resources, workers are at our service; we might find a job within the long chain of effort it takes to put a plane in the air and, with our wages, buy a ticket for one special trip to see the Nazca lines in Peru, visible from hilltops – or the air. The noise will not go away. We ride the dragons.

WILL WLIZLO

Endsickness in South Minneapolis

On a March morning, the air warmed and released a pissy drizzle. Rain fell on a foot of snowpack, which covered the still-frozen Minnesota soil. With no way into the dirt, the water wandered sideways. As I got back from a social hour that night, three inches of precipitation and melted snow lapped at our foundation block. Before dusk, a stream ran across the linoleum in our downstairs bathroom. By bedtime the carpet was absorbing the steady spill.

After about 48 hours, a sopping wet roll of carpet starts to smell like decay. As my girlfriend and I coiled slabs of the stuff into loose cylinders, the underside of the wet pad spattered little bits of tough white plastic onto our jackets and work gloves, in our eyelashes and nostrils, and like an alien dusting of dandruff, all over our scalps. We looked like passersby of a giant forest mushroom that had wheezed its spore load into the air. By day's end, 500 square feet of carpet sagged in a heap in our driveway.

About four years ago, we moved into a smallish bungalow with cracking stucco, lovely neighbours, built-in bookshelves and yard enough for a couple of garden beds and a clothesline. Previous owners finished the basement to keep an ageing parent close to her caretakers. Now it holds a writing desk, a sewing machine and a preposterous overstuffed chair. We changed the space but still associated it with comfort, leisure and security.

Fond feelings were scarce as we lugged the rug up our basement stairs, the smell of blooming mildew pungent on our hands and clothes. While the dead vegetable stench of fast-growing mold turned my stomach and tightened my throat, I've come to think I was also feeling the first symptoms of an ailment I couldn't name.

'These days all it takes is a little unusual warmth to make me feel nauseated,' writes Elizabeth Rush in *Rising: Dispatches from the New American Shore*. 'I call this new form of climate anxiety endsickness.'

I started reading *Rising* a few nights before the rain. The word 'endsickness' lashed me like water against a storm window. Rush tells the stories of communities around the United States who are being inundated by the steadily rising tide. During her reporting, she gazed queasily over the Atlantic, the Pacific and the Gulf of Mexico while fighting an incessant, building fever, fretting over the warming waters of the Earth.

Focused as she is on the coasts, Rush doesn't look inward to the continent's landlocked heartland. Concern about our changing planet has a different tone in the American Midwest. Far away from the unfathomable depths, the anxious small talk focuses on crop stress, boreal forest retreat, or weather-beaten refugees in county courthouses. Some folks even welcome a few degrees of average temperature increase given our wind chill's capacity for cruelty. We don't think about climate change in the same way as someone from Tampa, the Isle of Wight or Tuvalu.

When the water came for us, it came from above. The previous record for snow in February in Minnesota was 26.5 inches, set in 1962. Two feet of snowfall calls for many mornings shovelling before breakfast, but nothing like the amount of labour required for this year's new record. We notched 39 inches this February. The snow we removed from our driveway became a nine-foot-tall mountain that avalanched across our garden bed. By the end of the month, we could hardly fling snow to the pile's summit.

In the Midwest, snowstorms blow in from every direction – off the frigid Canadian taiga, across the Dakota plains, out of the Great Lakes Basin, and even up from the Gulf of Mexico. It was the latter variety of storm that buried us this year. Like hurricanes, these southern systems generate more power and gather more moisture above the warm waters of the Gulf. And the warmer the water, the bigger the blizzard.

This year felt like an anomaly but, when every winter is described as such, perhaps it won't seem anomalous for much longer. Imagining this 100-year winter happening again next season makes me dizzy.

'Like motion sickness or sea sickness, endsickness is its own kind of vertigo,' says Rush. It's 'a physical response to living in a world that is moving in unusual ways.'

My endsickness is recognition of my first direct loss to the warming Earth. Our dead carpet was the canary in our coal mine. Not that we were unaware of what was happening in faraway places. It's hard to miss the splashy magazine features and the peer-reviewed climatology meta-studies and the urgent fundraising letters from the Sierra Club. It's just that we had been protected by the luck of place and circumstance. But seeing a rising tide beneath our windowsill, and sensing civilisation's foundation shift ever-so-slightly under our bed frame, has tipped me into vertigo.

The carpet is gone and, trying to muster the best Midwestern-ness in ourselves we can, we are thinking of this as a blessing in disguise. (Good riddance, we never liked the pattern anyhow.) We spent several weekends installing a waterproof vinyl-plank floor. The reading chair is already back beside the egress window. We are privileged in that we can consider this trouble an inconvenience.

As we snapped vinyl planks together, presidential candidates were busy reassuring the residents of southern Minnesota and northern Iowa. They have less reason to feel lucky – the same melting snow set the rivers wild and left corn and soy fields underwater, levees broken and whole rural communities displaced. The crops will be resown, the politicians say, the crumbled infrastructure will be rebuilt, and these communities will thrive again. Each crest of hope in their speeches is matched by an undertow of new questions.

How long will the thunderheads rumble blackly in the distance before descending? After they do and the waters rise, will we ever find firm ground again? On what damaged shore will we stand at last?

Faced with these questions, Rush calls on something old and intangible to tackle this existential challenge: a reconsideration of the stories we tell. To replace the legends of human ambition mastering the docile landscape, she asks for new myths that match sea-level rise with a rise in the resilience of human character.

These stories require different tellers, disparate locales, new vocabulary. They're told in venues like suburban Staten Island's condemned townhomes, the moldering shrimp wharfs of Louisiana's disappearing coast, by down-and-out mobile home owners, weather-flung refugees, and indigenous leaders, such as John Bear Mitchell of Maine's Penobscot Nation.

'Our sacred petroglyphs – those carvings in rock that were put there thousands of years ago – are now being put under water by the rising seas,' says Mitchell. 'Our ceremonies and language still include the caribou, even though they don't live here anymore. Similarly, we know the petroglyphs still exist, but now they're underwater. The change is in how we acknowledge them.'

Mitchell's insight pricks me because his recognition feels universal: that the sacred and familiar are undergoing transformation and we must adapt our views of them accordingly. The old story of the world around us begs for a fresh copy edit, a roiling ocean of red ink. Wastebaskets shall runneth over with crumpled balls of paper.

To tell our story I need to listen to different teachers; imagine familiar places with a fresh perspective; try on a verdant new vocabulary. It feels like groping in a dark room, grasping for an invisible door knob and maybe a way out, worried the door will be locked. But as Rush writes, 'Sometimes a key arrives before the lock. Sometimes the password arrives before the impasse.'

The first password, for me, was endsickness. I don't know what secret doors the word will unlock or what lies behind them. It is, for now, a magic key in a parable about a city becoming a dimly lit sea. Even in Minneapolis, the coast is at our sidewalk, the ocean is at the door.

References

Rush, Elizabeth, *Rising: Dispatches from the New American Shore*, Milkweed Editions, 2018.

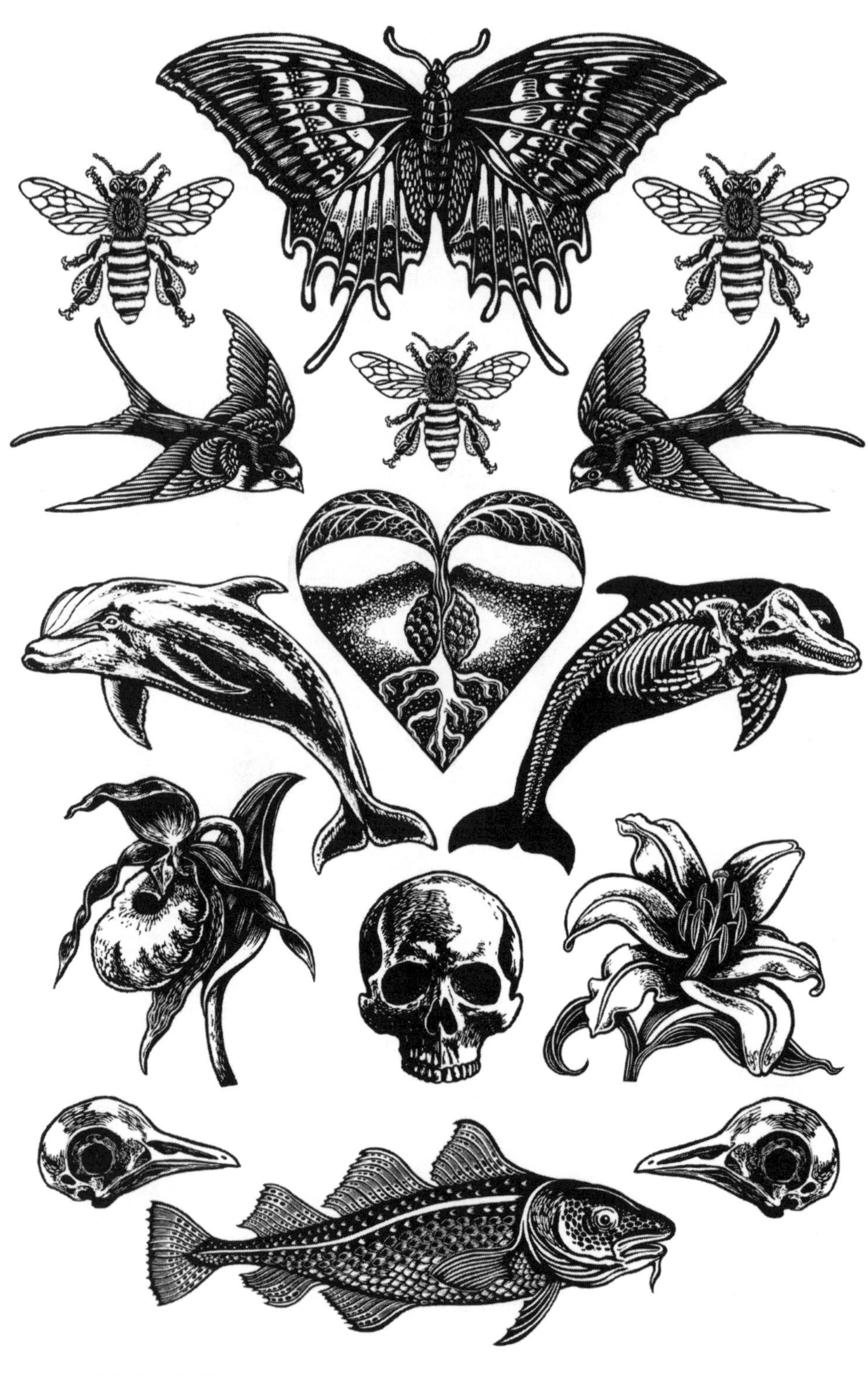

MILES GLYN

Various Linocuts 2018–2020

Designed for use on the human form, as part of the Extinction Rebellion project, as well as banners and flags. All these blocks are utility tools and continue to be

used. Made with Art Group discussion about the subject, while actively dwelling on our predicament and in direct response to the movement's needs rather than personal whim. All these images are available for hi-res download and can be used for any non-commercial use.

NICKOLE BROWN

Persimmons

My friend at Thanksgiving says it's already
happened. By *it*, she means *the apocalypse* –
the end come and gone but we just haven't
felt it yet, like a body that doesn't know it's
dead because the bones of the ear are the last to go,
sound still tickling the brain like wind chimes forgotten

in a dead tree. And I don't know what to say
but imagine saffron monks screaming
into the ears of their recently
deceased and wonder what they might say, maybe
something like, *It's already happened!*
or if they might also yell into dead
trees and what words I should belt out
to the beetle-killed hemlocks that barb
the mountains here, so many the canopy
creaks and sways the trail with a whole forest of little
more than widow-makers nowadays. And someone says,

Well, hell, pass the bourbon then, and I do, marvelling
how easy it is to pick up the bottle with my possibly
zombie arm, wondering if it's true – that we're living
off fumes, maybe already gone, but how would I know
because still I hear
the clink of soup spoons, the tink of the oven
working its heat around a turkey that is not
turkey at all but a miracle of manufactured protein
made to make hippies like us feel better about giving thanks
without dead flesh in our mouths but still enough to
give us that *flesh feel* – that pleasurable snap-back, craving as we do
the meaty fight real muscle puts up when chewed, because

we are animals who don't want to be animals but still enjoy
the vestige of animal like the foetal dream of a tail
or water-breathing gills once slit into our unborn necks.

It's already over, she adds. *The shortages haven't yet come, but they will.* And so the table grows quiet, and I hear all our little mouth
sounds, a soft-smacking not unlike the wet popping of fish
suffocating in the middle of I-40 month before last
when yet another hurricane
receded, the floodwaters leaving behind a city of underwater
life stranded miles from their home, a stench
that had to be blasted with even more water
from a fire hose. The sound grew until

someone asks, *Is that fake bird ready yet?* and I get up to
check, thinking of meat again, of starving
polar bears happy to sink their teeth into
dolphins fooled by a warm current gone
wrong; or how I read that octopus were numerous
enough to climb out of the sea and drip from trees
back when Homer was alive, but last summer in Greece, all I saw
were their severed legs drying on laundry lines.
I can hardly swallow

any of it, so my brain takes me
somewhere I can go – to a small thing I can
manage – a quiet panic over
persimmons, because petty as I am, I fret if
next month I won't be able to find them
at the store. It doesn't make sense other than to say
I never paid much attention to those little edible
carnelians, those dusty Ozark tomatoes, but now that
they might be gone, I'm suddenly homesick
for that stubborn country-girl produce, hard as they are
at first, always tongue-parchingly tannic long before
finally giving in and turning themselves into a slick kiss
of sweet hiding under that thick skin.

There's little else I can do, dead as I
might be, so I vow come December to fill my cart with them
once more, no matter how much they cost. I vow to do what
humans do – to greedily stuff into my body
the thing I want most to remember – and I will eat and eat and
eat them, making myself sick, testing
with my tongue the knowledge of fruit
that takes its sweet time to ripen, sometimes taking
months after it was yanked from its branch as if
it could live forever on the memory
of what it once was.

PETER FRIEDERICI

The Ends of the Earth

The announcement comes every few years, maybe more often in times of crisis. Back in the late eighties it was the Harmonic Convergence, some alignment of planets whose mechanics I never did quite understand and that, being rather young and unexposed to New Age ideas, I at first misheard as the name of some new and one would hope short-lived band, the Harmonica Virgins. As I recall the event was supposed to usher in a lasting new age of glorious peace and mutual well-being, which looking back now with pained gaze through the reigns of Bush and Trump and ISIS and Putin strikes me as one of the bigger miscalculations of the entire modern era.

Some years after that I was living in the Arizona heat as people were preparing for what they believed was going to be the entirely technologically instigated Armageddon of Y2K. An acquaintance of mine took to sterilising big jars full of grains and beans in the freezer, then transferring them to what she described as a hidden alcove out in the desert, a rocky place near a spring, so that she could survive there when civilisation went to hell.

It didn't. When the time came some friends and I, luxuriating in that period of late young adulthood before kids arrived, took some food and champagne and went backpacking off into the desert. We figured that it was saner to come back to reports of wholesale disaster than to live it in the moment. But in this too we were disappointed. Once we'd hiked back to the truck stop where we'd left the cars we checked a newspaper to find nothing more consequential than that Boris Yeltsin had resigned as the chief executive of Russia.

And the acquaintance? She had a hell of a lot of beans and rice and lentils to polish off. I never did hear too much about those meals.

By now, in my life experience, this has happened often enough that I recognise the pattern. There is, first of all, the aching sense that the end of things has got to come soon, real soon, before the end of our own all-too-short time on Earth, because how could that glory go to someone else?

There is the creation of an elaborate eschatology – the careful calculations of timing, the who's in/who's out assessments at least as intricate as the backroom political manoeuvrings of any Washington or Pyongyang. And finally there is the PR, the ready forgetting of any previously forecast ends of the world through a simple immersion in the obvious reality of the impending one just around the corner. As Bullwinkle would put it, 'This time, for sure!'

It hasn't ever been for sure, of course, and for me the most poignant time comes just afterwards. Some years ago when the end was supposed to come according to precisely worked out understandings of the ancient Mayan calendar a friend was driving west through Kansas and noticed skeins of people standing on the highway bridges.

'What's going on?' she wondered aloud when she stopped at the Quik-Mart.

'They think the end of the world is coming,' said the cashier.

'Oh, then I probably don't need to pay for my drink, right?'

'It ain't the end of *my* world, honey.'

And so she drove on, as did the economy of quick fill-ups and super-sized sodas and Slim Jim jerky bars. But what I wonder is what it was like to stand there up on one of those bridges as the afternoon wore on, as the sidelong embarrassed looks proliferated, and whether once the forlorn waiting for the call of trumpets or the opening of the heavens or (this being Kansas after all) some whirlwind got to be too much everyone just filed away silently. Or did they speak to one another? In some other place this might have been occasion for some profound French-inflected bit of wisdom such as *We can't go on. We must go on.* But in the American Midwest it was probably some foot-shuffling reflection like *Well, guess I'd better be going now – I figure the dogs must be hungry.*

This kind of thing has happened often and fervently enough that I have come to wonder if we just have the wrong idea about endings, and ends. Maybe the end of the world has come after all. A few years ago, a millennial sect made a remarkably but not uniquely precise calculation by adding up the extent of all the begats and reigns and wars in the various Testaments and came up with the announcement that the Rapture really was going to occur one 21 May, at 6pm Daylight Saving Time, which by the way is not evenly distributed throughout Arizona, where I live, and so if you want to get all nitpicky the event was slated to occur an hour apart on the two sides of a town that's split by the line between time zones. That would have been a pretty interesting hour.

But I digress. What, I wondered a day later when I read an AP story purporting that the end of the world had not taken place, what if it was not the *time* that was incorrect, but rather the *signs?* What if the end-times believers had been totally spot on? What if, like an oblivious diner refusing to see in the pattern of scorch marks on a piece of toast the clearly outlined, divinely placed visage of the Virgin Mary, it is just that we are too obtuse about what to look for? What if instead of giant earth-quakes causing the Earth to shake and split apart the long-looked-for signals were more like a delicious little shiver from nature, a tease rather than an ecstasy of destruction? Could it have been something as subtle as an unseasonably cool breeze shaking the nascent leaves and setting them to flutter in a way that no one had really paid sufficient attention to before, or a shower of gentle rain providing the perfect coda to a long drought?

What if the Rapture were heralded by a flurry of song from horny birds celebrating the lambent falling light of dusk – that undefinable quality of colour that is a depth, a saturation, rather than a nameable hue – or even by a particular young boy in Arizona, furiously concentrated, who managed to ride his red bicycle without training wheels for the first time?

What if the only sign of the culmination of God's grand design were something as simple as an asparagus stalk, taut with spring's irrepressible longing, flicking away the final covering of dirt particles (and let's not get into a discussion of exactly what *those* are) and emerging to sunlight at last?

What if that were the sign, and not only the notice of God's intent but His final word on the matter?

And what if not just you and I, but *everyone* had such a misguided notion of God's plan that in His eye-rolling offense at our failure of attention He decided that He would in fact be more comfortable for all eternity continuing to putter around alone in His house of many rooms, muttering to Himself as hermits will do about the iniquities of the world beyond the doors and enduring the occasional tedious visits from the impulsive Jesus and the wheezy Holy Ghost? What if it finally dawned on us, on all of us, that we are not invited to reside in that most opulent of mansions? What if it turned out that we have no reason to hope for the wild surmise of a new heaven?

Well, we might conclude that we're better off anyway without the draining seduction of an afterlife. Who wants to go live with an omniscient old fart Who has already done up the décor and promulgated all the rules? It would be like being a teenager again. Would you really feel comfortable there, padding around on stockinged feet, careful always to not make too much noise, tell an off-colour joke, or leave lint on the white sofas? What kind of music could you listen to? Would you be able to rock out to the Flaming Lips on discreetly hidden speakers, or only with the privacy of earbuds? Would you have to offer to help with the dishes? What's some tribulation at home compared to the perennial awkwardness of the pampered houseguest?

The real reason people long for the end of the world is that the world is constantly beginning, over and over again, and this reinvention comes in so many guises that just contemplating them can leave you as simultaneously filled and drained and exhausted as a new lover spent in the long slanting light of evening. Call me pagan, I guess, or a bad investor who wants to cash in his returns right now: I'll take the way the light swells or declines to something new, and the crows cawing their way back to the spruce for a night of restless sleep, and the kid riding his bike, immune not to falls but, far more priceless, to exhausting worries about endings. And I'll take living in a hilly place where a new bike rider, after panting his way up past the neighbours' house, gets to turn and take the ride of his life (so far), a magic coast downhill, earning the hard dividends of gravity that begin again, over and over, whenever you've put the work into the climb.

ALEX DIGGINS

Holy Island

In cities that
have outgrown their promise people
are becoming pilgrims again, if not to this place,
then to the recreation of it in their own spirits.
– R. S. Thomas

I wake with a start. Black shock; I am blind. I strain my eyes: nothing. Stumbling my fingers across the bedside table, I find the torch and click it on. Shadows loom and skitter in the corners of the unfamiliar room. My heart clenches.

I force myself up, cross the room and crack open the bedroom door, chasing the torch beam down into the kitchen. It's a big cold room, and the surfaces gleam queerly in the antiseptic light. Lit up like the set of a TV murder mystery. I try to push the thought from my mind.

I descend and cross to the front door, the flagstones biting on my bare feet. Pulling it open, I step out into the night. Quiet. The laboured churning of the generator next door has stilled. The only sounds are the susurrus of wind and the muted rip-and-roar of waves on the shore. No lights, except for my tiny beam and the red-eyed blink of the lighthouse in the distance.

I turn off my torch and look up. A stage of night: wind has swept the evening's clouds to the horizon. The sky is slurred with light. Stars crowd, thick and textured as though smeared on with a palette knife. Tang of salt on the air.

My first night on the island.

Bardsey Island – Ynys Enlli in Welsh, the isle in the flood tides – is a small place. Two miles long and just over a mile across its widest point, you can walk its coastline in a couple of hours. Or run them, as I discovered on one jubilant sun-spilt evening, in 45 minutes. Despite its snugness, it feels wild. The prevailing westerlies bring storms off the Irish Sea to hammer at your front door, and its rugged character is further emphasised by its most distinctive feature: Mynydd Enlli, the 584ft 'mountain'. Whale-humped and heathered, it looks like a Cairngorm mountainside miraculously transplanted to the sea off north-west Wales. In fact this resemblance is not fanciful: on the summit ridgeline you stand on 600 million-year-old Precambrian rock, some of the oldest in Britain. As in the Cairngorms, your boots press down on a once-mighty mountain range, planed down by ice and burying time.

But that is where the resemblance ends. Turn your back on the mainland and look out west, towards the stolid, candy-striped lighthouse, and Bardsey reveals a different character. The world falls away into neat squares of fields, half a dozen cottages strung out along the island's only track and, further off, the sheltered harbour of Cafn where the weekly boat comes in. It is a view both pastoral and theatrical – from this height other humans catch the eye, their amblings make for compelling drama. Drop a bit further down the slope, and the mountain's bulk cuts off any view back towards the Llŷn peninsula – phone signal dies as well – and mainland life abruptly vanishes. Bardsey is an island with its back turned decisively on the land. An enclave, a redoubt: a place set apart.

Thanks in part to this sense of isolation, the island has a long history of pilgrimage and retreat. Contemplatives and hermits have arrived on its shores since at least the sixth century, and probably far longer. Rough huddles of stone cells surface on the mountain's southern shoulder in autumn when the heather dies back. Early Celtic monks made their homes in these crude shelters, attracted by the promise of the landscape's austerity: a life ruled by the tide's gifts and deprivations, the mind kneaded to quietude by the pulse-beat of wind and sea. Written records from this time are patchy and sparse – and invariably braided with myth – and so it is difficult to determine what drove these first pilgrims. It is probable though that they were inspired by traditions of solitary meditation and retreat in Eastern mysticism. What is beyond doubt is that these *peregrini* felt keenly the yearning for a suitable desert. Migration's siren song was anchored bone-deep.

Wild and lonely places, especially islands, held particular attraction. They set a moat between the contemplative and the snares of everyday life. But islands also threw them back upon their own resources, physical and spiritual. The peregrini thus became castaways on themselves. For some solitaries though, these rigours were not enough. St Cuthbert, for instance, who ended his days on Lindisfarne, another holy island, built the walls of his hermitage so high that 'he could see nothing except the heavens above.'[1] Reading this, I was struck by the echoes in this image of the high-windowed cells I had seen in the Buddhist monasteries of Nepal, built so that they framed just a sharp strip of blue sky and blinding white peaks. There too, the astringency of the view was designed to still the mind's whirling sediments and purify thought – architecture as filtration for the spirit.

Even so, seclusion gnaws. My own week-long stay on Bardsey was shot through with jags of loneliness. The author R. Geralt Jones recalled a similar feeling during his first few days on the island. 'The sea is all around me,' he wrote. 'I cannot get away. There is only me. I have to live with this me all the time.'[2] By the end of his stay though, he began to negotiate with his isolation, perceiving instead the island's expansiveness, its sufficiency: '[It] seemed spacious, a big enough world, rich and full of minute variety.' In fact, in many accounts of island life, I met this same movement from scattering to stillness, the anxious edges of the writer's mind worn smooth by their encounter with the place. Sister Helen Mary, a contemplative nun who lived for 15 years there in lonely retreat, called it: 'The island of solitude where one is least alone.'[3]

The first Welsh reference to the island's monastics describes their dwelling as *Llan*, a common place name identifying a simple hut or enclosure. Even in early accounts, then, Bardsey brought to mind the balance between enclosure and exposure, shelter and the storm. It is a tension one still feels today: poised in the almost imperceptible shift from farmland to mountain heath, or thrumming in the ridgeline's crazy cavern of wind as you watch a trunk of rain approach over the sea, eyeing up the distance to your cottage.

When the weather is fine, I like to sit in the hide on the far western tip of the island. Perched on a cliff top, it faces the sea. It was built for watching – wildlife, weather, waves – but it works just as well for thinking. The inlet below is a mess of foam; suds fly off and catch in the nooks and crannies of the rocks like melting snow. More than at any other time, I feel the island as the prow of a ship, powering through the relentless working of the waves.

You enter the hide at a crouch, hunched, birdlike, forcing open the corroded metal hatch – more sea salvage than ironmongery. There is a floor of pebbles and a wooden bench corrugated with graffiti. The front panels unlatch and you can swing them down so you're given a rectangle of sea and cloud and sky. It's a frame; and like all frames it concentrates vision by constraining it. Mostly, however, I prefer to latch it back up, and wait for my eyes to adjust to the half-light that creeps through the slats. The dark is soft and muffled, but alert to every movement of the wind. A sounding box, an echo chamber, a weather window, and me at its heart.

But if you unlatch the window – and you have a little patience – your eyes adjust and you can catch the dip and dart of sea birds through the rhythmic churning of the waves. Bardsey is rich in bird life. Gulls, carrion crows, choughs and guillemots are all easily spotted on a walk of its coast and I would often see the black Jurassic silhouettes of cormorants perched on outlying rocks. The thousands of islands which halo the British Isles are some of the best locations for bird watching we have. That is because birds are among the animal kingdom's greatest migrants. Many species are almost entirely pelagic, spending their lives on the open ocean. And so the only places their lives intersect with our own are the frontiers of the land: coastlines, sea stacks, cliffs and islands.

Yet during my stay, I never saw Bardsey's most iconic visitor: the Manx Shearwater. At some 21,000 breeding pairs, the island has the largest population in the UK outside of Skomer and the Isle of Man. Their breeding season is between April and early September and so my trip, at the tail end of summer, just missed them. Still, their presence was inescapable: shearwaters are ground nesters and the slopes of the mountainside were honeycombed with their nests.

During the season, each breeding pair incubates a single egg in their nest. Once the chick has hatched, they will take it in turns to fish at sea or stand sentry. To avoid predators, the birds prefer to fly back at night, waiting offshore in vast rafts at sunset. And then, with the darkness, they return. The night thickens with phantom wing beats and their cries shaft through the dark, sounding uncannily human. The Vikings called them 'the Devil's birds', their voices those of the restless dead.

Towards the end of summer, the parents will abandon their chick to return to the sea. Swollen with sustenance, the chick will not be able to squeeze out of its burrow. Having fasted for a week or so, it can finally emerge into the open. Yet danger is everywhere and time is of the essence. Quickly it will note the position of the stars and begin its tentative, shuffling maiden flight to the sea. It will not return for four years.

When it does, it is to the same island, the same hillside, the same burrow. Navigating by the stars and inborn magnetic sense, it will have compassed the 4,000 miles to its feeding grounds off South America several times, returning home to the burrow it saw only once, a lifetime ago, on that first panicked dash.

Unlike Bardsey's first pilgrims, I knew where the shearwaters had gone. Yet, even so, their vanishing had the quality of a magic trick, leaving behind a sense of loss. I cannot believe those pilgrims failed to thrill at the sight of a lone bird threading the mountainous scarps of sea, the sun flaring chrome behind, convinced the shearwaters had returned. Fellow travellers, wingtips spread out against the light, crucifixes in flight.

On the island, silence and shadows strike a heavier, more plangent note. At night, the windows running with rain, I startle myself with my movements – filling the kettle, pressing the tap, the whump of the gas ring. Listening to the water begin to move in the kettle, catch, shiver and change pitch. A shift I feel in my gut. Back home in London, shadows are shrill, scattering. Any silence feels poised, tentative, wary of being cracked. But on Bardsey the dark and the quiet are great, blunt facts. I find I sleep lightly and my dreams are richly peopled. Faces and figures I have not seen since my school days chatter and accompany me. And I spend long reaches of the night awake – my normal rhythms pressed out of shape by the elemental black.

One morning, still muzzy-headed from my disturbed night, I wander over to the stables next to my cottage. Like most buildings on Bardsey, it is low-slung and solid, built of massive, close-fitting stones – designed to weather winter storms, not for elegance. I had seen transparent tarp over the windows and assumed that repairs were going on. I was wrong. I come around the back and am met by a woman in a homespun dress of muted green with bare feet and washed blue eyes. She moves slowly, carefully, with a dancer's poise. She beckons me in.

'Welcome to my workshop,' she says. 'I'm Carole, the artist in residence on the island.'

Carole is a mixed media artist and has been coming to the island for sixteen years, she tells me. First for a few weeks, then for the whole summer. She has few official duties, apart from producing a piece each season and encouraging visitors – especially small children and reluctant adults – to help her with the art. Mostly though, she is left to experiment and explore the island.

I step further into the room. It holds a glorious feeling of light and space. The tarps on the window now make sense – they allow illumination to flood the room but prevent the ever-present winds from making mischief. Art shines from every surface. Canvases are propped against walls; paint pots, brushes and buckets of iridescent water are piled crazily on stools and chairs; and the room is centred around a vast wooden table scattered with paintings in various stages of composition. Carole has been experimenting with natural dyes and materials. Charcoal is smeared across paper in confident, expansive strokes. Blackberries are mashed to an inky-black dye which stains everything it touches a washed-out purple. Willow wands from the beds just south of our cottages are stacked in sheaves against the walls to dry and are being stripped for paint brushes and styluses.

Something in the corner catches my eye. I walk over to take a closer look. It is a mobile made of seashells, hung on almost invisible wires from the ceiling so they seemed to float in the air.

'Ah, you've found my wishing Tardis,' Carole says, smiling. 'Go on – step inside. But careful, it's powerful.'

I part the curtain of shells and step in. The motion sets them swirling and tinkling, an echo of the sea's shifting. The column surrounds me; I feel as though I am deep underwater, looking up at light reaching down far beneath the surface while shells and other debris from the upper world drift slowly past, vanishing into the depths below. I stand there, sunk in its magic, until Carole begins to tell me the history of her workshop. It was a threshing barn, built like the island's cottages and school by Lord Newborough, Bardsey's Victorian landlord, for the resident families. During harvest in late summer, the barn became the heart of the community. Everyone gathered to thrash and strip the corn, ready for grinding into the winter's stores of flour. Standing there as Carole describes the scene, I can picture it: the metronomic thump of flails on the flagstone floor, counterpointed by sharp shouts and bursts of laughter; the air thick with drifting flecks of corn husk gilded by afternoon's low-slanting light. The workshop hums with history. Decades of care and discipline and patient practice have accrued here. A quiet human legacy laid, year on year, like the layers of paint on a canvas.

Just after sunset and summoned by its bell, we gather in the chapel. The pews face each other and candles cluster on the altar. Hunched, half-shadowed figures in a circle of buffeted light: I have the curious impression we are sat around an open fire in a cave. The effect is heightened by the wind, which rails at the windows with impotent ferocity. Inside the chapel, a shuttered quiet holds. Carole leads the service. She begins, her voice a thread of high, clear beauty:

Be still and know that I am God

Eyes closed, tasting the words as they leave the tongue, we take up the song.

In thee, O Lord, I place my trust

It rises and falls, rises and falls, in the incense-laden air. A tapestry of sound and breath and spirit; an act that is rooted, ancient, generous. It carries me up and out, through the phosphorescent storm of rain picked out by my head torch, and off, into the dark.

Our world is fugitive. We are in the midst of the largest refugee crisis since World War II. According to the campaign group Doctors of the World, 70.8 million people have been forcibly displaced. 37,000 people flee their homes every day due to conflict and persecution. The fifth and sixth centuries – the world of those Celtic wanderers – was likewise steeped in violence and scarred by continual migration and displacement. Successive invaders, the Anglo-Saxons, the Vikings, drove ordinary people before them. Many sought safety in the north and west, a centrifugal expansion away from the heartland towards the ragged edge of Britain. In the words of one contemporary source, they 'trusted their lives to the high hills and cliffs of the sea coast.'[4] These peregrini, then, were pilgrims – but also refugees. And holy islands like Bardsey summoned them with the promise of sanctuary, spiritual and physical.

As the climate crisis tightens like a noose, as governments dither and scapegoat, as our politics turns inward-looking and fearful, as walls become instruments of diplomacy, I wonder if these holy islands will once again begin to broadcast their call. Our current epoch delivers the present as warning and opportunity. Never have we been more aware that our choices, our actions, will continue to echo down to future generations, ricocheting forward into the depths of geologic Deep Time. Never have we been more aware of our responsibilities as ancestors. For those privileged enough to travel to places like Bardsey, these thoughts become difficult to ignore. Away from the roar of everyday life, you sense a shift, a turning, a widening of the gyre. Like grains of sand caught in a wave's infolding, you feel a great rearing of energy building towards collapse. Which way it will fall is harder to tell.

Crossing back to the mainland, I find autumn has arrived. Air pinches and breath pools. Climbing up out of the narrow, overhung harbour of Porth Meudwy, the air is cool and rich and green. Hedgerows are heavy with bird song. Behind clouds, the sun has a penny-sheen. As I climb, they break and warmth slants across the valley. I walk up, and out, towards the light.

Notes

1. Allchin, A. M. *Bardsey: A Place of Pilgrimage*, Bardsey Island Trust, 3rd Edition, 2016.
2. Jones, R. Geralt, *Bardsey: A Fortnight's Journal*, Tern Press, 1st Edition, 1976.
3. Chitty, M. *The Monks on Ynys Enlli, Part One: c.500 A.D to 1252 A.D.*, Self-published, 1992.
4. Gildas, *On the Ruin of Britain*, Manuscript, British Library (Cotton MS Vitellius A VI), mid-900s.

MONIKA KOSTERA

Lamentation

King Lear is dead
but miracles are still
likely to come.
The long march has halted,
the heart has fallen out
of the mouth of the city
and lies, like a small bloody animal,
at the crack of the curb.

Miracles are still possible.
Rain is falling on the homeless'
tent city. Should we weep now,
or have we missed the cue
long ago?

The King's crown of weeds
has been tossed in the air
like a bride's flower wreath.
He opens his eyes,
no dreams
want to come.

The tide rises, the tide falls like breath.
Miracles are still likely.

CALEB COHEN

When it Rains, Get Wet

September, northern Vancouver Island, British Columbia: I am one of 40 tree-planters working on a reforestation contract based out of a little logging town called Woss, on unceded 'Namgis First Nation territory. Across the island another dozen or so contracts are either gearing up or already pounding away for the home stretch of the planting season. Throughout the camp figures appear and disappear from tents, vans, truck top campers, fifth-wheels, SUVs, and tarp-rigged shanties. They dress in Stanfield sweaters, hi-vis T-shirts, Carhartt, Helly Hansen, Blundstones or rubber boots, fleece, wool and more fleece and occasional pieces of flair like a crocheted vest or a faux-sheepskin duster. Cigarette butts and beer cans lie in the dirt like scat or scratch marks, tell-tale signs of their presence.

The average age in camp is a bit past 30. The students and teenage vagabonds, common on spring and summer contracts in BC's interior, have all gone back to universities, cities or warmer, drier places. Left behind are the peripatetic career planters who began slotting trees in the ground in April or March or even February and will carry on well into October. Many of my co-workers are a decade into planting careers. Some are several decades in. Each season they follow the weather to bush camps across Canada to plant trees. There are surely many reasons they return year after year, but if you asked them most would only give one: the money.

Logging in British Columbia clear-cuts thousands of forested hectares a year – millions of trees. Since the 1930s the government has recommended that trees be replanted to replenish the timber stocks for future generations of loggers. In the 1970s the Ministry of Forests allowed open bidding on planting contracts and cooperatives of idealistic hippies replaced apathetic wage labourers. Early planters used heavy, cumbersome mattocks and hoedads. They would camp directly on the block and plant several hundred thousand trees in a season, most of which had bare roots and low survival rates. Over the next 50 years, the industry expanded and changed. Cooperatives gave way to small corporations. The recommendation to replant became a legal requirement. Innovations like the D-handled shovel, three-pouch planting bags, and root plugs increased efficiency and tree survival. Thousands of trees per season became millions. In addition to the relentless logging, forest fires, mountain pine beetle and pressure to act on climate change have led the province to launch the most expansive ramp-up of planting in decades. The number of trees planted in BC in the last decade has held steady at around 250 million per year. In 2020, it is expected to rise to 320 million. Some 500 new planters will be added to the existing 5,000 to make it happen.

Planters are paid by the tree. Here, on the coast, where the hills are steep and the slash (the logs and debris left behind by the loggers) is big, the tree price could get up to about 30 cents. On a good day on the coast, an experienced planter might put in 1,500 or more trees. In the flat, fast interior the price drops far lower, but that same experienced planter will put in three, four, or even five thousand trees per day. Convert that to an eight-hour work day and as far as an hourly wage goes, planting stacks up well against most trade or office jobs. Minimal expenses while in camp sweeten the paycheque, and the flexibility of seasonal work, the pleasure of working outside, the refuge from the press of urban life make it all the more attractive, or at least attractive enough.

For the next four weeks we will rise before the sun to the constant patter of rain, to dripping trees and spongy sphagnum and an ever-present damp. In the cold and dark we hobble to the mess tent; make a sandwich; eat some eggs or oatmeal, potatoes; then coffee, a cigarette and climb into a Ford F-350 pickup truck. Crews of six drive deep down logging roads, valley bottoms recede into the mist-draped mountain sides of the Island Alps. The second-growth forest outside the truck window is thick, but it suddenly cuts off and the savage, ravaged landscape of a cutblock surrounds us. Looking up impossibly steep hillsides, I see discarded trees strewn from one end to the other: western red cedar, *Thuja plicata*; western hemlock, *Tsuga heterophylla*; Douglas fir, *Pseudotsuga menziesii*; yellow cedar, *Cupressus nootkatensis*. They lie criss-crossed and piled across the block like pick-up sticks. Pieces of slash 100 feet long and four feet in diameter are common. Some, especially the cedars, shatter like fine china when they fall to the ground, but others are straight and solid and beautiful. If this is what the loggers leave behind, what are the trees they take out like?

Being on a cutblock is surreal. A fresh one looks like a war zone: stumps are flipped over with roots exposed, burnt slash piles leave black and charred scars, tread tracks could just as easily have been left by a tank as a feller buncher. The ground is muddy, pitted, scarred. The air is still. Year-old cut blocks are like abandoned graveyards. Stumps stand above the regrowth of grasses and shrubs, arnica and fireweed. Spread at even intervals, bleached and grey from the sun, they are their own tombstones. These old blocks, though, are full of life. I have seen countless fawns, baby rabbits and grouse nests. Generations of wildlife come of age in these altered landscapes.

As we plant we move methodically. We clamber over every metre of the block with our bags full of three hundred 20-centimetre seedlings and our dainty Speed Spade shovels. We work to a prescription: 1400 stems per hectare, microsite this species into that soil-type, all trees at least two metres apart, hide the seedling near a stump to protect from elk-browse and snowpack. Near each tree we hang a piece of blue polyethylene flagging tape so everyone knows: this spot has been reforested. Some days it rains all day and the temperature never rises past 10° Celsius.

The coastal contract is short. We only work 20 days in shifts of three days on, one day off. But it is my third contract of the year. The fifth or sixth for some of my co-workers. From March to September, from the Alaskan border to Alberta and Saskatchewan, we hustle to get in an 80- or 90-day season. Over and over and over, day after day after day, labour, putting new trees where the old ones had lived and breathed for centuries.

Swiss scientists claim that a trillion new trees could reverse or mitigate the worst of what's coming. YouTube stars and Instagram influencers urge viewers to go out and act by planting a tree. Social media campaigns ask for donations: one dollar you give equals one tree planted. Millennial American volunteers and Chinese and Indian army corps line up, shovels in hand, to plant trees. The prime minister of Canada, Justin Trudeau, pledged an extra billion trees to counter climate change, and a picture of him and his children contributing their three or five went viral. Like electric cars and paper straws, it's an attractive myth: planting trees can save us; there exists an easy solution. In this story of modern Johnny Appleseeds, of arboreal eco-warriors, the 5,000 career tree-planters in Canada are left wondering: where do our trees fit?

For us, planting is a Sisyphean task. It seems futile. We dart quickly but thoroughly across each cutblock, trying to colour in the great brown smudge with new green. Satellite images show it best; zoom in on any patch of BC and see little bubbles of brown and adjacent bubbles of dark and darker green: fresh clear-cuts and successive generations of plantations. We try to restore the homogenous colour the landscape once had, but always, across the valley, working more slowly but with equal tenacity, a team of fallers and skid-steer operators erases green and leaves new brown. Sisyphus strained and grunted against his boulder and planters earn each inch on the hill through sweat. Tree bags are heavy; the sun or rain or snow bear down; at every step slash grabs ankles, rocks trip feet, and alder spreads its limbs into fences. Sisyphus' boulder rolls back down the hill and always there is one more tree, one more bag-up, one more day.

Planting is also Sisyphean in its absurdity. In Kurt Vonnegut's *Slaughterhouse Five*, Billy Pilgrim describes the firebombing of Dresden in reverse. Fire and wreckage are packed into cylindrical bombs which are lifted magnetically into planes. The planes carry these cylinders back to the factories where they are disassembled and shipped to remote locations to be buried back in the ground. Ore, bitumen, oil, rare-earth metals, coal, petroleum for plastics, potash and lumber: all natural resources pulled out of the ground. Outside of Pilgrim's visions it is only lumber that is put back. Perhaps a cutblock is a worse scar than a tree plantation, but it is absurd to think that a replanted forest can match the bio-complexity of 500-year-old growth. This futility, the backwards absurdity that Vonnegut saw in war, the firebombing of Dresden, and the clear-cutting of forests, cannot be undone. The odometer does not roll backwards when a car is driven in reverse. It is absurd to think that Sisyphus can set the boulder atop the hill. It is absurd to think that planting can replace lost forests. For us, as individuals, planting only makes sense because each tree is money in our pocket.

I hated planting for my first three years. My friend Sean hated it for ten. It is gruelling work, physically and emotionally taxing. It is repetitive. Often planters work a piece of the block alone, only seeing other members of the crew at a shared cache during the ten minutes it takes to refill their bags every few hours. For eight hours a day, the planter is left with his or her thoughts. Relationship issues, anxieties, schemes for the future, regrets from the past, wild fantasies play out over and over in a spin cycle. I would spend days comparing myself to friends who worked in law firms or in finance. Inevitably though, the thoughts would turn to the work. Any environmental promise it held seemed hollow; the social value seemed worthless; there was no prestige. Planting did not fit well into a LinkedIn profile or on a glossy resume. It was something to do while I tried to figure out a better way to live. A way that fit more neatly into the mythic success story.

Then, after years of effort, a moment came where it transformed from grunting labour into sport. The movement became fluid, the ground became soft, the prices were good and I felt like an alpine ungulate browsing the new growth or a predatory bird striking shovel-beak after tasty grubs or worms. There was belonging. Nothing external had changed. Rather, after years of practice I had learned to exist within my own brain. The self-conscious negative-thought spin cycle faded. I learned how to prepare mentally and equipmentally for the weather. I learned how to suffer and in doing so, stopped suffering. After years of shared struggling, camp became an intimate world full of dear friends. Bush bacchanals and days off at hot springs and glacial rivers balanced the work. What was a monotonous chore reframed into a series of singular achievable tasks: put one more tree in the ground; prepare for tomorrow; laugh or read or play music because today's task is complete. Tree-planting became the best job, the best sport, the best lifestyle and the doubts about the value or purpose faded away. Bush life became something primordial and intuitive and intensely sane. There is value in the trees, a quantified cent amount, but there is also value in the experience of planting them, in interacting with the land, with each other and with ourselves. Push past the pay and planters start to admit that, of all the reasons they return season after season, it is the relationships and the lifestyle that truly brings them back.

I do not know if the trees my friends and I are planting here in Woss will grow big and tall. I do not know if they will die or if the ones we planted last year have already died because of drought or browsing or snow or because I left them shallow, with a bent root plug in the wrong microsite. Climate change or forest fire may kill them before they reach their predetermined death date at the hands of a sawman or feller-buncher. But, sometimes, I do dream that a few of my trees will slip through the cracks. Centuries will unwind and maybe, please, a few could become behemoths and leviathans and Methuselahs in the next millennium's old growth forests.

I know, though, that that secret hope is not the point. Reforestation will not recreate lost ecosystems. Centuries of logging and post-colonial development have given the land of British Columbia many scars. The muddy war-zones of fresh cuts and tombstone stumps of years-old blocks are not hard to find. The ghost of loss haunts them, and though young wildlife hides there too, the blocks are artifacts of the Anthropocene. So, we planters come and work; and when it rains we get wet, and in the rain, we bear witness; witness to the destruction, the transformation, the cycle of change taking place at our own hand, and we wonder for what end. Perhaps, when the last chainsaw powers down and the last seedling is planted, no one will ask about point or purpose; they will simply be.

SARAH MISSELBROOK

Inside the Forest

In June 2019 there was the worst forest fire in 25 years in the Ribera d'Ebre region of Catalunya, burning over 6,000 hectares of pine, olive and almond trees. As part of a creative initiative entitled 'Cendrart' – *cendra* meaning 'ash' in Catalan – I was invited to create a site-specific work for a temporary exhibition within the cremated forest. The initiative was to raise awareness of the fire and to give support to the fundraising group 'Rebrotem' – meaning 'we regrow' in Catalan.

I focussed on what I witness here in the mountains of Catalunya within nature. The ability of the fig tree to regrow after destruction, whether through controlled farming activities or forest fire.

The weekend of the 5th and 6th of October of that year was an intense period spent moving between the burnt trees of the Maials area in the Ribera d'Ebre region, one of the most badly affected areas of countryside.

Leaving my footprints within the deep ash floor, trying not to disturb the natural forms any more than had already been altered by the fire itself, I carefully placed 350 fragile plaster leaves, impressions taken directly from fig leaves which had dropped from a local tree.

The time spent in the forest was all-consuming. In the visual palette of greys and blacks, only the bright blue sky offered some relief. The fig leaves were a crisp, white, clinical offering to this place. However, with every movement and gust of wind, the ash soon filled the leaf veins creating a more beautiful nuanced surface. As if the leaves required this material to show them in their true beauty.

[opposite above] Sarah Misselbrook installing fragile plaster cast fig leaves at the base of a cremated pine tree in the forest of Maials, Catalunya, Spain.

[below] Plaster fig leaves are piled towards the lifeless tree in some kind of offering of restoration.

SARAH MISSELBROOK
[above] Detail shot of final installation showing plaster fig leaves enveloping the cremated pine tree.

[opposite] Inside the Forest
Collecting and cleaning the area of burnt branches and placing them within the metal cage as live performance, the artist's body shares the same surviving space within the cage.

JULIE WILLIAMS
Sculpting in the Pyrocene: A Disappearing Act
Video still

Within a eucalypt forest the artist performs a collaborative ritual with a burned tree. The tree central to the work was sculpted by bushfire on a mountain plateau; its deep roots remain steadfast, anchored within the regenerating landscape. The duo sculpt with a light filled net to unravel memory and history, poetically conjuring the past to the present to envision the future. They expose our vulnerability as a species in a collapsing world.

[opposite]
JORDAN TIERNEY
Purification Rite
Photograph

Interconnection of the earthly and the cosmos. Rusty auto parts and a perfume bottle found in an urban stream seem to distill the lowly into an airy state in the heavens. In the photograph my daughter, who is young enough not to fully grasp what we have done to our environment, uses a broken beer bottle as a chalice to perform a ritual known only to her and the stream.

CAROLINE ROSS

The Jacket

T'ai Chi master Mark Raudva bought this once-black jacket in London's Chinatown in 1988 and has worn it to teach several classes a week since then. In 2004 Frances, a long-term student and skilled seamstress, replaced the collar and renewed the cuffs where they were beyond darning. Since then Caroline Ross has been patching and mending the jacket with hand and machine stitching on a regular basis, and documenting the evolution of symbiotic wear and renewal. The jacket is still in weekly use, covered in visible mending, and is constantly being made and unmade.

CHARLOTTE WATSON

How to Fix a Bowl

Step 1

I imagine the bowl in its entirety, as an unbroken shape. Turning over each fragment I take note of the glaze, texture and the break itself.

Kintsugi is a kind of meditation. It requires full attention between the hands, ears and eyes. I gently turn over the curve of the bowl, using my fingertips to find hairline fractures. If I tug and they make a faint sound, or look as though they could continue to fissure, they're earmarked to be broken.

—

When the hull of the *S.S. Waikare* split on uncharted rocks, her captain knew they risked sinking into the depths of Dusky Sound. He ordered the crew to push the engines until she foundered on the shallows of Stop Island. All passengers disembarked and watched from their temporary camp as she rolled and gradually slipped below the water.

—

Retrieved from the sinking steamer was a lamp in the form of a spring nymph. Her arm was somehow broken and she was taken to a mechanic, the only local with the means to solder bronze alloy. But mechanics do not extend to anatomists, and she forever holds her swirling lamp outward from a double-jointed elbow.

—

Restoration is not always what we intend.

Step 2

With an eyedropper, I combine one part water to two parts flour until the substance is gummy and glutinous. Next, I add the brown *kiurushi* lacquer and mix. The combined substance, *mugiurushi*, starts to repel and spring back against the spatula. Mugiurushi is ready when it looks like chocolate cake batter but with the smell of old cheese.

Quickly, I apply a small amount of the paste to the connecting edges of the broken ceramic. I gently push the two connecting fragments, holding them in place once the edges touch. For the next 15 minutes, I'll hold and wait.

—

Urushi comes from *Toxicodendron vernicifluum,* a tree endemic to Asia. Various cultures have cultivated the tree over thousands of years, scoring the trunks for the sap that cures hard with a gloss finish. As the Latin prefix *toxico* suggests, it is poisonous, containing the compound 'urushiol' that is found in plants such as poison ivy. This substance can cause severe reactions simply from inhaling the oil within the sap.

—

A major allergic reaction is generally understood as a rite of passage amongst those who repair using the traditional kintsugi method. My initiation manifested as an angry, painful body rash, mitigated by a week of aloe vera and antihistamines.

Step 3

The ceramic segments are in place once they can tentatively support themselves. After securing the bowl with masking tape and rubber bands, I carefully place it into a *muro* – a box that maintains a stable 25°C for the urushi to cure. To be effective, a muro requires humidity and a small open space at the top for air to flow. I leave a damp sponge next to the bowl and leave the muro in a warm place, checking but not touching for the next two days.

—

Unstable temperatures threaten all sorts of apocalyptic outcomes. But in the world of my front garden it means scale, black spot and wilt. Sometime after the house was built, hybrid tea roses were planted under a thirsty paperbark in naturally acidic soil. If I had a choice – meaning, if my landlord was not so fixated on a certain cottage look – I would rip them all out and stuff the garden full of grevillea.

—

When I was a teen, an artist took my father and me through his native revegetation on the southern coast of Aotearoa. He walked us through Chatham Island flax and cabbage trees when we stopped near a low, fruiting bush with dark purple flowers. He said the farmers pulled it all out because it made cattle abort.

Years later, walking amongst local bushland on the other side of the Tasman, I realise it was *poroporo*, or in Australia, Kangaroo Apple. Bush Tucker.

Step 4

If the conditions allow, I can now trim back the thick edge of mugiurushi gum to the level of the ceramic. I move my scalpel carefully, aware that the mugiurushi is still soft inside, and the sections may fall apart again with little force.

Often, they do. I curse and start all over again.

—

I weed the brick courtyard out the back of my house every six months, mostly so the land agent will continue to let us live there. But in the in-between times, I let the native Sprawling Bluebells grow between the gaps so I can watch them sway from my window.

—

Restoration is not always a forward movement.

Step 5

Monitoring the muro over a few days, I ensure that the environment stays humid. Slowly, I repeat the previous steps until all remaining ceramic pieces are in place. There is no need for hurry.

—

Nearby is the Merri Merri ('very rocky') Creek. For the first time since European settlement, willow is being replaced by wattle to regenerate the area and improve water flow. A well-worn snake is painted on the concrete, warning incomers to the potential of any unidentified branches on the path between October and April.

—

I feel as though the Merri Creek is the only place in the city where hiking boots don't look over the top. In training for a long distance walk, I go further and further north into areas I haven't previously seen. But as my walks grow longer they also become slower as long-necked turtles, kookaburras and scar trees distract me.

—

In the studio, I listen to a botanist being interviewed about Hinewai Reserve, where an unconventional approach is being used to re-establish native bush over invasive gorse. He refers to the weed as 'nurse canopy' – the most generous term I've heard for a plant so regionally hated.

Step 6

Once the bowl is trimmed, I begin the slow layers of backfill. Using a fine brush, I gently apply pure kiurushi lacquer along the crack lines, focussing on areas that need filling in. This is repeated every day or two, covering my skin and face to gently sand back between layers.

—

In Melbourne, London plane trees line the streets, pollinating in spring with tiny trichomes that catch in the throats of the unsuspecting. Originally reminiscent of the settlers' former home, these trees have begun to die as Australian summers have intensified.

Step 7

The layering process is repeated with *kurourushi*, the glossy, black middle lacquer. This step requires many applications with sanding in between, to bring the repair line up to the level of the ceramic. I consider this process finished when I cannot feel the original break when running my hand over the bowl.

—

I restarted my vegetable garden after months of absence, both physical and emotional. This was forced, as someone gave me what seemed like a lifetime's supply of seedlings that needed immediate planting. Not one to let a plant die, they now sit in tidy rows and I sit with them, drinking tea.

—

Each morning, my cat runs outside to whack the dew droplets off the brassica's waxy leaves. The plants don't have a hope of producing heads, and I don't have the heart to ruin his fun.

—

Restoration is not only for ourselves.

Step 8

Once level and dry, I clean the break line of any residual dust or grit. To ready for the final layer it is important that I am fully present: no hunger, no phone and the door closed.

—

Living among the density and pace of Melbourne often leaves me feeling claustrophobic, longing for nature. But in Australia the grass is not always greener. Increasing temperatures combined with lower rainfall make the grass gold, the bush volatile, and I prune roses wearing a P2 mask.

Step 9

I turn the bowl over, considering how I will apply the final red *bengara* lacquer. Like all of kintsugi this step cannot be rushed, so completing the exterior may need to wait a day after completing the interior. The nature of the ceramic will dictate the process.

—

When I cannot stomach the news, I watch documentaries about food-foresters. One happened to live near the revegetation I visited as a teen. The forester described how growing food in this way had taught him to consider gardens differently. That what was required to 'fix' the problem was often more about changing his judgement or perspective, than intervening with nature itself.

—

To restore is to retract one's ego.

Step 10

I apply the sticky bengara lacquer with a fine brush. Moving very slowly, to take into consideration the curve of the bowl, I apply the lacquer with as thin a line as possible. Using the length of the bristles, I finish the tail of each stroke over the fine hairline fractures.

Next, I wait about 30 minutes for the lacquer to become tacky, before applying the gold powder.

Wearing the same P2 mask and using a fluffy, dry brush, I dip the bristles into the metal powder and hold the brush just above the fresh lacquer-line. Using my index finger, I gently tap the end of the brush so the powder falls onto the tacky bengara, being careful to not touch the surface with the bristles. I repeat this across the bowl until all of the lines are powdered, and then return it to the humid muro.

—

Occasionally on my walks I visit an old settler cemetery. I've always liked their quiet stories, being one of the few public spaces comfortable with symbol and metaphor for that which is beyond articulation.

I seek out the yew trees. Imposing and evergreen, they stand for immortality, able to grow anew from old wood. I wonder, planted here in this dry red earth, if they provided comfort for those who died far from home.

Step 11

A few days after all of the ceramic has been powdered and cured, I gently wipe the remaining metal powder with a damp cloth, taking care to not touch the break line itself.

Once clean, I leave the ceramic on a warm shelf. Though the repair is finished, it will be another one to three months before it's fully cured and ready for use.

To restore is to change our relationship with time.

JELLE CAUWENBERGHS

My Tooth

My left molar. What a strange thing it is; like something you might find on a beach at low tide: a bit of whalebone. Did it come out of its ear? I am thinking of those small bones we have in ours. I am thinking of all the particles we leave behind. I am thinking, *like an old car*.

But if it that is where it came from, what happened to the rest of the body, the whale fall, the pounds of plastic waste, some of it in the stomach so long it has started to calcify and is part of the whale and so alien at the same time it has forced the acid out through the lining of the stomach?

Hard and shiny like porcelain, from the Italian *porcellana* – 'cowrie shell'.

The sea is in everything. Our inner balance is water. Loop-shaped canals of fluid like the chambers of a shell. We hope that nothing breaks; that nobody will barge in like a bull in a china shop. Carelessness could tip us over the edge. It could make us homeless. 'Brush and floss regularly.' Action verbs. Polish the precious things: they will outlive us.

Most of my teeth are white. I have been lucky. But I am getting older. Time is starting to show in certain areas; my skin especially – like the bald patches in the fur of an old dog. I find scars, moles, all kinds of rat bites. What is it Tennessee Williams wrote? 'We all live in a house on fire, no fire department to call; no way out, just the upstairs window to look out of while the fire burns the house down with us trapped, locked in it.'

This tooth turned black. It did not hurt but I knew it would, eventually. I noticed a slight discolouration at first. I saw it become brown, tobacco-coloured. It turned coat like a disloyal partisan, slow but resolute in its betrayal. Then it spread. The stain grew more pronounced and hard to ignore. I knew it would gouge a cavity in the enamel and hold a candle to the nerve, at which point the whole tooth – or rather, the raw, exposed root dangling from the roof like a faulty electric cable – would need to be removed. At which point I would be forced to acknowledge the decay. I would be in agony and my tooth would be a cinder, a liability for its neighbours.

I went to see the dentist and he recommended a filling. I baulked at the cost. He said I could choose. A white enamel filling was expensive. A silver filling was cheap, but he would have to take out more of the decayed tooth. That is how he phrased it. He drew a red line on the screen to show how far he would have to go, how deep he would have to drill. The expensive filling nestled like a snowy owl in a lovely, shallow hole in the wall. It was a fuzzy pillowcase white. The grey filling was ugly. It looked like a cuckoo. A parasite.

Of course snowy owls do not nest in walls. And cuckoos are beautiful. All this is an allegory. It happened, but it is just an example of what takes place; in the mouth, in our forests, in every disputed dwelling-place. It is about acceptance and rejection, the onset of decay.

There must be a seismograph that has recorded every tremor. And what would be the equivalent for our natural history of decay?

I thought it was funny and incredibly sad. The clear demarcation. The dentist smiled. The whole operation seemed absurd. To save a tooth you hollow it out. You evacuate all the people but nobody can return; they are forever exiled. They have left the milk on the table, the cat outside, hoping she will be OK – she is not. When you come back there is nothing, just a fine mist over the clear-cut, the memory of a house. To stop the decay you demolish the tooth around the rot. Then you fill it with metal and you seal it, so the tooth can remain, seemingly a tooth, but really the façade of a house glued to an ugly, industrial skeleton; a bankrupt film set, a Potemkin village.

Potemkin was governor of Crimea during the reign of Catherine II. The story goes that he built mobile villages on the banks of the river Dnieper to conceal the ravages of war from the empress. He populated the villages with soldiers pretending to be peasants and moved the villages downstream once the imperial barge had passed. He disassembled the entire town and rebuilt it elsewhere night after night.

The line of the Wikipedia article that stayed with me reads, 'The tale of elaborate, fake settlements with glowing fires designed to comfort the monarch and her entourage as they surveyed the barren territory at night is largely fictional.' The tale is partly apocryphal. To me, it does not matter that it is fictional. I am interested in the power of storytelling. Even though Potemkin's villages may not have existed, the story illustrates our desire to be deceived. Potemkin's strategy of concealment may have inspired real, historical cover-ups; the concentration camp at Theresienstadt, for example, was used by the Nazis in propaganda films.

It had a zoo and a symphony orchestra, and it offered art classes to inmates. They would scrub it clean and hide the dead during Red Cross inspections. It closed in 1945, when the illusion was no longer sustainable, or necessary.

I wonder how many Potemkin villages there are in our time, to distract us from reality, to protect us – not from destruction, but from any awareness of the forces that erode us, the forces we have unleashed. Are there towns like this, frozen in time, living history museums for the human imagination, where nobody is hurt or lonely, where nobody ages or has cancer, where nothing new is ever invented or allowed in, where no radiation exists, where no telephones ring, where animals die without pain or fear of death, where humans live in firm denial of the wireless data that travels through their bodies, the clocks they cannot refuse?

There is no hiding from reality. According to an article I read, the primary limitation of wireless communication is the large transmission loss occurring when travelling through the human body. This occurs because of the conductivity and thickness of various tissues and organs. Like birds, our bodies respond to electromagnetism, and we absorb countless waves that travel through us like sunlight through leaves.

You age. Your teeth and body weaken. They soften. Nothing about your appearance will remain intact, none of it can be endlessly restored, repaired, rehabilitated; and neither should it be. It will not endure. Like the last wisp of a dream at daybreak, it must collapse. Because the body is a cavity and sometimes too much has been taken out and too much has occupied that empty black space.

I will be a found object. I will be an uneasy, soft sculpture. In a way, that is what this essay is – a diary of flesh. It is just not clear whose diary this is, and most of my recollections are inaccurate, ill-fitting; or they are someone else's words, and I have stored them in my cells, and I understand they come from a place deep within, a place beyond memory, a leaking storage space. And so many times, it is my porosity that provides the skeleton key for this house within me; I enter because I am already inside.

The poet Dorothy Molloy, while dying of cancer, wrote: 'The house has become strange. The doors don't fit.' That is what I feel when I see bears on thin ice. I feel like a door has opened in the house and a grey stranger has walked in: Mr Bones.

There is a painting called *Fragments* by Vasily Kandinsky. An amoeba-like form floats against a background of purple and yellow shapes. A tooth-like elephant. There are various other floating forms. They form a fidgety, fragmented whole, yet seamlessly flow into one another because each colour seems to fill a hole that would otherwise be silent; and one wonders what would be there instead, if left unsealed, radiating out from that nexus – that strange mute hollow. He painted it in 1943. Kandinsky, who said, 'I had little thought for houses and trees.'

I remember this fragmentation from my work in nature conservation. I once went to a forest in Poland to save a meadow and most of my work consisted in cutting down pine trees and mowing acres of tall grass and pollarding willow – evicting birds to let other birds in. The paradox of salvation: not everybody is saved; some are sacrificed. Like a tale where you give a tooth for a frog, a frog for a horse… and then what? What if that is not enough? The shoemaker wants a lock of hair, the hair of eternal youth. The empress wants a pearl, a perfect village.

To save the greater ecosystem of my mouth the dentist had to anticipate future destruction. He started a controlled burn to save the town from wildfire; he dug a trench and lit a match. The surgery felt like an invasion. He cut into my gums and made my skull rattle. It all felt very loose and metamorphic. I thought of the things I had lost, and I thought of the way that loss is absorbed by the body, lost in the great hall of the heart like a flock of homeless birds.

I had accumulated so much and parts of me were ripe for the dump; they would fall to the bottom of the sea, and some of them would wash up and some of them would not disappear for a thousand years. They would outlive me in shapes I could not anticipate – starlings murmurating – and perhaps that was more honest, that was a good way of looking at time and the way places and bodies changed, the way you had to throw things in the fire when they no longer held any promise of healing.

Things fall apart. We have always known this. That does not mean we stand by. That does not mean we must let it grow hollow; it just means we don't always know what will fill this vacuum, and sometimes we have to breathe in and out, like the child in the tale, when the last match goes out and the tooth goes black. It is night. You are very frightened. But you must learn to breathe in the dark.

JEMMA BORG

Flowering Tree Questions

All day, I'd walked with the insistent voice
telling me to lose myself in the woods.
Now it's 4 am and I barely have a mind,
only these derelict gardens at the windows
of a borrowed house where I watch the swan patrolling
like a question mark on the pond's loose mirror –
she can hear the slink-shriek fox nearby,
the one that tore her faithful husband's throat.
I'm listening too, husk of ear to the barrelling earth.
Who am I? Why am I here? All that sings
is the wind's voiceless tune; I remember nothing.
If you ask a question of a flowering tree,
it answers in a rain of blossom;
in the winter, it answers with a blackened branch.
A storm never ends, it only empties
then refills: the same stories shuffle, vessel
to vessel; one year ends, another begins.
Pay attention! says the wind, unmastering the trees.
And the house creaks like a ship, a pith
of moonlight lengthens along the timber floor,
ash stirs in the cold armour of the grate.
And I listen again – to the soundless work,
to the world being spun in a sleeping house.
Then the swan's bright sailing
                                        breaks out into wings.

BEN GREENLEE

Eidola

We noticed the first sculpture on a Saturday. It was thin and welded together in patches from scraps of rusted iron. The tallest of us came up to its shoulder. Yes, we knew it to be a shoulder. Despite the jagged gaps in the chest and lack of fingers on one hand and a jaw that was not there we knew it to represent a human body. We could see ourselves in the twisted iron; its awkward legs and elongated arms and stooped shoulders a parody of our own. It was composed in the act of bending towards a rose bush that had been growing in the park for years. A tree was shading that perpetual act. In that same tree birds were doing what birds often do. Some of us mimicked the sculpture from the opposite side while some of us merely watched, unsure of the sculpture's attention to the roses, its delicate bending of the body to not pluck the petals but merely get close enough to touch them. Some of us reached out and ran our fingers along the iron bones that held the body upwards, a fine red dust staining the tips of those fingers. Some of us only touched the smooth beading that held together the seams. Some of us put our hand in the hand that was about to feel the flowers. All of us wondered who had placed the sculpture there, had composed its body in such a way, brought to mind so many memories we'd rather not face. Many of us left the park and did not venture out of our homes until others asked us to. Many of us did not ask, could not, too involved with the clockwork of the how and why of the bending of an iron body. We were not prepared for that discovery on a Saturday afternoon.

The following day we were hoping for another sculpture. The first had populated our nighttime imaginations. We thought it was a piece of the town that had existed before we had. We proposed that the sculpture came first, then the sky, then the rose bushes, then us. We envisioned that those roses grew along the iron bones and fleshed out the gaps and set into the hollow skull a cradle of red petals that bees flew to on their invisible trajectories and that those bees carried away the sculpture's dreams and those dreams had names which were our names. We woke in the morning and told no-one of what we imagined though we could see it written across our faces as we searched for another sculpture, believed in another sculpture.

We found it in a field of wheat a mile outside of town. It was twenty feet tall and made of glass and was again a human body. It was facing the setting sun. No-one touched the sculpture; no-one got too close; no-one dared describe its construction. We sat in a circle around it. We could see through its thighs and knees and ankles to those on the other side, could see the way it both absorbed and reflected the light, how it became the light, a body of blinding light that could almost put out our eyes yet didn't. Those of us at the furthest edges could make out its every feature, even from so far away, as if it were a pebble that rolled across a palm. As the sun set the glass sculpture turned every shade of evening cloud until it gradually winked away into the darkness, either still standing in the field or not standing in the field any longer or straddling somewhere in-between. Some of us stayed for morning while some of us stumbled townward in the night, unable to stand the presence of the sculpture any longer. One of us refused its very existence, never believing in hope again. From our chairs and couches and beds, just before sleep, we considered the memory of our homes and the homes of our fathers and our mothers and remembered baked bread from the oven and the mineral-taste of well water and familiar songs from the radio and how the right blanket at the right time could sooth whatever worries the day had brought and how the pomegranate flash of a cardinal's wing signalled to our child minds that pure colour could, indeed, yes, fly. We went to sleep with possibility.

And we awoke to a citizenry of sculptures, an entire town refilled with what had once been lost. They were all human sizes now, unlike the giants of days prior, each of them different than the other. They were made from every piece of material ever imagined: broken pallets with their almost-white grains exposed; jacket buttons that stared like a hundred thousand peacock eyes; creek stones with their crooked edges; coffee mugs with missing handles; light bulbs and sneakers and soda cans and alarm clocks arranged nearly haphazardly and pillow feathers and yarn strung tightly together over who knows what and golden hay stuffed into sacks and papier mâché and ceremonial swords and car parts and the toys of children and half-burned logs and half-eaten watermelons and half-empty jugs of milk and carpet swatches and vinyl records and fibreglass and a few were made from books with their pages facing outward waiting to be read. Some were held together with nails or bent metal or 2×4s and some were held together with glue and some were held together by the melted edges of themselves and others were strung together by whatever hung loose: rope, shoe laces, twisted curtains, garden houses. One was simply the outline of a human body chalked against a brick wall. This is the one that made us pause.

We found the sculptures amongst the town, running errands, performing tasks, practising their numbers, huddled close together with perpetually cooled coffee cups in their ridged hands. They stayed in a line that started at the town mailbox. They waited patiently by the telephone in the office down the hall. They considered this can of beans versus that can of peas and we manoeuvred our carts around them. They walked in twos on the thoroughfares and up the stairs and down the rows of cabbages. They stood at the tops of slides contemplating the *whoosh* that might fill their empty stomachs should they let go. They conducted traffic at the intersections though the cars only flowed in one direction - we took the long route to work and didn't think twice about it. They put blankets over horses that had already moved away and shovelled gravel from a pile that never diminished. They stood at the registers and we decided whatever was to be bought could wait until later. They stood facing the library stacks forever indecisive and stood with paintbrushes in their hands, bristles dried fossil-hard. They stood facing front doors about to knock but hesitated. So, so many stood over graves on the hill in town and these are the ones we did not approach, each of them experiencing a more extended loss than even our own. They stood on the corners of streets and waved and stood on the stoops of businesses and waved and stood at the bases of trees and waved and it was because of those small recognitions that we decided to converse back.

We tipped our hats. We said *how do you do?* We spoke of pleasantries and superficial things. We described the shifting patterns of weather and when the rains would come and how much snow to expect in the long months and if it would be a good harvest. We told them how our plough had gotten bent on a particularly large stone buried deep in the field and how we had dug around the stone until it was exposed like a jewel and hitched up our oxen and lashed the stone tight with rope and leather and whipped those oxen to trudge forward while we and our sons and our neighbours heaved forward with our muscles and stout poles and eventually got the stone out of the pit and all of us quivering with fatigue and there it was having only moved a foot and now what? We told them how to make a cherry pie and when to place the eggs in the boiling water and how to mend a sock before it was too late. We told them of our playfriends with bronze skin and haloed hair and white robes that dragged behind them like a wedding train. *Can't you see them, silly? They're right beside you.* We walked them along the circuitry of a damaged TV, having removed the face to witness the crisscross of wires beneath that gathers electricity and magnetism like thunderclouds and how those wires lead to a small glass tube that projected images fast as thought and ah, there's your problem. Some of us felt ridiculous talking to them, like talking to a dog or a potato or an empty canvas. Some of us felt no worries at all perhaps for the first time in a long time, conversing with a plane of glass, a collection of wires, talking just to fill the empty space that had settled into our lives. One of us didn't say a word to anyone about anything and some us wanted to say so much more yet still couldn't as the sharp stab in the gut was still too fresh. Some of us got tired of looking at the expressionless hat boxes and assembled shoes and ceramic plates and so we dressed them like the people they were supposed to be and that was our downfall.

We opened boxes we said we would never open again. We took old sweaters from chests and aired them out in the sun. Drawers were emptied and their contents were washed and dried and folded, ready to be worn once more. Shirts and pants and dresses hung from lines and ghosted in the wind. We were thankful for the chance to re-clothe and re-fill what had grown so thin in our minds as to almost not be there at all. We whistled tunes of rejuvenation, with names like 'Life Has Two Doors' and 'My Gallant Darling' and 'There was a Birch Tree in the Field'. We greeted our neighbours sweetly, genuinely, openly for the first time in what felt too long, no longer hiding our shame and guilt and sorrow for having been left behind. We opened our hearts once more then went to work decorating the sculptures.

We found that many bent to our touch; that despite the wires and wood and rough edges there could be movement in the joints – some would never move, too set in their material for the hope of motion. We clothed them gently, careful not to disturb their delicate structures of cigar boxes, footballs, aluminium cans cut and layered and shining like fish scales. We sheathed one leg at a time and shortened the hems and tucked in shirt tails. We settled dresses over knees and tied sashes across middles. We covered them with hats and scarves and mittens though bitter wind had not yet come. We covered them as much as possible, masking the structure beneath, fleshing out the bones into something we could recognise, someone remembered, someone we could touch. Many of us applied powders and lipstick and paints of all colours. One of us didn't approve of such a thing but secretly wished we had thought of it first.

We began to reposition the sculptures, their original stances too familiar and rigid to suggest the mobility we knew they possessed. We shuffled them to the cupboard then the stove then the cutting board then back again, starting all over. We set them atop bicycles and staked the tires to the ground. *Be careful, now.* We put axes in their hands and asked for more wood. We put faded homework on their desks and told them we'd be back in ten minutes to check their progress and answer any questions. Some of us visited our neighbours and dragged them along. *You remember so-and-so.* A few of us brought out letters that had been hidden in a drawer and placed them in their laps. *Never had the courage to send these.* We set them at our dinner tables, elbows bent at their sides, placing fork and knife in hand though they themselves were made of forks and knives. We gave them the day's final coffee and filled empty plates and asked: *Wasn't that how you liked it?* We placed favourite desserts before them and waited patiently as they considered the first bite. We filled the sinks with water and submerged the plates and dried the soap with a cloth and placed everything back just the way they had it before. *You rest,* we said. *Everything will be taken care of.* We stood them on the back porch and put a pipe in hand or a cigarette in hand or a glass of wine in hand and hoped everything was alright when none of those diminished, simply glad they were back in our lives. Some of us eased them into favourite chairs and opened favourite books to favourite parts. Some of us played favourite songs and filled the house with music once more and waited awhile before we asked them to dance. Some of us told them stories about princes and princesses and far-off kingdoms and adventures and how they too could have a fairytale life now that they were back in the living. Another of us drew a bath, sat alone, and wondered what was happening in the other houses.

Almost all of us began to talk of our lives. Not the trivialities of earlier but buried things that had weighted our minds for all time and reminded us of how fragile and frightened and far away from ourselves we actually were. We discussed the mountains we'd never seen yet hoped to, and the pearl-smoothness of ocean wind against our faces, and the forest breath of pine needles in noonday sun. We spoke of dreams we had where blue horses ran around the egg of the world and how wings sprouted from children's backs and how these voices in a dark wood called for each other with names never heard before or since. *What could it mean?* We admitted how we admired the neighbour's wife as she painted the porch railing and how with every drop of paint that got away she'd laugh once, sharp and strong, and how that sound would crack open our very chests. Or maybe it was the librarian or the sheriff's deputy or the grocery clerk or half-a-face seen for half-a-second as a car drove past on Main Street that pulled us away from the direction we've travelled and wanted our entire lives, that heap of loneliness disrupting our trajectory of loving. We talked of those silent hours just before dawn when there's a need to get out of bed but the muscles won't budge and the colour of the world is vanished and the wind itself is a block of ice and what are we even doing anyway? Saying again to the walls around us, *what are we even doing anyway?*

Almost all of us at one point or another started a sentence with *Remember when. Remember when you brought that puppy home and I was so mad over another mouth to feed and you held it up to me and it licked my face and we named it Lolli right there? Remember when that tornado came through and lifted the neighbour's barn and flung its panels all across the field and we spent the night in the cellar wrapped in each other's arms afraid the same split would happen to us? Remember when those big flakes were floating through the night and landed on our shoulders and hair and I looked to you and your eyelashes were full of snow and I proposed without really thinking it through but never once regretted it, not now, not ever?* Remember this? Remember that? Remember when.

We lay them in our beds. We drew the covers over their bodies. We kissed them goodnight across their rigid cheeks. We turned off the lights. Almost all of us slept the best sleep that was humanly possible, thankful for just a little more time and high above us there was the Wheel of stars and space and stars again.

And just like before it didn't take long to grow frustrated with them. They got in the way of our cleaning. They got in the way of our mowing. They got in the way of the wooden animals we galloped across the kitchen floor. They'd interrupt the quiet time we had grown so accustomed to, standing in the doorway saying nothing, boots splayed awkwardly, rain jackets stuffed and lumpy and ridiculous, winter caps drooping across empty eye sockets. *What is it now?* They'd be gone for hours and hours and we'd worry our hearts raw until we thought we spotted them on the road facing our direction, a tiny figure on the horizon arrowing toward home to make us hopeful once again. They'd have someone else's cologne scented on their necklaces. They'd have someone else's lipstick on the inside of their white collars. They never said what they actually thought what they actually felt what they actually wanted. They did just about everything possible to annoy and hurt and damage us further. One of us knew this would happen, believed it into being yet never told a soul, saw in their mind the whole story unwind like thread from a broken loom that vexed every attempt to spool it tight again.

We'd complain to our neighbours. We'd complain to our fathers and mothers and little sisters. We'd complain to the priests and the rabbis and the elders who lead the sermons. We'd complain in the market and the hair salon and the hardware store and the playground and the ice cream parlour and the huts in the hills and in the fields where sheep only bent their faces to the grass. Just like before we'd complain to anyone who would listen and when some of us realised we were complaining to the ones whose eyes were painted open or who had straw coming from their necks or bits of wire hanging from beneath sweaters we'd stop talking and head home, peering close to anyone we crossed to determine who or what they were, how they'd break us further, splinter us in ways that suggested forever.

We hadn't anticipated the sculptures' ability to draw out the old fears the old worries the old loves. We hadn't understood them at all. We didn't speak to them at dinner. We didn't inform them about our day. We acted cold as stone. We asked them to sleep on the couch while we thought about things. We asked them for just a few hours before bed to have some time for ourselves. Some of us told them never to return. Some of us begged them to stay. Some of us said we forgave everything, both large and small. A very few of us decided to leave town altogether and never look back. Occasionally we think about those brick homes at the end of the lane where there was once joy and happiness and flaming logs in the fireplace and laughter in the sheets and a hug about the knees before school and we wonder to ourselves, because we are still alone: *What happened to the life that once was? How had it changed? Who are those people now?*

In the dark once more all of us thought about what tomorrow would bring.

What it could be.

How it could work.

Who would make it worthy.

And we awoke alone. The opposite side of our beds lay empty. The couches lay empty. The spare rooms lay empty. Folded sweaters and pants and shirts and dresses and scarves and jackets and socks and pajamas lay in neat stacks beside empty boots and sneakers and heels. There was no coffee in the pots or drying dishes in the racks. There were no chairs pulled away from tables and no lamps burning into dawn. Our front doors were bolted as they had been the night before. We emerged from our houses and saw as our neighbours emerged from their houses and their eyes, we know, were the same as our eyes, saying the same things as our eyes. They said *what a dream*. They said *it's all over*. They said *I hope not*. They said *you too?* And they said *of course, is there any other way*?

And one of us had not come out at all, instead, sat at the sculptors' bench early in the morning, tilting their head to inspect, guiding hands across wetted clay that shaped the minerals with pushes of the thumb and curves of the finger and a feeling in their heart like clear water rushing over river stone, watching a face emerge from the material, a face like yours or mine, saying to no-one or the only one, *let's see what this is about*.

Fellow wildtender Nikki Hill with a whole Yampah plant dug up,
Baker County, Eastern Oregon

KOLLIBRI TERRE SONNENBLUME

Weeds to Rewild You

Encountering Native American food crops

How could present-day America possibly exist if great numbers of people believed that the minerals in the ground, the trees and the rocks, and the earth itself were all alive? Not only alive, but our equals? If our society suddenly believed it was sacrilegious to remove minerals from the earth, or to buy and sell land, our society would evaporate… It is logical, normal, and self-protective for Americans to find the philosophical, political, and economic modes of Indian culture inappropriate and foolish.

– Jerry Mander[1]

Yampah, Luksh and Coush: these are three wild plants that Native Americans depended upon as staple foods. They were seeded, cultivated and harvested on The Hoop, a mode of gathering and hunting that dates back tens of thousands of years on the North American continent but which is now marginalised. People followed The Hoop in groups with the seasons, like the herds of mammals and the flocks of birds. The relationships among all these creatures – legged, winged and rooted – existed in a balance until the European Invasion. Genocide was perpetrated and is still perpetuated. Now fences, roads and borders criss-cross the land, preventing free travel along The Hoops. Private property owners can and do forbid trespassing. Public property administrators can and do prevent traditional harvesting and cultivating in national forests and parks.

Yampah, Luksh and Coush: these three plants are botanically classified in the genera *Perideridia*, *Lomatium* and *Cymopterus*. They can also be called weeds.

For a gardener, farmer, rancher or restorationist, weeds are any plant

Wildtenders harvesting Yampah seed by moonlight in eastern Oregon

that doesn't belong. This declaration is made regardless of any value the plant might actually have as food or medicine for people, or as a companion for the intended crops, or as a key player in a natural response to disturbance. The modern, control-obsessed mind, focused on goals, production and order, is unable to accept unplanned elements in a design, and must strike out at them. That this is a strike at life itself is unrecognised. The dire consequences of this blind-shooting, doesn't-belong philosophy – which include rapidly depleting resources, dangerously polluted water and air, and an increasingly top-heavy and unstable system of human consumption – were not only predictable, but actually predicted. We were warned, and here we are, grasping at straws of sustainability, when in reality the system cannot be sustained in any recognisable form.

By contrast, subsistence-based indigenous human cultures have a much different relationship to ecosystems and all their living creatures, including the weeds. If human life is to continue for many more generations at all, it will only be if this knowledge can re-seed within human culture at large, take hold, and grow. This is in much the same way that the isolated stands of old growth forest (and isolated stands are all that are left) might yet act to seed surrounding regeneration. But is there enough left? Of sustainable humanity, or of old growth forest? Or of coral reefs or of prairie or of steppe? That remains to be seen.

In the meantime, it is vital to learn as much as we can from the few and the little that remain. In the summer of 2012, I met a Shoshone-trained elder who has been living a traditional, migratory, subsistence existence for the past three decades out in the wilds, and I experienced joyful disillusionment with what I learned from her. I call the disillusionment joyful because being parted from my illusions was a positive thing.

The philosophy of dream it and it will happen, or if only you believe and have the right intentions every little thing's gonna be alright, so prevalent in American culture – especially in the New Age subculture – is pure hokum, and living that way can only be sustained by grand self-delusion. No, as humans, our intentions do not create reality. If they did, millions of people around the world would cease being starved, imprisoned and bombed (much of it on the US taxpayer bill) simply by having the right intentions to make it stop. Do not these uncountable suffering souls dream of an end to their torture? Does it continue because they are not pure enough of heart? Are only US Americans good enough to make it work? What a conceit.

The Shoshone-trained elder I met was named Finisia Medrano, aka Tranny Granny, and she would turn off many civilised folks, including the permaculture fans, with her obscenity-laced speech, anti-American screeds and down-to-gritty-earth common sense. What's ironic of course is that The Hoop is a permaculture quite deep, profoundly so. Too deep for most contemporary people to comprehend, due to cultural divides. Indeed, the chasm between the indigenous and techno-consumer cultures and their attendant viewpoints is likely uncrossable for all but a few. This, if nothing else, I learned from spending time with Finisia. There are ways of understanding life and all its relations that are quite simply beyond me and will most likely always remain so. Losing this illusion might have been her greatest gift to me, conveyed through the weeds she showed me.

I, and most people reading this publication who have been inculcated by what Finisia calls 'Occupied America', cannot and never will see the world the way that a native non-Coloniser can and does. We must simply accept this as the way of the world. Yet, if we are at all concerned about the survival of life on Earth, even just our own, we must pay attention to these alien (to us) and alienated (for them) cultures and their worldviews, and we must try to learn from them, even though much of it will go against everything we have been brainwashed to believe.

Yampah, Luksh and Coush: these are just three of the many plants that were food and medicine for the Native Americans which are now classified as weeds by the Colonisers because they are found in places where they don't belong, have no use, or are in the way. They live in farm fields, on livestock ranges, or mixed in with so-called invasives slated to be sprayed to death. They are illegal to plant on public land. These are three plants that Finisia introduced me to. Meeting them, interacting with them, and consuming them, did something to me that changed me. They touched me somewhere inside, awakening a hint of awareness that has long lay dormant. They are wild foods. Their growth habits, flavours and energetic punch are distinctly undomesticated. They gave me a small taste (pun intended) of what has been called rewilding.

Rewilding has been a buzzword for some time. Like all buzzwords – green, sustainable, permaculture – any meaning originally conveyed has been smothered through their popularity. Mummification through memeification, if you will. People use them to sound current, without concern for their own charade. We have whole clubs of naked emperors, with everyone tacitly agreeing not to point that out. In this context, Finisia is one of the few people I've ever met who is either proud of her clothes or proud of her nudity.

Regardless, when Finisia used the words rewilding and permaculture to describe the ways of The Hoop, I heard those words as if for the first time, because now they had meaning. No poseur is she, and for this she has lived a life of abuse. 'I'm the dog everyone loves to kick,' she has said. She has been harassed, jailed, threatened and chased off innumerable times, all for trying to follow the traditional, sustainable lifestyle of this land's original human inhabitants. The kind of lifestyle to which humans will have to return in order to avoid extinction. A lifestyle of seeding, cultivating and eating many wild foods, not only Yampah, Luksh and Coush.

Finisia does not limit herself to these native plants. She is interested in any edible plants that can be rewilded, including domesticated vegetables, and she has been experimenting with whatever she can get her hands on. The is-it-native? purity test does not interest her. She has seen the effects of invasive plants such as cheatgrass, but makes no efforts to eradicate them. She just seeds the Yampah in the cheatgrass, believing that it will take over again on its own.

There's no debate about Climate Change as far as Finisia is concerned. In her decades on the land, she has seen how ecosystems are changing and becoming inhospitable for what had been growing there previously. Therefore these plants need to be moved to places better suited to them. Of course, this means intentionally invading an area with a non-native, but in her view, these plants are 'refugees without legs', and we humans must be their locomotion. The picture she painted revealed to me the folly of restoration work that attempts to return a piece of land to its so-called pristine state before the European Invasion; first, because climate change means that the mix of plants from a century or two ago will no longer thrive there as they did, and second, because the restorationists almost always leave humans out of their ecosystems, even though the indigenous people were integral, inseparable elements. What are preserves preserving? We know what Indian reservations are reserving: exile and poverty. That's where we're trying to lock up our last best chance of communal survival, and ignoring it as hard as we can.

Finisia mentioned that – despite the ongoing genocide of the remaining Native Americans – Long House has declared that 'it is time to open the bundles'. As far as I can tell, this means that Native American elders have decided that skills and knowledge need to be shared with whomever will listen because the crisis facing the Earth is too great to keep secrets anymore. So, Finisia has been trying to teach. But, she says, she has an 'availability/credibility' problem. That is, she is credible only when she is living The Hoop, eating the native foods, remaining wild in the wild. But she is not available then. If she does make herself available, away from The Hoop, then she loses her credibility. The dichotomy of theory versus practice doesn't apply here because there is only practice, albeit one rooted in deep wisdom. Like the weeds that form the basis of the indigenous diet, one can know them only by giving oneself over to them and all that comes with them, which is feral. All else is casual disregard.

This view, that actuality of knowledge can only be found in experiential immediacy – a view that is understood by any number of spiritual and indigenous traditions – is completely and utterly at odds with the egocentric, superficial, virtual reality of life in the US. For example, think of the number of people you know who really believe that social media is a legitimate form of community. The notion is absurd. There is, as Gertrude Stein put it, no there there. Ones and zeros are producing shapes

Yampah roots in fry pan on foraging trip

on a screen, with no materiality, no vitality. The rest is in the imagination, which increasingly mistakes its pixelated illusions for real substance, to its own sad detriment.

Theodore Roszak put it well in *Where the Wasteland Ends:* 'The loss of transcendent energies in our society... has not been experienced as a loss at all, but as an historical necessity to which enlightened people adapt without protest, perhaps even welcome as a positive gain in maturity.' Indeed. And including pretentious Earth-based spirituality in a permaculture design course does service to neither permaculture (in its non-buzzword potentiality) nor to the dying flickers of transcendent energies we are snuffing out. Holistic comprehension cannot be attained by copy-catting rituals and sonorously murmuring magic words from a culture totally divorced from ours, especially when that separation is being enforced by us with such strident and perverse insolence.

Weeds, we spit with our speech whenever we see something that *doesn't belong*. We do the same to the people among us who don't toe the lines, even though those lines do nothing but mark the border of an entrapping cage where we are beaten into obedience. Most people are happy to crack the whip whenever they can, all the while convincing themselves that there's nothing else they can do, that it's for their own good, and isn't that what everyone else is doing anyway? The authentic is an endangered species because we are stamping it out. People like Finisia are few and far between because we are striving for their extinction. The train is going over the cliff, and we are urging the engineer to speed up. *Weeds!* we shout out, and reach for a sharp tool, a bottle of poison, or a social construct with which to eradicate them.

But we're not all dead yet. So for now, any individual can still dismiss daydreams and taste the tangible. That is what I, anyway, found when I met Yampah, Luksh and Coush.

References

1. Mander, Jerry *In The Absence of the Sacred: The Failure of Technology and the Survival of the Indian Nation,* Sierra Club Books, 1992, p. 227.

NINA PICK

Muhheakantuck

Muhheakantuck was the Lenape name for what is currently called the Hudson River. The river runs from the Adirondack Mountains to the Atlantic Ocean at New York Harbour. Its lower half is a tidal estuary.

The sky was fire,
and the river was water.
The river was dark
from the dams in the river.
The water was full of
dreams in the river.
The sky was fire
and the river was water.

The sky turned to water,
and the river turned to fire.
The rain dredged up
the stories in the river,
the stories from the very
depths of the river.
The river sang its stories
and the sky sang its water
and the water was river
and the river was fire.

The sky sang its stories
down to the river
and the river sang its stories
all through the water.
On the banks of the river
we watched as the river
turned from blue to purple to fire.

But we didn't listen to the
river's stories. We just took
of the river's beauty.
We took and took and
gave nothing back.
We forgot to pray to the river
and dance to the river
and say thanks to the river
and when the river asked
we did not answer
and when the river sang
we did not answer.

We even took the name of the river
and replaced it
with the name of a man.

And then we filled the river with washing machines
and rubber bands and plastic bags
and Coke bottles and PCBs.
And when the water grew sick
we were scared to touch it.
And because there was pain in the water
we were scared to touch it.
We wouldn't go near the water
because we knew
what was down there.
What we had put there
in the water. What we had put there
and forgotten. And not
forgotten. Meanwhile
the stones remembered and
the shore remembered and
the trees remembered and
the goslings remembered and
the eighty-year old sturgeon
in the water remembered.

His long whiskers touched the bottom
of the river
and he remembered.

We built museums to the river
sailed boats down the river
made maps of the river
and paintings of the river.
We were trying to touch the river
without touching the river.
Trying to praise the river
without facing the river.
We were trying to sing love
but had forgotten the words in the river's tongue
and were translating
from our language into nothing.

And now the sky of fire
and the river of fire
meet before us
in a wall of fire.

So now at last when we sing river
we sing its true name.
We sing pain
we sing grief
we sing unfathomable regret
we sing *Muhheakantuck*
the river that flows both ways

backward and forward
toward the ancestors and toward the descendants
toward the uncertain resolution or
restoration or
reparation
or revolution
by water or by fire

as our gasoline flows to the river
and our dishwashing soap flows to the river
and our saliva blood cum tears urine mucus shit sweat
flows to the river

and becomes river.

And as the water rises
and touches our cars our lawns
the front steps to our homes

we touch the river
for the first time.

We become river

we too
swimming in either direction
toward the future.

JAYNE IVIMEY

The Red List

Clay fired sculpture

An exhibition of 70 clay birds on the list of endangered British birds that is not only a celebration of the birds themselves but also a chance to pause and look at them, as they are and have been for so many millennia and could be again if we were to make their world a

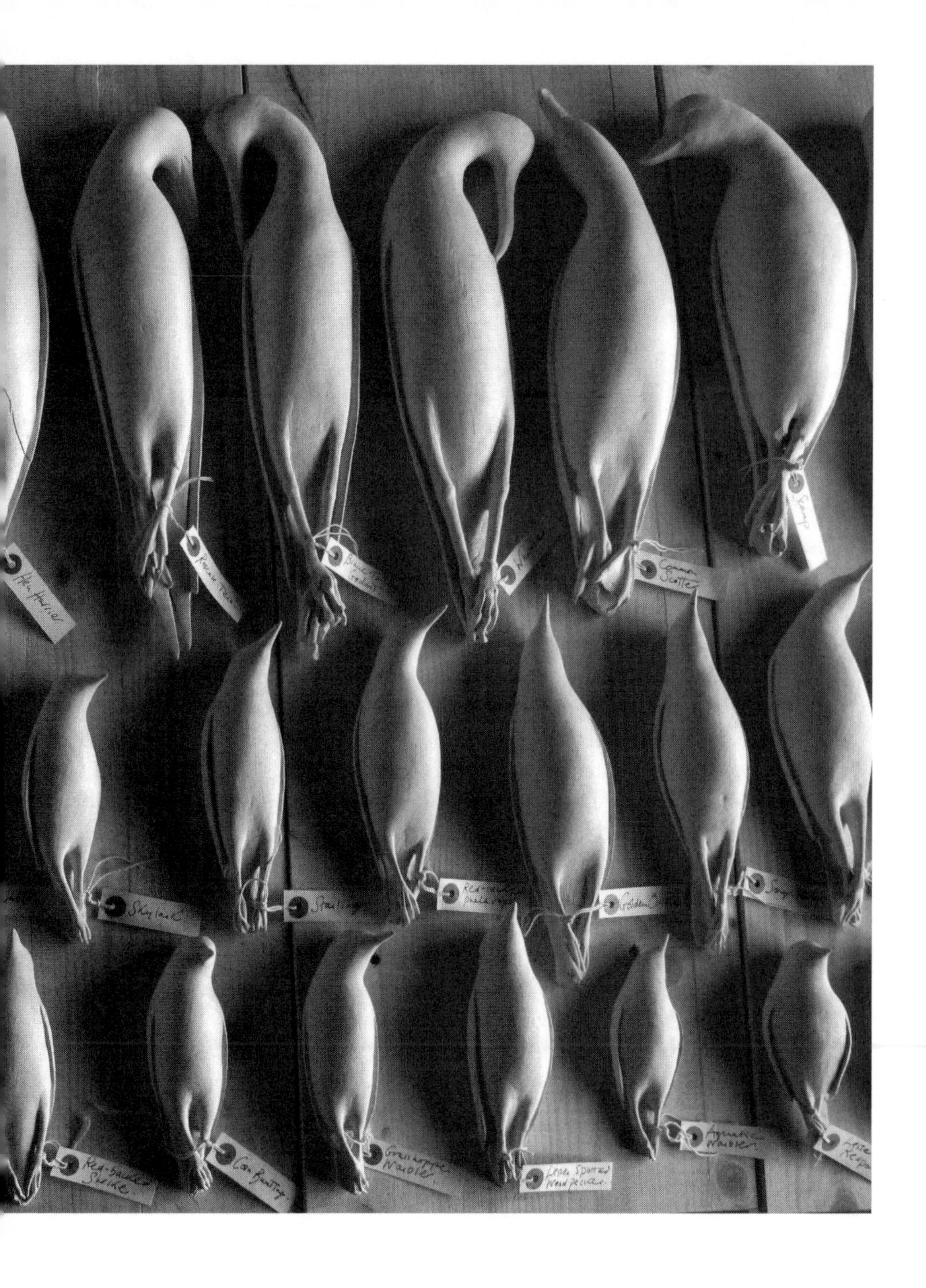

safer place. In 2009 the number of birds on the RSPB's red list was 52, their numbers having declined by up to 90%, as rural development and overfishing wreaked havoc with their habitat and food. Then the number rose to 70, 27% of the entire population of 244 species. Could rewilding help to reverse the decline of nature in Britain and offer a new way of looking at conservation? The simple possibility of leaving things alone and remembering that we are one species among many.

MATT MILES

Migrations

Actions and futures that were once unthinkable – because they were too wonderful or too horrible – are suddenly possible.

– Thomas Homer-Dixon

The first time they appeared, I thought I was dreaming. Flitting about the vegetable garden and alighting atop the fence posts were a pair of the most strikingly blue birds I'd ever seen. Their colour was so deep it seemed almost purple, and against the leafy verdure of the garden, their feathers seemed iridescent, lit from inside. They were electric, luminous, even on a bright May morning.

I'm still not quite sure which species of songbird I saw that day, but in the time since, I've watched indigo buntings, eastern bluebirds, and blue grosbeaks regularly come and go, stopping in the spring and summer on a migratory corridor that for some stretches up and down the US east coast and into the tropics in winter.

The American goldfinch, as vibrantly yellow as the indigo bunting is blue, began appearing here too throughout the year. Groups of the yellow-and-black birds bob excitedly through the summer air, resting on the trellis wires of the vineyard or nesting in the brushy margins of the woods. The goldfinches in particular are drawn back by the abundance of food plants that grow here – poppy seeds in spring, sunflower seeds in summer, and the remains of various natives that we've left to grow throughout the cold winter months.

Many of these birds are currently considered common, along with the robins, crows, blue jays, cardinals and others that thrive even among urban and suburban spaces in which I've spent most of my life, but I'd never noticed them here before our second year. As we built up our soil and applied the principles of regenerative agriculture to the landscape, this influx of songbirds seemed to us a signal that we were working with nature, rather than working to suppress it.

*

When Tasha and I first moved onto this property, it was in a very different state. The previous owners had spent much of their time keeping nature at bay on these two cleared acres. The steep hillsides on either side of our hollow had been regularly cut back to keep the adjacent forest from returning; the terraced slopes in front of the house were kept mowed in the semblance of a grassy suburban lawn; and the dirt paths through the bottom of the hollow that lead up into the woods – the remnants of logging roads – were rigorously maintained. The red dirt grooves funnelled torrents of water down the mountain in heavy rains, assuring no top soil could develop or plants take hold.

Nevertheless, the potential of this piece of land spoke to us. Beyond the damage done by logging and years of soil erosion, we tried to envision the place in its 'natural' state before it was disturbed by human interventions. While we couldn't turn back the clock, we could at least attempt to restore the property, to re-create a sustainable place both for ourselves and the non-humans surrounding and preceding us.

We worked to slow down the soil-destroying water by building swales, hugelkultur mounds, and diversion channels. We dug another pond and put in a greenhouse. We expanded the vegetable garden, planted a vineyard and dozens more fruit trees and perennial plants, and introduced chickens, goats, and ducks. And wherever we could, we stopped trying to hold off the natural succession we saw struggling back, especially at the forested fringes of the property.

But with the second year came the realisation that none of this would be enough to adequately restore the lost topsoil, without which nothing much would grow well. So we began applying truckloads of mulch, compost, and manure around the property. By the end of the second year, we noticed improvements in the soil and in the growth of many plants, and our erosion problems had largely disappeared. But we noticed something else around that time, too – the arrival of the birds.

Four years on, they are a routine but welcome sight in the pleasant days of late spring and early summer. As the light fades and the night begins to speak with frogs and crickets, there are new sounds – the 'whip-poor-will' of the bird that bears the same name, the cooing of a pair of mourning doves nesting in the vineyard, and as the night darkens, the unmistakable hoot of an owl.

On these nights when it's more comfortable to sit outside, we often talk of the day's events in the news – almost always bad news that happens in the world outside, which we feel ourselves to be less and less a part of here. When it's not a report of the latest outrage perpetrated by the Trump administration, it's bad news from the scientists – about the physical state of the planet and the non-humans that inhabit it. We try to put it in perspective, to balance it in terms of what we're doing here. So many things are beyond our control. But no matter what we do, conditions in the world at large are changing for the worse, it seems.

In September 2019, a study appeared in the journal *Science* showing that bird populations in North America have shrunk by 29 percent since 1970. Across the board, including species thought of as abundant such as sparrows and robins, populations are in steep decline. There are 2.9 billion fewer birds now than there were in 1970, just a few years before I was born, and this includes both native and non-native species. Warblers like the cerulean warbler – another magnificent blue songbird that lives mostly in the higher country to the west, perhaps the bird I first noticed in the garden – are among the hardest hit groups.

The study's researchers don't know the exact cause for the declines, but habitat loss – to expanding agriculture and human populations – is surely part of the problem. Other potential culprits are pesticides, like neonicotinoids, which don't kill birds outright but make it harder for them to gain the weight they need to manage seasonal migrations. Neonicotinoids are also thought to be a reason for the steep declines seen in honeybee populations in recent years.

The birds and the bees are more than just metaphors for life and its perpetuation – they are indicators of healthy ecosystems and vital parts of those natural systems. Without them to pollinate flowers, spread seeds, and perform all of the other roles so easily taken for granted, ecosystems collapse. Their absence is equivalent to the death of the canary in the coal mine; they are an early warning system sensitive to changes in the environment that will eventually kill us all, if we don't heed them.

*

It is a difficult space to inhabit – this place in these times – both literally and metaphorically. On the one hand, we are buoyed by the evidence we see daily that our efforts to restore this little piece of land are working – whatever 'restore' means in the reality of the non-native and, by some measures, invasive species we have brought onto the land to aid in its healing. On the other, the climate is changing in frightening and unpredictable ways. Here a season of record-breaking downpours is followed by months of drought when almost nothing grows unaided. Yet we are privileged to have been spared the worst. Not so far away, the climate is already causing intense disruption.

Last year, hundreds were dead or missing, and tens of thousands were left homeless in the Bahamas after Hurricane Dorian struck. Many refugees were denied entry to the United States. How they will survive on the Bahamas or the neighbouring Caribbean islands is unclear. The year before that, Hurricane Florence wrecked Wilmington, at the eastern edge of my own state of North Carolina. Friends who lived there told of whole neighbourhoods abandoned, when the better option was to move on rather than rebuild. And before that, in 2017, Hurricane Maria devastated Puerto Rico – two years on it is difficult to envision its full recovery. Where will these people go, to where will they migrate, now that their habitat is destroyed?

*

Last September, I returned to the area where I was born and raised, Washington, DC, to report on the first major Extinction Rebellion (XR) event in the US. Over a dozen climate and social justice groups blocked key intersections around the city. In the middle of one intersection not far from the White House, protesters from the newly-formed DC chapter of XR stopped traffic by fastening themselves to a pink and yellow sailboat.

Outside the police cordon, XR DC protesters held banners and chanted slogans. One of the more colourful among them was a man wearing, cape-like, a Puerto Rican flag. He told me he was studying at university here but was originally from Puerto Rico, and that he joined XR just a few weeks prior, after attending a protest outside the Brazilian embassy while the Amazon burned.

I asked about Hurricane Maria, and he told me how his family and community had been affected, how he worked to organise aid shipments that never reached the people they were supposed to help. He had already seen firsthand the horrors of a changing climate, met largely with indifference by the as-yet-unaffected in the global North. But he is hopeful still, and deemed the protest a great success.

Another scene lingers from earlier that morning: a woman who had chained herself to the boat, waving a handmade sign declaring 'Climate action is an act of love'. Below that, she had written names I presume to belong to her two daughters. As the media moved in closer to photograph her, she flashed a beatific smile.

*

We've entered an historical 'moment of contingency', to use the words of Thomas Homer-Dixon, where horrifying social, political and ecological outcomes that seemed far-fetched or absurd just a few years ago have become part of the fabric of day-to-day reality. But as Homer-Dixon writes, in times such as these, 'people's motivation to change their circumstances soars just as their opportunities to accomplish change multiply. Whether the outcome of this powerful confluence is turmoil or renewal hinges – in large measure – on how the situation is framed.'

While demagogues exploit the fluidity of this historical juncture to sow further turmoil, individuals like Greta Thunberg and groups like XR are working for renewal through acts of courage, commitment and hope. Though anxiety and despair may loom large, in these shimmering moments there is room for grace and beauty too – whether in the luminous smile of a protesting stranger, or in the song of a warbler in the garden.

Amidst the ongoing upheaval and increasing uncertainty of these times, it sometimes seems easier to succumb to the darkness and fear, to give up on the future and any hope, distant as it may be, of planetary restoration. For this reason, establishing and maintaining refugia – spaces dedicated to renewal, niches where species can survive extinction – is of vital importance. We must both preserve and work to restore these spaces on the landscape and in the spirit, where the wonder and beauty of life in all its forms might once again thrive.

It is from that perspective that we may be able to see a new way forward – if we can learn to view renewal through the lens of migration and adaptation. Ultimately our future depends on whether we as humans can leave behind the comfort, habituation and familiarity of well-trodden paths, and set out, bird-like perhaps, to face the terra incognita of a changing climate and an uncertain future.

SAM ROBINSON

A Stray

If I catch myself these days, it tends to be out on a hill, stuffing hay into a rack or fixing a line of fence, or sometimes standing quietly, waiting for Glynne and the dogs to bring the sheep over the top. And if I do catch myself here, I might trace the fresh thorn-cut on the back of my hand slowly beneath my lip, rubbing my thumb along a wool-softened finger, as the wind pulls at the corners of my eyes and the ground slopes tight to my feet, telling me how far I have strayed.

When it has come to putting pen to paper, I've never paid all that much attention to my own story. But as we tip into this new decade, looking back over the last one, it occurs to me that it might be worth sharing – that there are some threads in my story that others might find relevant to their own journey.

Ten years ago I was an 18-year-old schoolboy from Oxford, struggling to derive a sense of self from the individual struggle against conformity. I lost hours gazing at Caspar David Friedrich's painting *Wanderer above the Sea of Fog,* staring myself into the figure who stands alone on the mountain's peak looking down upon a clouded earth.

I pursued this vision to study philosophy at Cardiff University. One day, deep in the 2012 Six Nations, my friend Connor asks if I want to watch the Wales–England game. I tell him I don't do sport, that I consider national associations to be violent and delusional constructs I don't want any part in, but thanks anyway. Connor calmly replies, 'It's different here, butt. Come on we're going.' That afternoon I walk into the Albany pub as a reticent observer at best. Never having been one for the middle ground, by the half-time whistle I find myself howling for the boys in red.

Though I couldn't quite name it, something stirred in me that day that had long gone ignored. Allowing myself to feel it was like breathing meadow air after years in a stale dark room, which is an odd thing to experience in a pub rammed to the doors with boozing rugby enthusiasts. What struck me instantly, fresh out of an English public school, was how different being Welsh appeared to being English. English national sentiment, not yet divorced from its colonial past, seemed chiefly concerned with superiority over others, at all possible opportunities. Undoubtedly a disservice to other more grounded senses of Englishness, this was my received understanding of the nature of national identity, of what it meant to allow oneself to belong somewhere.

Match day in a Cardiff pub, encountering people with a sense of national belonging apparently unconcerned with such superiority, a crack appeared in my judgments. Here was celebration of a shared story and, at the final whistle – 19–12 to Wales – a blast of ancestral trauma exorcised in symbolic victory. But that horribly familiar compulsion to feel better than all others was nowhere to be seen, even when it came to playing England. And this crack was about to split open.

We were in the Mochyn Du, one of only a few Welsh speaking pubs in Cardiff, awaiting the Wales–France kick-off: a man walks in wearing a black beret, 'le Tricolore' draped finely across his shoulders, a garland of plastic garlic cloves around his neck, toy chicken in hand. As he tunes in to the unexpected cacophony of Welsh, the pen-drawn moustache above his lip begins to quiver. He turns for the door, but two old boys come straight over and grab him by the shoulders, march him to the bar and order him two pints. I don't think he paid for a single drink during that game. And every time France scored, the entire pub cheered with him.

Hiraeth is a Welsh word that has no cognate in English. A contraction of 'hir aeth', 'long it-went', hiraeth refers to a peculiar depth of longing. It is longing for a home that is lost and will likely never return to you. And it is uncertain. Perhaps it is for the home of your childhood. But then again perhaps you never actually knew it yourself; perhaps it was lost before living memory. Or is this a longing for something that came before home, a connection yet more primal or ultimate? Just beyond every poet's attempt to hold hiraeth in words, something of it eludes.

After Cardiff I went west. Shortly after moving I came back to visit Michael and Rosemary, my great uncle and aunt. They had moved to Cardiff in 1962 following Michael's appointment as a philosophy lecturer, and during my studies we had become close friends. As I was telling them about life out west, Michael said he thought his grandmother, my great-great-grandmother, had come from somewhere out that way. He retrieved a marriage certificate from deep in a drawer. Born in 1869, she grew up on a farm near the Pembroke–Carmarthenshire border. At the age of 23 she met a tenant farmer from Northamptonshire, perhaps at a drovers market on the borders. They were married at the Tabernacle

Chapel in Whitland before moving to England, where she remained for the rest of her life. Her name was Hettie Owen. Welsh was her first language, but she rarely spoke it again, and didn't pass it on to her children. I had just moved to Pembrokeshire, aged 23. I was working on a farm 11 miles from where she grew up, and had just begun, tentatively, to pick up the language.

There was a photograph dated 1936, making her 67. She is standing by a wall in the garden looking straight into the camera. In her eyes, I saw that I had known hiraeth my entire life; that *her* hiraeth had welled up in me through the generations of scattering. I saw myself clearly then. Unable to name this disorientating loss for what it was, I had tried to resolve it in unyielding attachment to intellectual abstractions, in desperate aspiration to that point-in-thought above the clouds, when, I am now convinced, all I had ever been calling for was a sound placement on the earth, and roots there.

What does it mean to belong? Are distant blood ties essential to verify one's relationship with a place? I think presence with people and with the land takes precedence. And yet: while ancestry doesn't mean everything, I cannot say it means nothing.

From Pembrokeshire I drifted north, the unmeetable longing for origins bringing me here to the Dyfi Valley, to begin anew in my life as a shepherd. Running up and down these hills, feeling my heart enveloped in the wind and the fall of water, I have let go into this place. Let go the fear of stillness. I have sweated into this ground, and shed tears for its grief. I have sung its songs long into the night, and I have never stopped howling for the boys in red. I have even taken to the rugby pitch myself, and joined the local choir of course. I continue to learn Welsh, *Cymraeg* by its own name, a language that sings the leap and flow of the water-blessed hills it was born of. And I am shifting with that flow, as this new old tongue takes hold of me and suggests its own sense of who I am. As this place claims me, I take care to remember how I may have benefitted from the same forces of colonisation that have hounded it and its people over the centuries. With this in mind, I begin the slow journey of coming to belong.

So I have strayed. I have gone into the west, certainly. But I have also come down; down from the clouded mountaintop and onto the hillside, eye to eye with the land that nourishes me in body and in heart, waiting for Glynne and the dogs to bring the sheep over the top before we gather them down the hill towards home, crying like buzzards as we go.

ROBERT MCGAHEY

The Blade of Wheat at the End of the World

Ah Death, thou comest when I had thee least in mind
– Everyman

'Swamiji, what happens to the Creator's desire for creation to know him through attaining self-realisation as human beings if an irreversible wave of climate change leads to the extinction of our species on this planet?'

There were audible gasps in the full hall of listeners. Mine was a frightening, yet reasonable question.

Answering in Hindi, Swami Paramanand, supposedly a realised being, responded: 'Do you know creation?'

Chastened by the recognition of all that I did not know, I replied, 'Sounds like what God said to Job out of the whirlwind.'

Swami Parmanand proceeded to mime a stalk of wheat. 'What happens when the stalk ripens to maturity?'

'It is harvested', I replied.

The Swami nodded his head; just so the world when it has run its course, and thus our species when its race is run, whether the divine *lila* – the game that God plays by hiding Himself in all creation, as the Upanishads detail – is fulfilled or not.

As Swami Paramanand held his forearm to the sky, I was struck by the homology with the Eleusinian Mysteries, where the priest holds up a blade of wheat to be sacrificed, Demeter sacrificing her daughter Persephone, to be reborn as spring. Both the Dionysian and Christian mysteries replay this ritual. I suddenly realised that the swami was extending our local imagery – local to the West and the planet – to the universal dance of death and rebirth, universe after universe.

The swami continued: 'Do you know the purpose for which you were born?'

Damn. They always come to this, these teachers. Even the Hindu fellow-traveller on the train would casually ask, 'And what is your purpose, my goodsirruh?' My purpose, from the standpoint of *Advaita Vedanta* and a line of sages stretching back thousands of years, was the Hindu version of 'know thyself'. Become realised yourself, and stop worrying about creation, the Earth I was trying to save.

'Swamiji, I understand what you are saying. But I don't accept this with the same equanimity as a realised being.'

Swami Paramanand nodded again, smiling. At least the aspirant knew where things stood.

*

Human extinction and ecological faith

For many years now, I have been periodically visited by Death. He wears a heavy dark cloak, hooding his face, and carries a big sickle. Though formidable, the scythe is not so unwieldy that he can't nimbly move over obstacles. He has big hands, a farmer's or blacksmith's. I imagine his face as I write now – long, thin, bony, intelligent, cunning – but I have never actually seen it. He is crossing a boulder field. Nimbly. He only stops occasionally to sharpen his sickle, then springs to his feet and moves steadily on towards me. He has me in his sights.

I went to India on a Fulbright grant right after college graduation and spent a year teaching English and studying North Indian classical singing with a master. I was enthralled by the culture, especially the belief, strongest in rural areas, that spirit was paramount and material life secondary. I felt deeply at home for the first time in my life, with my introversion and mystical tendencies fully valued. I took on the persona as well, letting my hair and beard grow, dressing in *kurta* pyjamas. It was always confusing to my fellow train-travellers that such a fellow was a lecturer at Indore University. As one said, 'But sirruh, you must be being Amrikan hippy-saddhu – see how you dress.' As for death, after being protected from it for my first 22 years, I got a full dose in Hindustan, where it is out in the open: at the burning ghats, in the gutters, at the train station. That year turned my world inside out.

And now, with our dream of progress at its apogee, Death stalks our entire species. For we are unaware that the myth of progress, like all dreams, is simply a swinging arc, and on its return, the arc becomes that scythe blade. We are the first creature not only to foresee personal death, but to foresee species death, the death of its very form.

Death certainly threatens global civilisation, whose Herculean expenditures of energy and natural capital have created a towering, unsustainable potential for self-destruction. The inexorable logic of population dynamics shows that, like any species, we are limited by our food supply, and even though we have systematically stolen other species' habitats, harvesting virtually the whole arable planet, we continue to reproduce as if the Earth had no limits. Though most of us steadily and blissfully ignore it, this is elementary. Our species crossed the boundary of planetary sustainability in 1986, when we consumed 100% of the planet's annual biotic output. So we have lived on her capital for more than 30 years, gouging deeper and deeper. Meanwhile, we have edged closer to another boundary, a thermodynamic one.

At some level, we are all desperately fighting to avoid collapse. At the species level, when we say that we are fighting to 'save the Earth', what we really mean is that we are fighting for human survival. We want to maintain our own species' ascendance in this, the Cenozoic era of mammals, our niche amplified by the social and material forms we have grown accustomed to. But this context is a rapidly changing one, for our tool-extensions have become the monstrous technological onslaught by which we are commoditising the Earth. Despite an awakening to the reality of climate change, our continued maintenance of unsustainable lifestyles – culturally accepted greed multiplied by human numbers – is tearing huge holes in the Earth's fabric. We have become a 'planetary power' whose collective action is sufficient to alter the entire system.

Let's face it; not only the Holocene epoch, but the Cenozoic era, the age of flowering plants and mammals, is at risk. Of the total number of species – perhaps eight million – 20% are doomed, even if we act quickly to mitigate climate change. The more likely levels are 50–60%. The sixth great extinction in Earth's history is underway. We do not know if our species will perish during this event, but it is very possible, for much that we depend upon will soon be gone.

Death will certainly come, to us and eventually to the Earth, but, like Everyman, we want it to be delayed as long as possible. What seemed infinitely far away a few decades ago now appears right on the horizon. I look at my young grandsons and toddling granddaughter, calculating the scant generations left, no longer numberless as the sands.

It is not likely that Gaia will see the likes of another intelligent ape again if we suffer extinction – but it is possible; life, multifarious life, eventually leading to big-brained great apes, survived the Permian extinction of 250 million years ago, when more than 90% of species disappeared. Evolution is a powerful agent working within the body of Gaia, still occupying a sweet spot in the known universe.

Since the Renaissance, our faith has been in human ingenuity, in reason: 'Man is the measure of all things.' But at a time when the Earth faces yet another die-off since the inception of life 3.5 billion years ago, it is imperative to ground ourselves in a faith which reaches deeper than our own anthropocentric self-regard. Ecological faith is faith in Gaia and her ability not only to endure, but to thrive as long as the conditions that allow her to self-organise persist. Life on Earth will continue until the endgame of our solar system. And, depending on the extent of the Sixth Extinction, it may flourish yet again, attaining a degree of complexity in creatures we cannot imagine.

*

The regenerative universe: cosmogenetic faith

Swami Paramanand's answer to my question about human extinction helped me expand an ecological faith to one reaching beyond this universe to the infinite nature of Brahman, beyond time and the particular forms we know. Hindus believe that the universe has been created and destroyed many times and that this process will continue ad infinitum. Some Shaivites believe it happens every microsecond.

Hindu sages have traditionally explained the birth and death of countless universes in terms of a divine cycle of introversion and extroversion. During the introverted stage, the divine sinks into its own essential nature, and the universe rests as potential form. Sages call this the 'sleep of Brahma'. During the extroverted stage, e.g. the Big Bang and its aftermath, it displays itself in a magisterial panoply of material forms in evolutionary flux. In the Hindu cosmology, divine creation is not constrained by the limits that Big Bang cosmology carries like an eschatological seed – a terminator meme that lurks within its elegant, but space-time bounded theory.

The Big Bang theory is the cosmological mirror of our ideas of linear progress and the endless ascendency of human reason. I watched it come to dominate our thinking as I grew up, but since around 1990, the germ of a new paradigm has begun to sprout. In a Scientific American article from February 2017, 'Pop Goes the Universe', the authors describe an accumulating body of new data from orbiting instruments beyond the smudged glass of Earth's atmosphere, which cover the full octave of wavelengths rather than just those derived from visible light, which form the basis of the Big Bang theory. The data derived from visible light alone shows an unimaginably rapid initial inflation of the universe, to explain which Big Bang proponents must invoke special conditions. The authors suggest the data is more plausibly explained by an expansion following a previous period of contraction – a 'big bounce', the repetition of which could well go on indefinitely.

The idea of a 'continuous creation' has a more nuanced variant named the 'regenerative universe'. Rather than an overarching pattern of cycles of expansion and contraction, the regenerative theory postulates an environment where structures and boundary conditions form and reform across many scales. Based upon the fundamental ubiquity of electromagnetic forces rather than gravity, the theory postulates ongoing creation from electric plasma, painting a picture of long, twisted paired filaments from electromagnetic pulses. These electromagnetic forces, 39 times stronger than gravity, and acting over hugely greater distances, obviate the need for 'dark matter' and 'dark energy', which are postulated by Big Bang theorists, but have never been observed. Instead, in the regenerative scheme, long plasma filaments connect galaxies and superclusters of galaxies. The largest known observed filament is ten million light years long. And a hypercluster nicknamed the 'Great Wall' could well be 10 billion light years across! In the electromagnetic universe, everything is connected rather than being seen as empty, dead space. This is a vision that Nietzsche intuited in an unpublished fragment, of the world as a 'colossus of energy, without beginning, without end … that does not expend itself but only transforms itself … not a space that would be 'empty' anywhere, rather as force everywhere, as play of forces and waves of forces …'

The terminator meme required by the Big Bang ('You only go 'round once') is not derived from experimental, observable science, but rather is another instance of mythical thinking in the supposedly objective realm of science, despite the brilliance of the astrophysicists who elaborated the theory. It is telling that some of the same scientists who worked on the Manhattan Project blithely transferred the metaphor of a huge explosion to the dominant cosmological theory of the 20th century. The old mammalian politics is manifest in the power struggles among scientists over who gets to publish in the distinguished peer-reviewed journals. The steady-state folks lost out decades ago, and the ascendant Big Bang theorists have kept them at bay until now. But a treasure trove of new data that the Big Bang gang struggle to accommodate has forced the debate into the open.

I am convinced that it is only a matter of time before the regenerative theory becomes the norm in Western cosmology. Emergent modern scientific cosmological theory is a welcome affirmation for those of us influenced in the '60s and '70s by Eastern metaphysics, especially by the confident assumption of the infinite possibility of cosmogenesis. Deep intuition now has theoretical ballast, supported by a rich set of new observations. What fascinates me about the regenerative universe theory is not only that it recognises that 'in the beginning there were multiple beginnings', as Robert E. Messick, Jr. has put it, but that it meshes with Hindu sages' purely metaphysical intuition about cycles of creation-dissolution and dormancy: the sleep of Brahma. It is an intuition that the ultimate restoration, outlasting the ecocide of the Sixth Extinction, might be the regeneration of the universe itself, beyond the horizon of the heat-death of the Sun.

*

Shards of Brahma's handiwork

Deeply moved by a workshop on despair and empowerment with Joanna Macy, I retired from academia in 2000 to focus on the global ecocrisis. I became a trainer in Macy's network, taught climate science in churches, marched in the streets, and was twice arrested for civil disobedience. But after leading a workshop on 'Collapsing Consciously', I collapsed myself – and it took years to recover. I learned I could not live without hope, but most of the hope I saw around me was dishonest. Encountering the theory of the regenerative universe has given me comfort that, though we may well fail in our efforts to awaken humanity to its collective madness, the process of creative evolution is ongoing. It does not mean I turn away from the work of uncivilisation, and the temporary bulwarks against collapse like regenerative agriculture and the mutual aid society that I support in my southern Appalachian river valley. But it does remove the burden of *saving the world.*

A few years ago, my wife and I circumambulated Mount Kailash, the mythic abode of Shiva, god of destruction – both of the individual ego and of material creation itself. Kailash is considered by Hindus, Buddhists and Jains to be the centre of the world. Once in that moonscape, what drew me was Lake Manosarovar, the shimmering ethereal place where Brahma reflected creation into being from its characteristic greenish glacial melt. I found its shores strewn about with stones of all sorts. 'A geological mess', an expert geologist friend commented as I showed her my samples. They looked to me like the shards of Brahma's efforts at creation. Many appeared to have writing on them, intricate cracks and seams forming complex patterns, reminiscent of Tibetan *Mani* stones, deposited everywhere in Brahma's landscape of creation.

Who will read those stones when we are gone? What does it mean for the Earth, or perhaps even the universe, to lose what may be its premier locus of self-reflection, not only sentient, but conscious of its creative process, its beauty and complexity? Such a loss points beyond an ecological faith to the sense of mystery and reverence expressed in the words, *made in God's image*. Can faith abide at a moment when we face not only permanent losses in the fabric of life, but its observer and celebrant as well?

As the tsunami of consequences begins to break upon us, ending a magnificent geological era in which our species arose and upon which all our earthly hopes rest, my Gaian hope is for complex life to continue to evolve in Earth's remaining time. We know that the Earth will outlast us and endure until her time, too, ripens. But it took a universe and time to evolve the magnificent Cenozoic. What kind of progeny will thrive on an ageing Earth which has been blasted by a thankless, reckless child? Nevertheless, if I am faithful to what I know, acting with integrity, then I will live as if to sustain the fabric of the Cenozoic, even as it tatters and collapses under the stresses of the Anthropocene epoch.

It is mind-boggling to think that our place in the Great Dance of Creation may soon vanish, but the Hindu metaphysics of my hippy-saddhu youth has permeated me. Beyond this field of dharma, Kali Yuga, the end time of Earth's Cenozoic era, my deepest hope and faith are in cosmogenesis, the unquenchable and infinite possibilities of the Source of this universe, which even now prepares its rest from the battlefield of cosmic striving. Entropy, expressed in the second law of thermodynamics, is universal, yet it is offset by the syntropy of limitless Creation, implicit in the very fabric of possibility, even beyond space-time. *You're right Swamiji, I do not know creation, so I won't presume to predict the outcome of the dance – though you have pointed me to a possibility that may not require metaphysics.*

But if it is humans that you love, and other mammals, and the wildflowers of spring, and the fishes and frogs, and the birds and magnificent forest remnants of this earthly time, then look upon those faces and forms you love best with the gaze of a dying man hungry for every moment of consciousness, and commit them to soul-memory. If the soul transmigrates not only between lives in this bounded universe, but between universes, perduring through the long sleep of Brahma, then she will remember, and our images will be everlasting in a way the seed of our species can never be.

Rest well, O Brahma. May your great works continue to prosper, in universe after universe. And you, my loves, my friends, my children and grandchildren, live the best life you can, as if this world would always remain in pristine, balanced perfection.

KERRY PRIEST

Womb

I am looking at a tree.

I regurgitate my tea and the water rushes up into the tap. It's getting earlier and earlier. Soon, we are reversing around the Dordogne as summer flies unpick themselves from the windscreen.

Mum and Dad's ashes turn to flesh in Rotherham crematorium as they go back to exhaling cigarettes and un-watching *Crimewatch* in a series of bungalows. Meanwhile, at the London Olympics everyone is running backwards. Fewer and fewer people are tapping at computers which are getting slower and slower, as their modems get louder and louder. East London is getting worse, Camden Town is getting better. Canary Wharf is getting lower, Brixton is getting blacker. I go back to university, unmeet my husband, the millennium comes in an implosion of fireworks.

In Berlin, spray paint peels off the wall, liquefies, is sucked into a can. The same thing happens in New York, where everybody is breakdancing. Suddenly, a lot of my friends are getting really small. They are stuffed back, scream-inhaling into the wombs of their scream-inhaling mothers. Somehow, I am still here and hair is being cut longer. The Beatles are back together and all their records are spinning backwards. Except the ones with hidden satanic messages, which are spinning forwards.

Soon, my mother is pushed back into grandma's womb and women everywhere leave factories and start unpicking their knitting. Hemlines get lower and lower and dresses suddenly puff to a sheen as everything gets slower and slower, but there are still wombs. Marie Antoinette finds her head. Men wear wigs, then tights and Columbus or the Vikings lose America. The Mongols and Muslims and Goths and Christians and Romans retreat, retreat, cities disappearing. Cleopatra brushes off her make-up. Wheat fields grass over. Ceramics turn to clay, stone circles are dismantled, cave artists brush ochre back onto pallets and it's wombs and wombs all the way until the last few people hop back across the savannah, their arms getting longer and longer.

The trees welcome them back.

KATE WALTERS
Tree as Artemis, Mountain, or Mother
Watercolour on Saunders Waterford paper

I've been growing my hair as an act of resistance; and seeing my hair as an extension of my psyche, connecting me to wild spirit children. When I paint these thoughts they become tree branches, and my body the trunk; milk appears as the manifestation of bodily and divine love to all the hidden ones, the seeds in the dark earth.

Mountaineers

Monique Besten is an artist, writer and educator based in Barcelona and Amsterdam. She makes long-distance performative walks through Europe and researches slow ways of being, connections between artistic media and different fields of life. She teaches performance art and artistic survival skills at the HKU University of the Arts Utrecht, NL. moniquebesten.nl

Chris Booth left London in 2016 to live and work as an artist in Rye, UK. His drawings are made from millions of tiny dots stippled over several months and they often revolve around dilapidation and an imagined held breath before the plunge towards renewal and restoration. Instagram @christopherjbooth

Jemma Borg won the Ginkgo Prize for Ecopoetry in 2018 and the RSPB/Rialto Nature and Place Poetry Competition in 2017 and is published in magazines including *The Poetry Review*, *Oxford Poetry*, *Plumwood Mountain* and *The Hopper*. Her first collection is *The Illuminated World* (Eyewear, 2014). jemmaborg.co.uk

Nickole Brown is the author of *Sister* and *Fanny Says*, and most recently, two chapbooks of eco-poetry: *To Those Who Were Our First Gods* as well as her essay-in-poems, *The Donkey Elegies,* published in 2020. She lives in the US where she volunteers at three different animal sanctuaries. nickolebrown.com

Anne Campbell is an artist and photographer living and working in Aberdeenshire, Scotland, where she teaches analogue processes at Grays School of Art. She loves peripheral landscapes, all things north and feeding the badgers at her back door. annecampbell.photography

Jennifer Case is the author of *Sawbill: A Search for Place* (University of New Mexico Press, 2018). Her essays have appeared in journals such as *Orion*, *Michigan Quarterly Review,* the *Rumpus,* and *Fourth River*. She teaches at the University of Central Arkansas and serves as the Assistant Nonfiction Editor of *Terrain.org*. jenniferlcase.com

Jelle Cauwenberghs was born in Belgium, grew up in France and currently lives in Glasgow. His poetry, essays and short fiction have appeared in various journals and independent magazines and he is a regular contributor to *Caught by the River*. He is currently working on his first poetry collection, *The House of Last Refuge*. Twitter @kingfisher_noah.

Cate Chapman is a poet and freelance editor based in the UK. Her work has been featured in several Dark Mountain issues and a number of other print publications including *Walking on Lava* (Chelsea Green, 2017) and *Letters to the Earth* (William Collins, 2019). Cate currently works as poetry editor for the Dark Mountain Project. @wordbird_

Jane Cipra is a Californian biologist (working in botany and wildlife) and an artist (working in oil paints) combining the two disciplines to convey the complexity and beauty of our vanishing ecological systems. Instagram @ballnjane

Mike Cipra has lived and written in landscapes ranging from Death Valley to the old-growth redwood forests of northern California. He is honoured to be included among the writers, artists and thinkers involved in the Dark Mountain Project. mikecipra.com

Caleb Cohen is based in Victoria, British Columbia, though he grew up in Vermont. He studied at McGill University and has worked variously as a farmhand, trail builder, ski hut cook and tree planter. To date, he has planted about a quarter of a million trees. His favourite is the white pine.

Sylvie Decaux is associate professor in English studies and communication at the University of Paris. Her research interests include ecopoetics and environmental humanities. She is involved in the *Collectif pour le Triangle de Gonesse* and the Transition movement.

Alex Diggins is a writer and critic based in London. He has written for *The Economist, The Spectator*, *TLS*, *New Welsh Review*, *Island Review* and *The Clearing*. He is published in *The Los Angeles Review of Books* and *Rife: Twenty-One Stories from Britain's Youth* (Unbound), and is currently working on a book about holy islands and the climate crisis. Twitter @AHABDiggins

Paul Feather is an animist farmer living in Georgia, USA. His recent work is to translate his animist and ecological perspective into the language of Cartesian mechanical science. He works closely with his wife Terra, and some of their work may be found at paulandterra.com

Tim Fox lives with his family in western Oregon. His writings appear in *Walking on Lava*, *Forest Under Story*, and *Dark Mountain: Issues 4, 5, 9* and *11*. He recently completed a young adult far-future trilogy, *Afterlands Convergence*. Watch for his forthcoming essay collection, *Wild Integrity*. wildintegrity.blogspot.com

Alex Freilich is a multimedia artist, living at the southern reaches of the Salish Sea in so-called 'Olympia, Washington'. He makes reverent ambient music as Cedar Dreamer. This is his first published piece of writing. cedardreamer.bandcamp.com

Peter Friederici gardens, scrounges for streetside fruit, and listens for birds in and around Flagstaff, Arizona. He does most of his writing while walking trails in the mountains and canyons nearby. Read the results at peterfriederici.com

Siana Fitzjohn lives in Canterbury, Aotearoa. She has a Masters in Science Communication, spends much of her time as a climate activist, and thrives in a cold ocean, with her animals and on outdoor dance floors.

Miles Glyn has worked on the EXTINCTION REBELLION project since its inception, applying his background as a craftsperson and fine artist to create social change by working cooperatively. He previously collaborated with Clare Farrell on the #Bodypolitic project, reclaiming the human body as a place for radical creative expression.

Ben Greenlee teaches English at Colorado State University where he earned his MFA. His work can be found in *Green Briar Review* and the *Citron Review*. This is his first published work of fiction.

Ranae Lenor Hanson's grounding place is the north-eastern wilderness watersheds of Minnesota. She teaches writing and global studies at an urban community college and works for climate justice with students, her local Transition Town, Minnesota 350.org and Quaker communities. Her book *Thirst and Fog* will be published this year. ranaehanson.com

Nick Hunt is an editor and co-director of the Dark Mountain Project. He has also authored two travel books, *Where the Wild Winds Are* and *Walking the Woods and the Water*, and a work of gonzo ornithology, *The Parakeeting of London*. He is currently working on a collection of short stories and a third travel book. nickhuntscrutiny.com

Neale Inglenook is a contributing editor to the online edition of Dark Mountain, and his fiction and essays can be found in the pages of its books. He lives on the California coast he grew from, along with his parents, wife and daughters. digital-material.net

Artist **Jayne Ivimey** has returned to the landscape of her native East Anglia over many years in a quest to understand its geology and ecosystems. Seven years in New Zealand working in bird conservation alerted her to the global problems in the bird world. Her book *Bird by Bird: The Red List in Thought and Image* is written by Julia Blackburn. jayneivemey.com

Emily Joy is a UK based visual artist making sculpture, installation and performative work. She has exhibited throughout the UK and Europe. Emily is also a teacher, facilitator of creative community projects, a slow traveller and gardener. giftsformothermnemosyne.wordpress.com

Sue Jowsey is a founding member of the F4 Collective and Senior Lecturer at Auckland University of Technology in New Zealand. She explores how magic, when folded within a modern Western perception of reality, can disclose a multiplicity of worlds within the animating force of the more-than-human. Her work draws on a spectrum of disciplines from the digital to the handmade. jowseywilliams.co.nz

What **Obi Kaufmann** is: a naturalist, a California native, an artist, a historian, a cartographer, sometimes a journalist. What he is not: a scientist, a politician, a lobbyist, a lawyer, a farmer. He is the author of the best-selling *California Field Atlas* and lives in Oakland, California. coyoteandthunder.com

Monika Kostera is Professor Ordinaria at the Jagiellonian University, Poland and Professor in Management and Organization at Södertörn University, Sweden. She has published over 40 books and numerous scientific articles. Her current research revolves around organisational imagination and ethnography. She also publishes poetry in Polish, English and Swedish. 'Lamentation' features in the poetry collection *Going to Delos* (erbacce-press). kostera.pl

Michael Leung is an artist/designer, urban farmer and writer. He was born in London and moved to Hong Kong in 2009. His projects range from collective urban agriculture projects such as The HK FARMers' Almanac 2014–2015 to researching Insurrectionary Agricultural Milieux, territorial struggles and communities connected by wormholes. studioleung.com

Rob Lewis is a poet, writer, activist and house painter, working to bring the power of language to the defence of the more-than-human world. His writings have been published in *Dark Mountain*, *Cascadia Weekly*, *Manzanita*, *The Atlanta Review*, *Southern Review* and others. As owner of Earth Craft Painting he also works to revive the use of local wild clays to paint our work and living spaces.

Jane Lovell is an award-winning poet whose work is steeped in natural history, science and folklore. Her latest collection is *This Tilting Earth* published by Seren. Jane also writes for *Elementum Journal* and *Photographers Against Wildlife Crime*. She is Writer-in-Residence at Rye Harbour Nature Reserve.

Anna Mayo cultivates her artwork through an awe of the wild. Deepening her connection to the lands she wanders by creating her paints and inks from their rocks, leaves and flowers. Her art is born from journeys in South America, Spain and the UK. Anna is based in Sheffield, UK. instagram.com/_silvestria

Robert McGahey is a Quaker ecologist, retired college humanities teacher, longtime steering committee member of North Carolina Interfaith Power and Light, and member of Celo Community, the oldest non-sectarian community land trust in the US. Author of *The Orphic Moment* and his memoir, *India: A Love Story*, which will be published in May. ecospirit.blogspot.com

Richard Metz is an environmental artist and activist, who seeks a deeper relationship with nature. He lives just outside Philadelphia, Pennsylvania. Having just retired from teaching art for 30 years, he now tries to spend several days a week in the woods, creating work, leaving himself open to what may be present.

Matt Miles is a North Carolina-based writer, journalist and poet whose work appears in *Dark Mountain*, *Earth Island Journal*, *Hakai Magazine*, *Modern Farmer*, *Minding Nature*, the Garrison Institute's 'Lineages' column and elsewhere. clippings.me/mattmiles

Perching in the forest of Catalunya, **Sarah Misselbrook**'s research-based practice concerns the transient nature of material and environment. Fragile installations break down, mirroring devastation of floods and fire. Performing obsessive acts of repetition, whilst making and installing the work, the artist searches for something other. An offering of hope for restoration.

Mari Fallet Mosand runs the crafts business Krokvokst in Norway, making traditional handicraft and offering courses in woodwork and willow weaving. She also creates art and makes her own paints and inks from earth pigments and other natural materials. Her work often explores the force of life in nature and in us, and how that force has manifested throughout the ages. krokvokst.no

Eric Nicholson is a retired art teacher who lives in the north-east of England. He finds he has one foot planted firmly in city culture and one planted in the countryside, where he especially enjoys the serendipitous encounters with wildlife. erikleo.wordpress.com

Samuel Osborn is an independent scholar and writes about antique theology and Iron Age religion. He lives in Boston where he is an avid runner and climber in the mountains of New England.

Mat Osmond's a writer and illustrator based in Falmouth, Cornwall. In April 2020 he and the painter Kate Walters are publishing a pamphlet of poems and pictures, *The Black Madonna's Song*. Mat is convener for Art.Earth's November 2020 creative summit at Dartington UK, *Borrowed Time: on death, dying & change*. borrowed-time.info

Kathleen Palti writes about connecting with nature in the Anthropocene. She has a PhD in medieval literature and is inspired by deep ecology, yoga and myth. She lives with her family in Munich, Germany. @KathleenPalti

Nina Pick is the author of two chapbooks, *À Luz* and *Leaving the Lecture on Dance*. As a teacher, editor and oral historian, she seeks to restore an embodied reverence for our ancestors and the Earth. She lives in New York along the Hudson River. ninapick.com

Dan Porter is a photographer based in England. His first book, *You Would Be Earth* (with Meral Güler), was published in 2015.

Kerry Priest is a poet and sound artist living on the edge of Dartmoor. Her poetry has been anthologised in *The Best New British and Irish Poets 2018* (Eyewear) and *Anything That Can Happen – Poems About the Future* (Emma Press). She was formerly a lecturer at Humboldt and Eichstätt universities in Germany. Kerry is an emerging playwright at the Minack Theatre in 2020. Kerrypriest.com

Sam Robinson lives in the Dyfi Valley in west Wales where he works as a shepherd. He is a coordinator with LWA Cymru, a branch of the Land Workers' Alliance, a union founded on the principles of food sovereignty and agroecology. He plays on the wing for Clwb Rygbi Machynlleth.

Christy Rodgers writes essays and tales about biocide, remnant mythologies and struggles for justice, some of them inspired by working and journeying in Latin America for three decades. She lives in San Francisco and on Whidbey Island, Washington. christyrodgers.wordpress.com

Caroline Ross is an artist and t'ai chi teacher living on the River Thames. She makes her tools and art materials from wild-foraging and from what other people discard. She has contributed to Dark Mountain since *Issue 8: Technê*. She teaches art and the use of wild materials in the UK and Europe. carolineross.co.uk

Robert Lee Thornton has had poems published in *descant* journal and the *Writers in the Attic* anthology, and has reviewed poetry collections for *Cloudbank*, Broadsided Press and *Gulf Coast Online*. He has several unpublished novels, all of which boil down to 'people find weird stuff in the North Idaho woods'. down-from-the-hoodoos.blogspot.com

US artist **Meridel Rubenstein** began her professional career in the early 1970s, evolving from photographer of single photographic images to artist of extended works, multi-media installations and social practice. She maintains her art studio in Santa Fe, New Mexico while directing the Eden in Iraq Wastewater Garden Project in southern Iraq, under the umbrella of NGO Nature Iraq, Iraq's pre-eminent environmental group.

Lucy Ann Smethurst weaves slow steps and deep words exploring life in death, motion in stillness. Her writing responds to encountering the fragility and wonder of the human and other-than-human in endangered wild places. Lucy shares an ensouled life in Cumbria with her partner and the trees. jointhedotsjourney.wordpress.com

Kollibri Terre Sonnenblume is a writer, photographer, tree hugger, animal lover and dissident, at large somewhere in the western United States. He is the author of several books including, *The Failures of Farming & the Necessity of Wildtending*, *Roadtripping at the End of the World* and *Adventures in Urban Bike Farming*. macskamoksha.com

Jordan Tierney wanders forgotten and abused tracts of urban wilderness. Based in Baltimore, USA she carves found wood and assembles flotsam and jetsam into poems about their overlooked beauty. Jordan loves when her artwork provides a transformational experience suggesting the one she had out in the woods while creating it. jordantierney.com

Kate Walters is based in Trewarveneth Studios, Cornwall and published by Guillemot Press. Time spent in wild places – Shetland, Orkney, Italian national parks and the Hebrides – inform her painting and her writing. Most recently she has been working on a poetry pamphlet with Mat Osmond in response to a dream of an ancient sacred feminine force, *The Black Madonna's Song*. katewalters.co.uk

Anna M. Warrock has lived in the North American eastern woodlands most of her life. Her latest book, *From the Other Room*, won the Slate Roof Press Chapbook Award. Her poems have been choreographed, set to music, performed at Boston's Hayden Planetarium, and inscribed in a Boston-area subway station. AnnaMWarrock.com

Charlotte Watson is a New Zealand-born visual artist and writer. Her work looks at the stories that inhabit the land, and how place inhabits us. She is currently based in Narrm Melbourne.

Lori Michelle Wells is a writer who is immersed in modern animism and integrated creativity. She grew up in the Arizona desert, wandered the west coast, and now lives with her husband in the hardwood forests of Ohio. lorimwells.com.

Julie Williams is a photo-media artist living in the Vale of Clwydd, New South Wales, Australia. She utilises self-portraiture to immerse herself within the landscape to highlight the search for reconnection. Her work queries the spirit of place and how humanity can inhabit a place more fully. juliewilliams.art

Kate Williamson lives in a nature reserve in the South Island of New Zealand surrounded by native trees, birds and rushing water. Williamson describes herself as 'a humble cave painter trying to capture the unrivalled splendour of Nature (the real artist) on canvas' at a time when the body of Gaia, our home, is under threat of collapse. katewilliamsonart.com

Will Wlizlo is an active transportation advocate in Minneapolis, Minnesota. His writing has appeared in the Minneapolis *Star Tribune*, *Rain Taxi Review of Books*, and *The Millions*. Find peace and light at wwolfgangw.com.

Miek Zwamborn is a Dutch author and artist based on the Scottish Isle of Mull where she is involved with the rewilding project Tireragan. She has published three novels: *Oploper* (2000),*Vallend Hout* (2004) and *De duimsprong* (2013), and a seaweed anthology *Wieren* (2018) which will appear in English this summer.

DaRk
MOUNTAIN

Roll of honour

The publication of this book is made possible by the support of subscribers to the Dark Mountain Project. The following subscribers have provided financial support beyond the call of duty. We are very grateful for their belief in our work, and for that of all our subscribers across the world.

Bob Archer
Keith Badger
Kay and Wahhab Baldwin
Jeff Blackburn
Carolee Bol
Paula Boyle
Bruce Campbell
Sandra Carey
Ben Carpenter
Jonas Caufield
Theo Clarke
Peter Culp
Kate Davis
Brook Dickson and Kurt Navratil
Simeon Gallu
Jack Gates-Browne
Lorien Goodale
Alexander Grant
Jan Ernst de Groot
Christopher Hall
Colin Harper
James Heal
Rebecca Henderson
Victoria Hill
Ann Hine
Henrietta Hitchings
Christoph Höhn
Rachel Holstead
Nathaniel Holdsworth
Michael Hughes
Andrew Hurley
Erik Jacobs and Dina Rudick (Anthem Multimedia)
Mary Strong Jackson
Atlantis Johnson
William Johnson
Howard Jones
Andrew Junius
Max Kloosterman
Rebecca A. Knittle
Lark
Shabehram Lohrasbe
Jennifer Loewen
Deirdre McAdams
Ian McCleave
Peter McDonald
William Maxwell
Johan Meylaerts
Brian Midtbo
Todd Moore
Sarah Murray
Stephen Nally
Noor Ney
S. Nate Pochan
Simon de Quincey
Johnny Rath
Bonnitta Roy
Helen Sieroda
Sara Solnick
Susie Unseld
Hans Vermaak and Eileen Moyer
Celia Fulton Walden
Elizabeth Watson
Gregory Webster
Jacob Williams
Julia Winiarski
John W. Wolf
Robin Zykin